THE ROYAL MALADY

THE ROYAL MALADY

CHARLES CHENEVIX TRENCH

HARCOURT, BRACE & WORLD, INC.

NEW YORK

TO PHYLLIS MANN

*who, to questions about the eighteenth century,
generally knows the answer and always knows
where to find it.*

Contents

List of Illustrations

(Between pages 108 and 109)

LIST OF ILLUSTRATIONS

'FILIAL PIETY'

> From the cartoon (1788) by Rowlandson in the
> Department of Prints and Drawings, British Museum

'BLUE AND BUF LOYALTY'

> From the cartoon (1788) by Rowlandson in the
> Department of Prints and Drawings, British Museum

FANNY BURNEY

> From an engraving after the portrait by E. F. Burney

BETSY SHERIDAN

> From the portrait in the possession of W. Le Fanu, Esq.

COLONEL GREVILLE

> After Ozias Humphry

ACKNOWLEDGEMENTS

I must first express my thanks to Sir Randle Baker Wilbraham, Bt, for his great kindness in allowing me to use the diary of his ancestor, Sir George Baker, and other unpublished papers at Rode Hall; and to reproduce Sir George's portrait. I am also most grateful to his daughter, Mrs T. G. Kirkbride, for copying these papers; and to Miss Phyllis Mann, who so expertly guided me through the eighteenth-century maze.

I have received valuable help, advice and documents from Mr L. M. Payne, Librarian of the Royal College of Physicians; Mr E. J. Davis, the County Archivist at Aylesbury; Miss W. D. Coates, Registrar of the National Register of Archives; Mr I. R. Christie; Mr F. T. Baker, Director of Lincoln City Library; Mr Charles Garton, of the University of Durham; Mr G. U. Illingworth and the Hospital House Committee of The Lawn, Lincoln; the staffs of the London Library and the Reading Room and Department of Manuscripts of the British Museum. Mr William Le Fanu and Messrs Eyre and Spottiswoode have very kindly allowed me to quote from *Betsy Sheridan's Journal*; and the Bodley Head have let me quote extensively from *The Diaries of Robert Fulke Greville*, edited by F. M. Bladon. The Editors of *History Today* have allowed me to reproduce parts of my article on this subject published in that magazine. Dr John Charters gave me valuable advice on the medical aspects of the case. To all these I offer my sincere thanks.

INTRODUCTION

King George III's attack of insanity in 1788–9 has been considered by most of the historians and biographers of the period. These have, however, drawn mainly on secondary sources, hearsay and gossip. The only authoritative eyewitness accounts of the King's ailment available to most of them have been the physicians' evidence given before the Parliamentary Commission. For reasons which I hope to make plain, in a matter of such delicacy and political importance the physicians were not altogether frank with the politicians, and their evidence was coloured by ambition, by professional etiquette and jealousy, by political prejudice.

For the truth about the King's illness, we must look to the *private* diaries of two of his physicians, which have escaped the notice of historians. These are the diaries of Sir George Baker, the King's only doctor during the early stages of his illness; and of Dr John Willis, who with his father was in immediate charge of the patient for some three months until the King's recovery.

The original of Sir George Baker's diary is in possession of his descendant, Sir Randle Baker Wilbraham, Bt, who in 1952 allowed a copy to be made and deposited in the Library of the Royal College of Physicians. The diary of Dr John Willis was acquired from a member of his family by the British Museum in 1929. The volume of the Catalogue of Additions in which it is indexed and described was, however, not published until 1959; which perhaps accounts for its neglect.

Filling a gap of some five weeks between these two diaries, is that of Colonel Robert Fulke Greville, an equerry who had daily access to the King from about the date on which Sir George Baker's diary ends until the arrival of the Willises. This diary, published in 1930, does not seem to have been available for study before that date. It has subsequently been briefly noticed by one or two writers; but it is of uneven value and must be handled with care, a sharp distinction being made between events at which Greville was present, and those of which he heard through palace gossip.

I

Although the present book deals mainly with the King's insanity in 1788-9, this must not be seen in isolation. In 1765 he had a mysterious illness which was probably a mild and early onset of the same disorder.[1] Dr Willis's cure in 1789 was not permanent: indeed modern psychiatrists would say that psychotic disorders cannot be cured, though they can be so brought under control that the patient lives and works normally for years, perhaps for the rest of his life. It was Dr Willis's achievement that he brought the King's ailment under control. It remained under control for twelve years. In 1801 and 1804 there were comparatively short and mild attacks, the latter followed by blindness. In 1810 the King had another attack, from which he was never to recover. In the unbecoming words of his son, 'We have turned the key on the King. He'll come back no more. That I'll promise you.'[2]

I am not, however, writing of this later insanity, because it was devoid of political interest. The conditions which produced the Regency Crisis no longer existed: the King's part in government was small and spasmodic; the Prince of Wales, though still on singularly unfilial terms with his father, was no longer the leader and patron of a united and unscrupulous Opposition; the nation, fighting for its life, could not spare these matters much attention. No one pressed for a Regency before 1810; and after 1810 no one disputed it. The malady produced no crisis.

The events of 1788-9 are of far greater interest. Their immediate result was the Regency Crisis, which displayed with clarity and exactitude the mechanics of the eighteenth-century political system just before it collapsed under pressure from the French Revolution. The conventional picture, diligently reproduced by generations of Whig historians, of a virtuous Whig party engaged in ceaseless struggle for liberty against the crafty encroachments of George III and the Tories, has been somewhat blurred by modern scholarship: it remains, however, the image which most people retain of the reign. Nothing displays more clearly the discrepancies between fact and Whig legend than the history of the Regency Crisis.

After this illness, George III was never quite the same man. He had to take things easy, to bring to an end his ceaseless and fussy interference with the day-to-day details of administration. The royal malady had, therefore, an effect analagous to George I's convenient dislike of the English language: it reduced the work and influence of the Crown just when the nineteenth-century political pattern was taking shape.

CHAPTER I

The Onset of the Royal Malady

In the spring of 1788 King George III's health was a cause of anxiety to his physicians. The bile, they considered, did not flow correctly; and as he refused to take any of the medicines they prescribed, his 'up-and-down condition' defied their skill. 'A pretty smart bilious attack', he informed his Prime Minister, Mr Pitt, 'forced him to take to his bed, as the only tolerable posture he could find.' It was even suggested that they call into consultation Dr Monro, physician to Bedlam Asylum. In the event, however, they followed the usual custom of eighteenth-century physicians when puzzled by a case: despite the King's notorious moderation in food and drink, they diagnosed gout; and prescribed a regimen without riding, to which His Majesty refused to submit, and the mildly purgative waters of Cheltenham, to which he consented.[1]

He set off in July in a holiday mood, for such a jaunt was an agreeable novelty. In twenty-eight laborious years, the King had so burdened himself with the cares of his own and his Ministers' offices that he hardly ever took a holiday. There was nothing he liked better than riding round incognito, a kindly, inquisitive Harun al Rashid, prying into his subjects' cottages, asking fussy questions about their health, crops, religion and private affairs: but such benevolent attentions had been bestowed hitherto only upon those who had the felicity to live near Windsor or Richmond: the vast majority of His Majesty's subjects saw nothing of their sovereign, nor he of them. Now, however, the political horizon was tolerably clear: he could safely leave the ship of state for a few weeks to young Mr Pitt and, obedient to his physician, Sir George Baker, abandon himself to the bucolic pleasures of the most beautiful land he had ever seen, 'the colliery country near Stroud'.*

* *Sic.* Either His Majesty was misinformed, or the royal handwriting was misread. There were no collieries there. Perhaps he meant 'clothieries'.

On 12 July, the day of their departure from Windsor, the palace staff were up at five in the morning. There seems to have been a certain failure in organization, some delay in the necessary preparations; for the noise and confusion were prodigious, and the palace resounded with 'people stirring, boxes nailing, horses neighing and dogs barking'. Stopping for breakfast at Henley-on-Thames, for 'a sort of half-dinner' at Oxford, they passed through almost unbroken crowds from Oxford to Cheltenham. Every four or five miles they encountered bands of 'the most horrid fiddlers, scraping "God Save the King" with all their might, out of tune, out of time, and all in the rain'.

Bays Hill Lodge, which the King had borrowed from Lord Fauconberg, was a square, white box of a house so small that Fanny Burney, junior Keeper of the Queen's Robes, could not bring her own maid, and was obliged to take tea with her cronies in a passage. Here the King settled down happily to the life of, almost, a private gentleman. A skeleton staff, a mere handful of equerries accompanied 'the Royals'. Their Majesties actually condescended to dine with the equerries, whose gratification was modified by their opinion of the royal diet of 'regular mutton and potatoes', lamentably varied by *Sauerkraut*. The equerries liked to eat well, and to linger over their port; but the King, with a horror of the family inclination to obesity, ate very little, seldom drank more than half a dozen glasses of a sort of lemonade dignified by the name of cup, and left the table long before Colonel Gwynn had taken even the edge off his considerable appetite. As for the claret, it was execrable until the Prince of Wales, at one of his rare dinners under the parental roof, pronounced sentence upon it.

Many loyal Britons, themselves martyrs to excess, feared that their sovereign carried abstinence to dangerous extremes. His indisposition, they thought, would have exhausted itself in his extremities in the shape of gout had he drunk like almost any private gentleman: but His Majesty preferred other, perhaps less judicious, remedies. Rising while it was still dark, and long before his staff, he bustled down to the Spa, only three hundred yards from the Lodge, for three full bumpers of the purgative water. After a walk, he refreshed himself there again. Such quantities had a violent effect; but the King was never one for half-measures, and in his letter to Sir George Baker could not 'sufficiently express the benefit he finds from this salutary spring. He has never been in the least heated. He finds a pint and a half the proper quantity to give him two openings, these only clear him without any sinking, on the contrary he finds himself in better spirits and has never been obliged to take the rhubarb pills.' The Princess Royal contented herself with three-quarters of a pint; but Princess Elizabeth was obliged to have recourse to the rhubarb, and was not allowed to get up until eight o'clock breakfast lest she fatigue herself. His Majesty was deeply interested in the health of all his household, and commended Lady Weymouth for being ready always before six to take the waters with him: 'if she continues this mode of life, she will certainly never want dandelion nor any other specifics to remove the byle.'

He went for day-long drives with the Queen, visiting, perhaps, a clothiery making red cloth for army uniforms, or a group of farms. One of these jaunts was to Hartlebury and back, a sixty-mile drive—not very prudent, one would think, for a convalescent. More often the King rode alone, which he most enjoyed, 'though the rides', he informed his physician, 'require going slower than in other places, therefore though the King is resolved to be very prudent, yet the country would not permit him to act otherwise'.

Plainly dressed, with no escort, he came upon a farmer in a muck-sweat.

'So, friend,' said the King affably, 'you seem very warm.'

'I came a long way,' the farmer replied, 'for I want to see the King.'

'Well, here is something to refresh you after your walk.' A guinea was graciously bestowed.

'But where, worthy sir,' asked the farmer, 'can I see His Majesty?'

'Friend, you see him before you!'

Another yokel, casually encountered, asked, 'Have you seen the King? 'Tis a good sort of man, but dresses very plain.'

'Aye,' said His Majesty, 'as plain as you see me now.'

This, and a score of similar instances of royal condescension

6

delighted the country folk and fixed George III in their affections.

The King and Queen dined at four o'clock; in the evening they walked on the walls. Nothing could be more domestic than the sight of this bulky middle-aged gentleman in the ugly Windsor uniform of blue and red, arm-in-arm with his wife who so distressingly resembled a monkey, bowing and taking off his huge hat to anyone he thought he recognized, while the five little princesses trotted alongside. The good people of Cheltenham turned out in hundreds to see this affecting spectacle; and George III remarked genially to his Queen, 'We must walk about two or three days to please them, and then we may walk about to please ourselves.'

After dinner, Their Majesties watched the Lodge servants play cricket, using bats and balls which the King had himself provided lest they sicken through lack of exercise. They attended a display of magic, and condescendingly allowed the conjurer to cut out, and replace, a piece of the Queen's gown.

They made excursions further afield, to Tewkesbury where the townsfolk stood crammed even on the parapets of the bridge to cheer them as they passed. 'My good people!' he called, 'I'm afraid some of you may fall—don't run such hazards to see your King! I'll ride as slowly as you wish, that you may all have a sight.'

So they huzza'ed him all the louder.

The Duke of York, the King's best-loved son, was able to tear himself away from his military duties (which, according to his senior officers, were neither onerous nor efficiently performed) and pay a visit to Cheltenham. As there was no room for him at Bays Hill Lodge, and the King could not bear to be parted from him, a wooden house at the far end of the town was dismantled, carried up to the Lodge and there re-erected with prodigious trouble and expense. The Duke stayed in it one night, and hastened back to London.

When the royal tourists honoured Lord Coventry with their company at dinner, 'everything which taste and elegance could accomplish was displayed for the occasion'. The cellar doors were opened, and a multitude of onlookers were regaled with good October. Amply refreshed and defying the postilions, some waggish young farmers insisted on clambering on to the royal coach, from which eminence they saluted their wives. The equerries were not amused, but His Majesty laughed heartily, commending their spirit and civility.

Moving on to Worcester, he took especial pleasure in being shown the town and battlefield by a great-grandson of Oliver Cromwell. Among all the cheering crowds, the Quakers conspicuously kept on their hats. The King picked them out for special attention, uncovering and bowing very low. 'Fare thee well, Friend George!' they cried.

He honoured the mayor and corporation by a visit to the town hall, where an elegant cold collation was provided. Having heard of the King's idiosyncrasies, the mayor offered him a jelly instead of a glass of wine. However, His Majesty genially replied, 'I do not recollect, Mr Mayor, ever in my life drinking wine before dinner; yet upon this pleasing occasion I will venture.' He then downed a glass of rich old Mountain, with the toast, 'Prosperity to the Corporation and citizens of Worcester!'

He consented to sit for a portrait to be placed in the town hall; and attended divine service in the cathedral where, since the royal presence would stimulate local piety, the nave was filled with chairs 'to accommodate the large assembly expected on this interesting occasion'. The next day the King and Queen were again at the cathedral, listening to a selection from the works of Handel, and His Majesty was observed beating time to *Messiah*. They also attended a charity performance at the College Hall, where the 'sum of the Collection [£602–7] was not very large, considering the numerous attendance [about 2,000] at the meeting, and that it contained the liberal donation of £200 put in the plate by His Majesty'. The audience, however, got a good view of this 'amiable and beloved family. The King was dressed in his blue and gold uniform, and the Queen and Princesses in royal purple gowns with silver tissue petticoats. Her Majesty's head-dress was a cap decorated with purple ribands, studded with beads of polished steel no less brilliant than the finest diamonds.'

Next door to Bishop Hurd's palace, where the royal couple stayed, a house was being converted into a porcelain shop. This fascinating spectacle drew the King like a magnet: soon, accompanied by the Queen, he was picking his way through the big rooms, over tools and plaster, wood-shavings and rubbish, asking the masons and carpenters a thousand fussy questions. Not content with their answers, he decided to inspect the work himself, and climbed the stairs to the very top floor. 'Come, Charlotte', he said to the Queen, 'come and sit down, for I'm rather tired.' Down they sat on the dusty top stair, laughing heartily at their situation.

Although the visit to Worcester was such a happy occasion, certain features of it gave rise to anxiety among those in the know. Since his youth, the King had been lamentably addicted to early rising; and his rousing the Dean from bed for a visit before dawn to the Cathedral might indicate no more than an unusual elevation of spirits. But surely it was more than eccentric of the King to go to his equerries' lodgings while the maid was still washing the front door step.

'Good day! Good day! Pray show me where the fellows sleep, what? what?'

Colonels Gwynn and Digby, apprised of their sovereign's untimely visit, leaped from bed as though surprised by an enemy. But by the time they were dressed, His Majesty was off, bustling along the riverside and making himself painfully conspicuous.

'This, I suppose, is Worcester New Bridge?' he asked some early-morning loafers.

'Yes, please Your Majesty!'

'Then, my boys, let's have a huzza!'

And a fine shout there was.

Worse still, he displayed a marked and embarrassing admiration for Lady Pembroke, an old flame of his repressed adolescence who, still beautiful, still chaste, unhappily and insecurely married to an incorrigible rake, was spending the summer at Cheltenham.

It might almost be said that madness was the fashionable complaint of the late eighteenth century. To take two random examples—European monarchs and English literary men—the Emperor of Russia, the Kings of Prussia, Spain, Denmark, Naples and Portugal were all more or less mad; Cowper, Gray, Smart, Johnson, Boswell, Blake and Lamb all admitted, even

9

boasted of mental affliction; Sterne could hardly be described as normal. The greatest Englishman of his time, the elder Pitt, descended for years into the shades of melancholia. An extraordinary number of English gentlemen were markedly eccentric, and among these must be included King George III.[2]

It is difficult to see any reason for so much abnormality. A person superficially acquainted with the eighteenth century might think it not unconnected with too much high living, too much of what was euphemistically called 'pleasure'—in short, too little self-control. But this facile explanation hardly fits the case of, say, Dr Johnson, or of George III. Probably people often diagnosed as lunacy what would now be called a nervous breakdown. Perhaps the general improvement of medical science showed up, by contrast, the treatment of mental disorder, which was generally crude, brutal and sensational.

In his youth George III was indolent, timid, indecisive, pleasure-loving, dilatory and highly sexed. Driven by an able tutor, Lord Bute, he forced himself to correct every one of these shortcomings.[3] He became painfully diligent, self-immersed in details of administration that should have been left to Under-Secretaries. His guiding principle in public life was never to change his mind, never to give way to persuasion or pressure, because that would betray the hidden weakness of his character. Time and again he displayed a stiff courage, physical and moral. He forced on himself (and on his groaning Court) a regimen that included hard riding or walking for hours a day, a minimum of food and drink, the most Spartan discomfort in his draughty, under-heated palaces. His Court and domestic life ran as regularly, and as tediously, as clockwork. He was faithful to a singularly plain and unamiable wife. Miraculously he succeeded in transforming his character, but at what a cost! Thirty years' resolute, unremitting effort imposed upon him too great a strain.

As King, he had had a rough passage. He had seen his beloved tutor hounded from public life for serving him exactly as he wished to be served. Ill-advised by his Ministers and driven on by his self-assumed obstinacy, he had maintained for the first half of his reign an undignified feud with Mr Wilkes, the most adroit demagogue England had ever known, from which he gained nothing but ridicule and hatred. Actuated, he persuaded himself, by the best of motives, to maintain the authority of Parliament, he had involved his country in a war with the rebellious colonists which should easily have been won but for his Ministers' ineptitude and the nation's, in the end, losing its nerve: and everyone blamed him for it, as though he should have presided with equanimity over the dissolution of his Empire!

Nor could he contemplate (as an agreeable contrast to the political scene) the felicity of a virtuous family life which, heaven knows, he had done everything to deserve. His sister, the Queen of Denmark, had been imprisoned for improper relations with a physician; one of his brothers, the Duke of Gloucester, had married the illegitimate daughter of Sir Edward Walpole by a mistress he had 'fairly dragged off a cinder-cart'. Another, the Duke of Cumberland, had first been sued, in conditions of uninhibited publicity, for crim. con. with Lady Grosvenor; and had then married (lest worse befall) a woman with the shadiest background, of whom it was said that, after half an hour's conversation with her, one felt like washing out one's ears. His eldest son had abstained from nothing that would injure and humiliate his father: he headed the political opposition, in company with his profligate crony Charles Fox; his debts were mountainous; he had been involved in scandal after scandal, culminating in his illegally marrying a Roman Catholic and keeping the secret so badly that it had been debated in the House of Commons.

The King was noted for mannerisms and a way of speech that invited ridicule, parody and no doubt a good deal of exaggeration. The royal conversation was liberally punctuated by meaningless questions, 'What? What?' or 'Hey? Hey?'—for which he seldom awaited an answer.

'Thank you, thank you, thank you!' said the King to a passer-by who helped him when his horse stumbled. 'Who are you? What? What? Who are you? Who are you?' He then rode off before his helper could reply.

Sometimes he received an answer he did not expect. 'How do matters go, hey?' he asked a maid of honour, in love. 'When did you last hear from him, hey?'

'Well, now,' Lady Cecilia tartly replied, 'what's that to you?'

What was one to make of his remark to Fanny Burney? 'Was there ever such stuff as great part of Shakespeare? Only one must not say so! But what think you? What? Is there not sad stuff? What?' Modern readers may consider the royal observations to be fair comment; but contemporaries gave them a less flattering interpretation.

A multitude of such tales[4] created in the public mind the image of a monarch who was kindly, well-meaning but eccentric. Undoubtedly the mannerisms and way of speech were symptomatic of that timidity and sense of insecurity, displayed in his early correspondence, which in manhood he sternly suppressed.

There were other reports which may not have been true but, true or not, spread a vague idea that the King was far from normal. It was considered significant that before he was thirty he had shaved his head, an operation reputed to relieve pressure on the brain. He displayed a morbid interest in insanity, of which he had an unusual horror; and almost expressed a wish for the death of acquaintances in whose family there was a hereditary taint. In 1765 he had had an illness about which the Court was very secretive. The Prime Minister called it a cold; but it was sufficiently serious to raise the question of a Council of Regency. It was either a nervous breakdown, or an early attack of insanity.[5]

According to a pamphleteer called Withers, who exploited the public interest by writing *A History of the Royal Malady, by a Page of the Presence**, the King, while driving with Her Majesty in Windsor Park, alighted and, approaching a venerable oak, seized one of the lower branches and shook it with the utmost cordiality and regard. At the Queen's request, the page approached and found His Majesty in earnest conversation with the oak-tree, which he imagined was the King of Prussia.

'Don't you see I'm engaged?' he said testily.

'Your Majesty', said Withers, 'Her Majesty the Queen desires your company.'

'Good lack-a-day! That's true. Run and tell Her Majesty I am hastening to her.'[6]

---

* How much is Withers to be believed? The question is important, because he claims to be one of the few eye-witnesses to the King's insanity. He

On another occasion in Windsor Park the King, after complainingly vehemently of the horse brought to him, at last mounted and set off at full gallop, crying, 'Tally Ho! Miranda, Tally Ho! Halloo, Hector! . . . This way, Your Majesty of Prussia, this way!'[7]

However, despite some uneasiness about his behaviour at Worcester, it was generally felt that the holiday had done the King good. He, at any rate, thought so, as he drove away from Cheltenham through the streets thronged with cheering subjects, gentles on one side and commons on the other, the town band blaring out 'God Save the King'. But some people thought he looked ill when he arrived at Kew.*

September, with Parliament in recess and Charles Fox enjoying with Mrs Armistead the delights of Switzerland and Italy, was a quiet month. But in October, the King had a severe attack of hives, showing his family an arm covered with weals 'as if it had been scourged with cords'. On the 16th he tried to shake off a slight indisposition by walking four hours in the rain; then, although the water poured from his boots when he took them off, he refused to change his stockings before going to St James's; and at night he consumed four large pears. Not surprisingly, next day he had a bad chill, with violent spasms in the stomach and bowels which Miss Burney found 'nothing, I hope, alarming, though there is an uncertainty as to his complaint not very satisfactory'.[8]

was, by his own boast, a political pamphleteer. He was probably *not* a Page of the Presence nor, indeed, any Palace employee, for he is mentioned by neither Mme d'Arblay, Mrs Papendiek nor Colonel Greville, the three Palace diarists. He claims, in his book, to have witnessed 'through a chink' an intimate scene, culminating in a quarrel, between the Prince of Wales and Mrs Fitzherbert; the story is almost certainly untrue, because the Prince would never have brought her to his father's palace, nor would the King's page ever have been admitted to the Prince's or Mrs Fitzherbert's house. He was later sued for libelling Mrs Fitzherbert. On the other hand, he was a strong partisan of Pitt, and therefore (for reasons set out hereafter) politically inclined to minimize, rather than exaggerate, the King's symptoms. Probably he can be set down as a scandalmonger whose stories are founded on fact, but embroidered to help sell his vile little book.

* Half the royal household seem to have had 'flu during the summer. Perhaps he caught a belated infection.

13

He was, however, well enough to write personally to his physician:

> The King had this night a spasmodic bilious attack, though much slighter than in the month of June. He therefore wishes to see Sir George Baker as soon as convenient, and desires he will bring one of the opium pills in case the pain should not have entirely subsided. He has as yet taken nothing but a pint and a half of warm water from thinking there was an inclination to vomit; but this had no effect, and the inclination proved nothing but wind on the stomach.[9]

Sir George found His Majesty 'sitting up in his bed, his body being bent forward. He complained of very acute pain in his stomach, shooting to the back and sides and making respiration difficult and uneasy. The pain continued all day and did not cease entirely until the bowels had been emptied.' His Majesty complained also of being tormented with cramp and rheumatism; and of a rash, which Sir George thought trivial. It has been alleged* that Baker gave his patient a purge so violent that it had to be promptly counteracted by laudanum, 'and repeated this therapeutic juggling act no less than three times in twenty-four hours'. Baker's detailed diary does not confirm this story, which seems to be one of the many spiteful and untrue rumours circulating to Sir George's detriment.[10]

There was, and is, a tendency to blame Sir George Baker for deficiencies in the eighteenth-century treatment of psychotic cases. He was, in fact, exceptionally well qualified. Not only had he over thirty years' experience of general practice, but he had written a specialist book on mental disorders. His failure (as will be seen later) seems to have been in controlling an exceptionally difficult patient: either his personality was not strong enough, or his authority was weakened by the very fact of his being a familiar figure about the palace. Moreover he was not robust enough to bear alone, for three weeks, the strain and responsibility later shared with half a dozen colleagues. To complete his portrait, it should be added that he was a man of charm, scholarship and culture, to whom Gray paid the high

* By Guttmacher, whose source I am unable to trace.

compliment of dedicating the 'Elegy Written in a Country Churchyard'—but such qualifications counted for little in the royal household. He may be compared to British generals who are unfortunate enough to be in high command at the *beginning* of a war: his reputation was not enhanced by his treatment of the royal malady; but it recovered enough for him to be chosen, presumably with the approval of the King, for the highest honour in his profession, the Presidency of the Royal College of Physicians.

As the only physician in attendance, he found himself in a position of extraordinary difficulty, writing a few days later:

> Let me take leave to interrupt the thread of this journal. The shade by which soundness of mind is to be distinguished from some degree of insanity is often faint, and in many cases hardly perceptible; and nothing is more embarrassing to families as well as physicians than the condition of persons half-disordered, whom the law will not confine, though they ought not to be at liberty. Such appeared to me to have been His Majesty's case.

His colleagues, called in later, had a much easier task: by the time they arrived, it was accepted that the King was not in his right mind.[11]

To rest, to go to bed for a few days to relieve the ache in his swollen joints, would have been to give way to pressure: the King would *never* give way, and insisted, on the 19th, on going for a long ride in heavy rain. For the next four days he suffered various physical discomforts—stomach-ache, swollen feet, cramp and bile. Palace rumour reported his speech as rambling and disordered; the Queen was uneasy, but would not speak of it; and Miss Burney was terribly alarmed. Sir George Baker's diary, however, does not mention as yet any derangement; and on 20 October the King was able in the evening to write to his Prime Minister: 'I have not been able to answer Mr Pitt's letter sooner, having had a very indifferent night: but the medicine which Sir George Baker found necessary to remove the spasm has greatly relieved me. Indeed, I think myself nearer getting rid of the complaint than I have been since the attack.' There followed some sensible observations on the imprudence of intervening in a quarrel between Sweden and Russia, thereby damaging the nation's finances which, 'if our pride will allow us to lie quiet for a few years, will be in a situation to hold a language which does not become the having been driven out of America'. Nothing could be worse for the King than brooding over disasters seven years old, but he admitted to Mr Pitt that he had never, 'day or night, been at ease since the country took that disgraceful step. . . . I am afraid Mr Pitt will perceive I am not quite in a situation to write at present; but I thought it better to write even as loosely as I have than to let the box return without an answer to his letter'.[12]

On the 22nd the King's spirits were low: his 'agitation and flurry of spirits gave him hardly any rest'. Nor, alas, did Sir George who, the bowels being costive, ordered in the morning what *he* called a gentle purgative. The royal observations on this treatment were expressed with warmth and displeasure.

In the afternoon [wrote Sir George] I was received by His Majesty in a very unusual manner, of which I had not the least expectation. The look of his eyes, the tone of his voice, every gesture and his whole deportment represented a person in a most furious passion of anger. One medicine had been too powerful, another had only teased him without effect. The importation of senna ought to be prohibited, and he would give orders that in future it should never be given to the royal family. With a frequent repetition of this and similar language, he detained me three hours. His pulse was much quickened, but I did not number the strokes. Having no opportunity of speaking to the Queen, I wrote a note to Mr Pitt immediately on my return to town, and informed him that I had just left the King in an agitation of spirits nearly bordering upon delirium. Mr Pitt called on me that evening, and I had an opportunity of giving him a full description of His Majesty's condition.[13]

It was now that Sir George first suspected the painful truth, and consulted a medical friend.

As far as it had appeared to *me*, there had been no incoherence in what he uttered; but his talking had been perpetual, and with such an excess of vivacity and eagerness that it was impossible for me not to suspect a derangement of his understanding. Yet so

delicate was the situation in which I was placed, that I did not
dare to communicate my suspicions, or take any decisive measures
in consequence of them. I hoped indeed that retirement to His
Majesty's favourite place of residence [Windsor] and a total
relaxation from business would in no long time have restored
strength to his body and composure to his mind. In the mean time,
I thought it prudent not to raise an alarm of such public importance while it could be avoided.[14]

About this time Mrs Siddons, the actress, was surprised
to receive a cheque, blank except for the royal signature.[15]
Obviously all was not well with the King, and his household
unobtrusively got ready for whatever might befall. Kew House
was prepared, with singular inefficiency, in case it should be
needed as a sanatorium. At Windsor perfect quiet was ordered,
and church bells were silenced. The equerries were reinforced;
three gentleman-porters were posted at the entrance-gate and
four sergeant-porters at the park gate to turn away inquirers.
The doors leading from the King's suite, of solid mahogany,
were strengthened; and the royal family were moved into one
wing of the castle which was cleared of outsiders, except for the
equerries and those of the staff who might be needed in an
emergency. Arrangements were made for food and hot drink to
be available at any time for the pages and others who had to
attend His Majesty's person; and camp-beds were placed in the
ante-room for those off duty.[16]

In public, the Court put as good a face on it as possible, to
check the rumours which were being diligently spread through
well-informed circles. There was much anxiety about the Levee,
arranged for the 24th. Should the King go, or not? If he went,
how would he behave? If not, how could his absence be
plausibly explained? The little Princess Augusta wrote to Sir
George:

I am ordered by Mama to desire if you find it necessary to prevent
the King's going to town tomorrow, that you would advise His
Majesty to remain at Kew until he is better. 'Tis not her partiality
for this place that makes her wish for it, but your being nearer to
us in case anything should happen again that we might have your

advice immediately. Mama desires you would express it *not* as hers, but as a wish of your own.[17]

Sir George advised the King to remain at home: but, in a singularly ill-timed transaction, he happened at this moment to sell £18,000 worth of stocks 'to take advantage of a favourable mortgage'. The spectacle of the King's physician apparently unloading stock at this time started a panic among holders of gilt-edged. In great distress Baker hurried to Kew to confess his error, informing the King that the funds had consequently fallen ten per cent. His Majesty, though languid and uneasy at the prospect, felt obliged to attend the Levee in order (he told Mr Pitt) 'to stop further lies and any fall in the stocks'.[18]

This brave effort had exactly the opposite effect. His clothes 'exhibited strong proofs of absence or oblivion', and the Chancellor had privately to advise His Majesty to retire to the Closet to adjust his dress. No one could fail to notice his agitation as he harangued Lord Thurlow: 'You, too, my lord, forsake me and suppose me ill beyond recovery. But, whatever you and Mr Pitt may think and feel, I, that am born a gentleman, shall never lay my head on my last pillow in peace and quiet so long as I remember the loss of the American colonies.'[19]

The King was unaware that he had shown anything worse than bodily stiffness, and next day promised to 'desire Sir George Baker to call in at Downing Street that Mr Pitt may know exactly how Sir George found me. . . . I am certainly stiff and weak, but no wonder. I am certain air and relaxation are the best restoratives.'[20]

Next day, after a good breakfast, he left Kew for Windsor. Elated at the prospect of moving into his favourite residence, he commanded Sir George not to attend him there until summoned. On arrival he was rather over-excited, but calmed down in the afternoon, visited the stables, dined with his family and attended a private concert in the evening.[21]

On Sunday, the 26th, in the middle of matins, he 'frantically embraced his wife and daughters'. 'You know what it is to be nervous', he exclaimed, 'but was you ever as bad as this?'*

* The story is of doubtful authenticity. According to Fanny Burney, he was persuaded not to attend Chapel that day.

Next day, at another Handel concert, he laid his hand on the conductor's shoulder and said, 'I feel, sir, I shall not long be able to hear music. It seems to affect my head, and it is with difficulty that I bear it. Alas! The best of us are but frail mortals.' Such, at least, was the fashionable gossip: but Sir George, keeping in close touch with the Palace, 'was not informed that either in the course of this, or the preceding day, any other observation was made concerning him than that his spirits were uncommonly agitated and that he talked with more than usual rapidity and vehemence'.[22]

Miss Burney met him outside the Queen's room. He went on about his health for nearly half an hour, talking hurriedly and continuously as though in fever. 'I *never* sleep, not one minute, all night!' He begged the Queen a hundred times not to speak when she was in his room: but, far from needing this advice, the distraught woman uttered hardly a syllable. In his inconceivable agitation, he was still pathetically anxious not to give trouble to others.[23]

This morning, [wrote Sir George on the 27th] he took an airing in the chaise. His great hurry of spirits and incessant loquacity continuing now gave great uneasiness to the Queen; and Her Majesty sent me a private order to go to Windsor this evening; to say nothing to the King on the subject of physic, but to inform Col. Goldsworthy [an Equerry] of my opinion. When I arrived the King was at the concert. He at first seemed much disconcerted at my attending him without orders, but was very soon satisfied, having conjectured that I had acted under the Queen's direction. During the whole music he talked continually, making frequent and sudden transitions from one subject to another; but I observed no incoherence in what he said, nor any mark of false perception. His sleep and appetite had been natural. His pulse in a room much heated with company, fire and candles was only at 84. He was lame, and complained of rheumatic pain and weakness in the knee, and was sitting and rising continually.

Tuesday, 28 Oct. He had slept quietly, his pulse at 72. The agitation of his spirits and inordinate flow of words continued almost as yesterday; and it was with some difficulty that I could prevail upon him not to go to the Levee the next day, but to be contented with seeing the Ministers at Windsor. This morning he visited a family in the neighbourhood, with whom he stayed two hours and half. I have authority to say that, during his visit, no one of the family observed anything extraordinary in His Majesty's look or manner. The conversation turned on the wars in Germany; and the King showed great curiosity on the subject, and appeared much amused.[24]

The King's stiffness, his hoarse voice and incessant volubility alarmed all about him. He complained of a heaviness in the head; but on the 29th, in search of 'air and relaxation, the best restoratives', he rode for five hours, received Mr Pitt and ate with a good appetite. He now complained to Sir George (whose medical advice he had not followed) that his vision was confused by mist floating before his eyes whenever he tried to read. He also mentioned, 'as a cause of great distress, that having in the morning selected a certain prayer, he found himself repeating a prayer he had not proposed to make use of'.[25]

For the next two days there was no great change in the King's condition. Despite his complaints of insomnia, Baker's diary shows that his sleep was continuous, though unquiet. He was observed to be rather childish and trifling in his actions, and endlessly loquacious. On 1 November he insisted on hunting, though he walked like a man with gout and his voice was so hoarse it was painful to hear.

'My dear Effie!' he cried, meeting Lady Effingham for the first time for some weeks, 'you see me, all at once, an old man.'

'We must all grow old, sir', she replied with admirable composure. 'I'm sure I do.'

He showed her a walking-stick. 'I can't get on without it, Effie, my strength diminishes daily. . . . I take the bark, but the Queen', he cried, 'is my physician, and no man need have a better. She is my *friend*, and no man *can* have a better.'

As for the Queen, she was in a terrible state, and often in tears. 'How nervous I am!' she exclaimed. 'I'm quite a fool! Don't you think so?'

'No, ma'am', was all Miss Burney dared reply.[26]

Up to this date, the Court had contrived to conceal their fears. Three days after the disastrous Levee Sir Gilbert Elliott, an ardent Opposition MP, thought 'the King is certainly in a bad state of health, but I fancy nothing material. They make a great mystery about it.' On 29 October, Burke told Elliott that the King 'had been in extreme danger from his late illness . . . violent spasms in the stomach . . . speechless for one and a half hours'. Burke never heard distinctly what the complaint was for which he had to go to Cheltenham, 'a great mystery and secrecy having been observed'.[27]

It was thought right to summon the Prince of Wales from Brighton, whither the royal patronage had brought 'all the gayest and prettiest women of a certain class to market on the Steyne'. With him came the Comptroller to his Household, Captain Jack Payne, a naval officer whose gallantry in action was overshadowed by social and financial irregularities so glaring that, though proposed by the Prince himself, he had been blackballed for Brooks's. The Duke of York also came, released from his military to perform his filial duties; though not with the happiest results, for his suggestion that the Guards bands be equipped with Turkish musical instruments and embellished with Turkish horsetails and crescents had the worst effect on his father.[28]

On 4 November Elliott had some more colourful detail, but still did not suspect the truth:

> After the Levee he returned to Kew, where the Queen wished him to take something cordial; but Georgy Boy liked his own way best, and ate a pear* and drank a glass of cold water. . . . A violent thing in the stomach rendered him speechless and *all but*. . . . The Queen ran out in great alarm in her shift or very little clothes among the pages and sent for an apothecary. . . . The King was kicking one heel against the other which, though swelled, was soft and yielding to the kick. 'If it was the gout, how could I kick this without any pain?'†

His Majesty had, Sir Gilbert heard, 'a dropsical swelling'.[29]

---

* Sir Gilbert at least got one fact partly right, though the date quite wrong. See p. 13.

† Compare this with Sir George Baker's account of the day after the Levee, when the King left Kew for Windsor. See p. 18.

The King would still not admit that there was much wrong, writing on 3 November:

> The King thinks it must give Mr Pitt pleasure to receive a line from him. This will convince him that the King can sign warrants without inconvenience; therefore he desires that any that are ready may be sent. . . . He attempts reading the despatches daily, but as yet without success. But he eats well, sleeps well, and is not in the least fatigued with riding, though he cannot yet stand well and is fatigued if he walks. Having gained so much, the rest will follow.[30]

Sir George Baker, however, thought otherwise, and was right, for this was the last letter from the King to Mr Pitt for many weeks. On that day, Sir George brought a colleague, Dr Heberden, to see the King, 'which I had in the course of the past week often in vain solicited'. The doctors were told that the King had that morning 'given great pain to his attendants by his very incautious manner of riding'.[31]

It has been stated by various historians that on that day, 3 November, the Duke of York called in to inquire after the King's health. ('So good is Frederick!' exclaimed the fond father.) After his ride, the King is said to have burst into tears and sobbed out to his favourite son that he wished to God he might die, for he was going mad. The story must be accepted with reserve, for its source, Captain Payne, is thoroughly muddied.* But something of the sort may have happened, for Baker records that day, 'It was now too evident that his mind was greatly disturbed. All the marks of it before mentioned appeared with aggravation.'[32]

On the 4th His Majesty was all smiling benignity; but he gave so many contradictory orders to the postilions, got in and out of his carriage so many times, that the Queen was not in the least reassured. In the evening fearful rumours circulated through the Palace that the King had seized the Prince of Wales by the throat, thrust him to the wall and demanded in a hoarse whisper, 'Who will dare say to the King of England that he may not speak, or prevent him whispering?' The Prince

* See pp. 65–8.

22

nearly fainted, and had to be revived by rubbing Hungary water on his temples and by bleeding. The Queen had hysterics and, for the first time in their married life, slept apart from her husband.[33]

The secret could no longer be kept, for the Prince of Wales and the Duke of York were two of the most zealous members of the Opposition to their father's government. As soon as word got round of what had happened, every politician realized that here was a major political crisis.

To explain why this should be so, a digression is necessary into the political conditions of the time, and the history of the previous seven years.

CHAPTER II

The Political Scene

In the English Constitution it was the King who governed the country. He did so with the aid of Ministers whom he generally consulted individually in his Closet, treating them rather as Heads of Departments, and discussing with each Minister only his own subject. That, at least, was his intention, modified by George III's inability to stick to one subject at a time, and by the Ministers' habit of concerting their opinions while waiting in the ante-room, at country-house parties and at meetings of the 'efficient' Cabinet at which the King was not normally present.[1]

The King had a right to demand his Cabinet's advice on any subject, though it was doubtful if he was obliged to do so. At the beginning of his reign, his Ministers tendered advice only on matters which he referred to them. But by 1782 they were claiming the right to give advice unasked. The King did not like it: 'The Minister of the Department', he protested, 'always used to ask permission of the King to lay such a point before the Cabinet . . . then the advice came with propriety. . . . Certainly it is quite new for business to be laid before the Cabinet and consequently advice offered by the Ministers of the Crown unasked.'[2] However, by 1788 the Ministers had pretty well made good this claim.

That the King was constitutionally bound to take the advice so offered was even less certain. Burke in his *Thoughts on the Causes of the Present Discontent* might maintain, in conveniently imprecise terms, that the King's powers should 'be exercised on public principles and national grounds, and not on the likings or prejudices, the intrigues or the policies, of a Court'.[3] But it is doubtful whether any Hanoverian king would specifically have pledged himself always to be guided by his Ministers. The question is, however, an academic one: for George III, while

24

never conceding the principle, did, in fact, always take his Ministers' advice except on semi-domestic matters such as the Prince of Wales's allowance, and on the details of patronage and regimental promotions.

From this it might seem that the King was merely the instrument of his Ministers: but his strength lay in the fact that he (and this applies equally to the first three Hanoverian kings) made the Ministers. So long as he did not make an outrageous choice, he was universally admitted to be constitutionally able to choose anyone he wished. Henry Fox maintained that 'The House of Commons has a right to accuse a Minister and make it very inadvisable for a prince to retain him in his favour. But I do not remember that they ever undertook to say who should succeed him.'[4] This was the orthodox view, accepted by almost every eighteenth-century politician. The doctrine that the King must entrust the government to the party leader who can command a majority in the House of Commons is a product of the nineteenth century. It is irrelevant to conditions in the eighteenth century, when the King was expected to provide his Ministers with the majority necessary for them to conduct his government. How this was done is discussed later in this chapter.

The King not merely made the Ministers, but subjected them to constant, nagging supervision. He found it far more difficult to delegate a job than to do it himself: having delegated, he interfered. The volume of his official correspondence was formidable; and it was supplemented by discussion on endless departmental details. His Majesty never rested, never took a holiday from what he felt to be his duty; and worked himself far harder than he worked his Ministers.

There was a general opinion, surviving from the political struggles with the Stuarts, that the main, indeed the sole, function of Parliament was to prevent the despotic use of the Crown's powers.[5]

For two reasons, the House of Lords played but a minor part in this spoiling game. Firstly, the Crown patronage could there be employed to the best effect, for the Lords of the Bedchamber and the Scottish peers were notoriously venal, and the Bishops were seldom so imprudent as to 'forget their maker'. Secondly, the great majority of peers, who seldom attended Parliament, could always be rallied to the King's support if they felt his honour or vital interests to be at stake.

Traditionally the main check to the Crown was provided by the House of Commons; but its efficacy was limited by its composition and by the methods of election. The 1761 House of Commons contained (among its 558 Members) 204 paid directly by the Crown. A list of placemen in the House (including Ministers, Civil Servants, naval and military officers, Court officials, Government contractors and holders of miscellaneous sinecures) for 1774 shows 173 names.*[6]

It should not be assumed that eighteenth-century politicians were unduly venal. Politicians must live; and these, unlike their modern counterparts, had no Members' salaries, no company directorships nor trade-union emoluments. The main difference between politicians of the eighteenth century and those of today is not that the former were paid for their services, but that many were paid *by the Crown*.

MPs were divided by the most expert parliamentary manager of his day into five categories:[7]

Members for English counties	80
Members for English open boroughs	232
Members for English close boroughs (i.e. pocket boroughs)	177
Members for Welsh seats	24
Members for Scottish seats	45

Of these, 254 English and Welsh Members each represented an average of 23 voters; the Scottish Members represented an average of 49 voters. Detailed calculations show that 106 borough-mongers, of whom 51 were peers, nominated 192 members; and the Administration nominated 32 more.[8]

Generally, ambitious politicians liked to sit for close boroughs, because whenever an MP was appointed to any 'job' under the Crown, he had to stand for re-election—an expensive business

* The 1761 list includes ten holders of Secret Service pensions, which are not included in the 1774 list. Nevertheless there is an apparent overall reduction in parliamentary placemen and pensioners over the very period when, according to orthodox Whig history, George III was industriously multiplying parliamentary corruption.

in a county or open borough for a careerist who hoped for promotion or a new appointment every two or three years. So many members of the Lower House were related to peers, that Pitt called the Commons 'a parcel of younger brothers'.[9]

Figures now available confute the Whig historians' stories of control by crude bribery. The expenditure of money from the Secret Service and Special Service funds, and the Civil List, shows no general increase during the reign of George III; and its total is surprisingly moderate.[10] Parliamentary control was exercised not by bribes, but by patronage.

Pressure could be applied in two ways: directly on the placemen, pensioners, and Members for boroughs controlled by the Admiralty and other Government departments; indirectly through the borough-mongers who expected to be supplied, not only for themselves, but for their friends, relatives and dependants, with regiments and bishoprics, colonial governments and Court sinecures, Government contracts and innumerable petty jobs as postmasters, riding-officers, tide-waiters, surveyors.

Many borough-mongers steadily supported the Opposition; but the majority could be induced, by 'civility', 'bustle', 'management' or, in a last resort, 'expense' to side with the Crown, whose resources of patronage were unrivalled.[11]

Besides the power of patronage, the King could count, in a real crisis, on a very large number of people, in and out of Parliament, who still had a vague feeling, lingering on from the previous century, that *any* formed and planned opposition to the King's Government was in some measure disloyal and dishonourable. Lord Mansfield, in the previous reign, 'would far rather not exist than join in this time factiously in opposition to the King, whomsoever he employs'.[12] The elder Pitt, disagreeing with George III on almost every issue, was nevertheless, said Burke, intoxicated by the least peep into the King's closet. This sentiment, except briefly in 1782, sustained George III throughout his reign.

Connected with this feeling in favour of *any* Ministry supported by the King, there was a strong preference, held equally by George III and by the country gentlemen, for coalitions, or 'broad-bottomed administrations', rather than party governments.

27

A contemporary analysis[13] of the House of Commons in May 1788 shows it as consisting of:

1.	Party of the Crown	185
	This party includes all those who would probably support His Majesty's Government under any Ministry not peculiarly unpopular.	
2.	Party attached to Mr Pitt	52
3.	Detached parties, supporting the present Administration	
	Dundas	10
	Lansdowne	9
	Lonsdale	9
	East Indians	15
4.	Independents or unconnected	108
5.	Opposition	
	Mr Fox	138
	Lord North	17
6.	Absentees and neutrals	14

Nothing can more clearly demonstrate the fatuity of reading the politics of the day in terms of political parties as they were understood in the reigns of George IV, or of Queen Anne. Nowhere in this list, nowhere in the full and detailed *Parliamentary Papers* of John Robinson (Secretary to the Treasurer and George III's most able political manager) are the terms 'Whig' and 'Tory' even mentioned. Gentlemen are described as 'steady friends', 'generally connected with the Administration', 'under the protection of the Duke', 'coming in on Lord Oxford's interest', 'good voters', 'more than hopeful', 'might be talked to', 'his attachment to Lord North made him vote for the Bill though averse to it'.[14] No great differences of principle distinguished the various 'parties', which were held together by personal attachment to a leader such as Charles Fox, by ties of friendship, by family and territorial connections, favours given and received—by all that the eighteenth century termed 'interest'.[15] Nineteenth-century historians give the impression that the reign of George III was a period of constant struggle between liberty-loving Whigs, and Tories who supported the royal prerogative. In fact almost all of George III's Ministers up to 1789—Bute, Grenville, Chatham, Townshend, Grafton, Sandwich, North, Pitt—called themselves Whigs. The General Warrant of 1763 was issued by Whigs; Wilkes was exiled, imprisoned and forbidden his seat in Parliament by Whigs; the American War was provoked, bungled and lost by Whigs. The expression 'Whig' was applied, generally by themselves, to half a dozen parliamentary groups whose divergent policies were purely empirical, who vaguely professed a 'love of Liberty', an 'attachment to the principles of the Revolution'.

The Tories were an even more nebulous body. They were no longer in sympathy with Jacobitism; but they could hardly look back with pride on the part they had played in the Glorious Revolution because, basing their creed on devotion to Church and King, they had in 1689, in order to save their Church, assisted in the expulsion of their King. So far as they can be defined at all, they were simply a section of the landed gentry who wished to see a respectable government carried on with economy. Their behaviour on specific issues was quite unpredictable: Boswell, a Tory, was opposed to the American War; in the King's prolonged feud with Wilkes, more than half the Tory MPs voted for the Radical, atheist libertine; and the organizers of the Petitioning Movement, nourished mainly on the grievances of Mr Wilkes, found most of the younger Yorkshire Tories 'very hot for petitioning'.[16]

With no party system to check the power of the Crown, was this power supreme, unchallenged? No. 'The trees do not grow up to the sky.' The Crown's system of parliamentary management carried within itself the seeds of its own defeat. No Hanoverian King could fail to win for his Prime Minister an election: his troubles began later, when he had to satisfy the claims of his 'steady friends', 'to find pasture enough for the beasts that must be fed'. Disappointed politicians, failing to get 'places' from the King's Ministers, flocked to pay tribute to the King's heir, to obtain places 'in reversion', i.e. on his succession to the throne. 'Everyone', said Walpole, 'comes to Court to *get*, and if there is nothing to be got at present, it is natural to look for reversions.'[17]

Collecting around him these disgruntled groups, each Hanoverian Prince of Wales became in turn the leader of the Opposition. As the King grew older or iller, reversions became more sought after, the stream of desertions to the Opposition increased until the weakened government was forced to buy back some of the deserters and a coalition was formed.

This process was repeated time and again in the eighteenth century. It was well understood by all its practitioners, and worked tolerably well so long as there was an old or ailing King and a young, healthy heir. But when in 1760 George II died, the startled political world was confronted with a novel situation— a young, healthy King and for an heir his unamiable uncle, 'Butcher Cumberland'. 'There is now', Lord Hardwicke sounded the alarm, '*no reversionary resource*'. Burke made the same point: 'Coming to the throne in the prime and full vigour of youth, as from affection there was a strong dislike, so from dread there seemed to be a general averseness from giving anything like offence to a Monarch against whose resentment opposition could not look for a refuge in any sort of reversionary hope.'[18]

It is this lack of a reversionary factor, far more than his own alleged leaning to despotism and the growth of political corruption, that inflated the power of the King during the first twenty years of his reign. The Opposition, deprived of their only effective counter to the Executive, were helpless. But from about 1780 onwards, with the King now middle-aged and the Prince of Wales an adult, active and unscrupulous Opposition leader, something like the traditional pattern of eighteenth-century politics reasserted itself.

The political game was not quite as it had been in the days of George II, Henry Fox and the Duke of Newcastle: the American War divided in passionate disagreement those who instinctively sided with authority against those whose instinct was for opposition. For a few years questions of principle positively intruded into English politics, producing temporarily a semblance to a two-party system, but with Whigs on both sides. When the war was over, however, no difference of principle divided Mr Pitt's Ministerial Whigs from Charles Fox's Opposition Whigs; and for a few years—until the French Revolution gave meaning to the expressions Whig and Tory—the politics of the eighteenth century enjoyed a brilliant autumnal flowering. The expressions 'reversion' and 'reversionary factor', so commonly employed by the previous generation, seem to have dropped out of use: but the situation and political tactics were as they had been thirty, forty, fifty years ago, with the reversionary factor dominant at the onset of the royal malady.

CHAPTER III

The King, Mr Fox and Mr Pitt

News of the surrender of Yorktown reached London on 25 November 1781. The Prime Minister, Lord North, took it like 'a bullet through the breast'. 'Oh God,' he moaned, "'tis all over!'—as well he might, for this defeat ended not only a war, but a political epoch. For twenty years the King, unhampered by reversionary opposition, had contrived to keep in office Ministers entirely of his own choice. Now, with the revival of the reversionary factor* and with party passions aroused by a disastrous war, George III's system was shattered. Seventeen months' intricate manoeuvring between rival Whig factions produced a coalition government, owing allegiance to the Prince of Wales, every member of which the King detested.[1]

The Coalition was a partnership between the popularity, fire and genius of Charles Fox, and the votes controlled by Lord North. It was a marriage of convenience, inspired by pure opportunism. Fox required North's 120 votes in the Commons; and North, after a year and a half out of office, needed fresh injections of patronage to keep his wilting party alive.

For years Fox's favourite theme had been Lord North's corruption, Lord North's duplicity, incompetence, treachery, fraud. He had threatened Lord North with the scaffold, described him as 'a lump of deformity and disease, of folly and wickedness, of ignorance and temerity . . . it being hardly conceivable that so much pride, vice and folly could continue to exist in the same animal'. He had opposed a pension for Lord North, who had 'ruined his country'; and declared that, should he ever make terms with a 'Minister void of every principle of honour and honesty, he would rest satisfied to be called the most infamous of mankind'. With such insults fresh in the

* The Prince of Wales was a precocious nineteen.

memory of every gentleman in Parliament, it might be thought that the prospects of a smooth-running partnership were remote.[2]

North, however, was 'irreconcileable to no man'. He would never initiate a policy, but could follow competently one devised by a stronger character. For twelve years he had followed his sovereign's lead from one disaster to another, begging all the time to be released from an onerous duty; now he was content to take a lead from Charles Fox.

He had intelligence of a high order; and was a first-class House of Commons man, meeting violent attacks with placid good-humour or a wry, self-deprecatory aside that convulsed the House. But his sloth, his complacency, the tears to which he was often reduced, made him a target that no hostile orator could resist. One of these, in a passionate harangue, fumed at the spectacle of the Prime Minister apparently asleep on the Front Bench. Lord North opened one bulging, gummy eye. 'I wish to God I was', he murmured, and closed it again. After another debate, in which Fox had flayed North's colleagues, 'Boreas'* cheerfully remarked, 'Charles, I'm glad you didn't fall on me today, for you was in full feather.'[3]

As for Charles Fox, it was not (he himself said) in his nature to bear malice or ill-will, 'my friendships are eternal, my enmities not so.' In or out of office, he was by far the most popular man in politics and, except in one of his rare sulks, the most lovable, 'Charles' to everyone from the Prince downwards.

Now aged thirty-four, swarthy and Hebraic in feature, he was ludicrously fat but capable, when he wished, of tremendous physical effort. A few years before, he had been a famous macaroni, dressed (on credit) to the nines.

> But Hark! The voice of battle shouts from far!
> The Jews and macaronis are at war.
> The Jews prevail, and thundering from the stocks,
> They seize, they bind, they circumcise Charles Fox!

But now he affected the most careless attire, dirty and negligent, generally in his party's colours, buff and blue, the colours of Washington's army.

* Boreas—The North Wind—was North's nickname.

He lived for the thrill of racing and, even more, of gaming. But his ill-fortune was proverbial and, in an age of high play, his losses were regarded as prodigious.

> In Brooks's of pigeons they say there are flocks,
> But the greatest of all is one Mr Fox.
> If he takes up a card or rattles a box,
> Away fly the guineas of this Mr Fox.
> He sits up all night, neither watches nor clocks
> Ever govern the movements of this Mr Fox.
> Such irregular conduct undoubtedly shocks
> All the friends and acquaintance of this Mr Fox,
> And they very much wish they could put in the stocks
> And make an example of this Mr Fox.
> Against tradesmen his door he prudently blocks,
> An aversion to duns has this Mr Fox.
> He's a great connoisseur in coats and in frocks,
> And the tailors are losers by this Mr Fox.
> He often goes hunting, though fat as an ox,
> I pity the horses of this Mr Fox;
> And certainly all must be lame in the hocks,
> Such a heavy-tailed fellow is this Mr Fox.

This picture, drawn some years before, still portrayed many aspects of his fascinating character; though *embonpoint* increasingly compelled him to substitute for hunting a few weeks every year of puffing, blowing, banging-off-in-all-directions partridge-shooting.

He was, unhappily, a sponger, whose friends were proud to provide for him. After one subscription raised on his behalf someone, anxious lest he be offended, asked, 'How will Charles take it?' 'Take it?' replied George Selwyn. 'Why, quarterly, to be sure.'

But one of Fox's bond creditors, warned that debts of honour must have priority, at once tore up his bond. 'Now, Sir', he said, 'it is a debt of honour.' Such was his trust in Charles Fox's integrity.

Fox would walk barefoot over broken glass to help a friend—or even an enemy in distress, with the sole exception of George

34

III, against whom his rancour was implacable. Above all, he had matchless charm. Asked by a Frenchman how the English nation could submit to the rule of such a roué, Pitt at once replied, 'Ah, you have never been under the wand of the magician!'

He was a lover of women but not, as a rake, in the same class as Wilkes, or the Prince of Wales. Nor was he incapable of Platonic friendship with beautiful women: he adored, and was adored by, the great political hostesses, the Duchess of Devonshire and Mrs Crewe; but no whisper of scandal touched their relationship.

By nature slapdash and idle beyond words, when in office he forced himself to be industrious and accurate, even to the point of taking writing lessons. He was a master of impromptu oratory. Although his speeches were ill-prepared, or not prepared at all, although their logic was often doubtful and their construction faulty, his well-known voice, rising to 'a shrill, energetic squeak', pouring out a torrent of violent (but never malicious) invective, wit and generous wisdom, always held the House entranced.

George III gave a hostile, but shrewd and not unfair judgement of Fox. 'He is a man of great parts, quickness and eloquence; but he lacks application, and consequently the fundamental knowledge necessary for business; and above all, he is totally deficient in discretion and sound judgement.'[4]

The titular head of the Coalition was neither of these able men, but the Duke of Portland, ornament of an august house traditionally devoted to 'the principles of the Revolution'. His elevation to office had reminded George Selwyn of the Puritan tract, 'A Shove to a Heavy-breeched Christian'. Horace Walpole calculated that, before this, hardly a hundred men in England knew he existed; and deprecated not so much the claim of a few great families to the exclusive right of giving their country a head, as their insistence that it be a head without a tongue.[5]

The Duke was, indeed, 'a fit block to hang Whigs on'; and his Chancellor of the Exchequer, Lord John Cavendish, the indispensable representative of another great Whig house, was scarcely more intellectually gifted; but no Ministry which in-

35

cluded Fox, Burke and Sheridan could be said to lack ability. Burke held only the minor office of Secretary to the Navy, but his influence in the party's counsels was immense. Sheridan was found a place on the pay-roll as Secretary to the Treasury, though his real job was liaison with the Prince of Wales.

His Royal Highness was a poor advertisement for old-fashioned methods of bringing up children. Through boyhood and youth he had been ruthlessly educated, disciplined, lectured, moralized at and subjected to the dreadful tedium of his father's Court. When he or his brothers transgressed any of the innumerable rules laid down for them, they were held up by the arms and whipped like dogs—a chastisement which their father, the kindliest of men, felt it his duty to superintend. The flogging was no more severe than any of his contemporaries suffered at Eton or Westminster; but the boredom of Windsor and Kew was insufferable: and as soon as he escaped from it, the Prince plunged with zest into the pleasures of London.

He was handsome and well-proportioned; but displayed a flaccidity of muscle and a rotundity of outline unbecoming a Prince Charming. His pink and white complexion and mass of fair hair added to his slightly feminine appearance, as did his liberal use of scent and cosmetics. His manners were captivating, and he was excellent company; he had a passion for music, a true appreciation for art, and a talent for mimicry and anecdote to which his father's eccentricities gave ample scope. He danced well and rode adequately, without sharing his father's passion for horses and hunting. No member of his family could lack native courage; but his was not kept in trim, like his father's, by a Spartan and active life.

Inevitably he displayed a precocious interest in feminine frailty, and his amours were conducted with neither inhibition nor discretion. At eighteen, complained his father, he 'got into an improper connection with an actress and woman of in-different character*, through the friendly assistance of Lord Malden. He sent her letters and very foolish promises', the return of which cost the King £5,000. At twenty, he acknow-ledged two illegitimate children.

* Perdita Robinson, an actress of beauty, charm and a variety of accomplishments.

He could hold his own in any drinking bout, and treated his excruciating hangovers by profuse blood-letting, often opening the vein himself.[6]

As heir to the throne, he had naturally assumed the leadership of Charles Fox's party when they were in opposition and clustered round him like wasps on honey; they were constantly at Carlton House, and he at Brooks's.

His tastes were expensive and since, by a happy coincidence, his dear Charles had attained office just as he attained the age of twenty-one, he expected to be provided with the means of gratifying them. By a clumsy and discourteous oversight, nobody consulted the King, until Portland calmly suggested that, while Parliament provide £50,000, the King make the Prince's income up to £100,000 from his Civil List which had already been lopped by Burke's Œconomical Reform Bill. His Majesty 'could not find words expressive of his utter indignation at these proposals to gratify the passions of an ill-advised young man', which only went to show 'how ill-founded are the principles of economy in those who have so loudly preached it up'. Eventually, however, rather than permit 'a shameful squandering of public money', he agreed to give £50,000 a year from the Civil List, to which he added, with a very bad grace, £12,000 a year from the Duchy of Cornwall. Parliament provided a lump sum of £60,000, half to clear Florizel's* princely debts, and half to set up his own establishment. With some difficulty the Prince was induced to accept this compromise and release Fox from more generous promises; but it rankled, and he made no effort to restrict his expenditure to a paltry £62,000 a year.[7]

The Ministry were confronted with tougher—though less recurrent—problems than the Prince's financial difficulties. Having obtained office by the agreeable process of pulling to pieces an unpopular peace treaty negotiated by the Earl of Shelburne, they were now confronted with the more exacting task of improving on it. It is not easy to win a peace after losing a war, and Fox's peace contained no discernible improvement on Shelburne's.[8]

By an extraordinary reversal of fortune, the Ministry's patron

---

* The Prince's current nickname.

was now the Prince of Wales; while the King made it clear that he greatly preferred the Opposition. At the Levee where the Coalition kissed hands for their places, 'the retiring ministers were overwhelmed with royal condescension, the incoming Administration treated with undisguised aversion' by a monarch who 'turned back his eyes and ears just like the horse at Astley's, when the tailor he was determined to throw was getting on him'. This determination, this aversion, were further displayed by a refusal to nourish his enemies, Fox complaining that the King gave them 'no peerages, no marks of support, but civility enough'.[9]

The Coalition included all who, since the retirement of Mr Wilkes from active politics, were most abhorrent to their royal master. For Portland's and Cavendish's modest abilities he had nothing but contempt. Lord North, whom he had loved since their boyhood, had not merely betrayed him, but had carried his political secrets over to the enemy. Sheridan was drunken, a playwright and the Prince's evil genius.

Burke, an Irishman equally devoid (in the King's opinion) of principles and of property, had set himself out to oppose every royal wish for fourteen years. Recently, for the sole and express purpose of emasculating the Crown's political power, he had enforced economies in the Privy Purse:

> the only fund from which I pay private bits of benevolence and every improvement to my gardens; nay, many articles of convenience for the Queen and myself. The grating clause that the Crown should be furnished for its table, household furniture, etc. by open contract as a hospital, I am certain must revolt every mind. Lord Shelburne has seemed very solicitous for my health, which undoubtedly is much interested in this business.[10]

Finally, there was Charles Fox, who seemed to have been created solely to plague his sovereign. As a young man, though profligate in a life which was far from private, and an incorrigible gambler, Fox had at least played a useful part in the campaign against Wilkes: he had even filled, very creditably, a junior ministerial post. But he had suddenly resigned, in protest against a measure on which the King felt his personal honour depended, the Royal Families Marriage Bill, described by this insolent young man, with infamous impertinence, as 'a measure giving the Princes of the Blood leave to lie with our wives, while forbidding them to marry our daughters'. Since then he had, the King considered, 'so thoroughly cast off every principle of honour and honesty that he had become as contemptible as he was odious'.

It was bad enough Fox being the heart and soul, to say nothing of the wit, of the King's enemies: far worse was his political seduction of the Prince of Wales, who looked for advice only to his dear Charles and daily attended the *lever* of this roué whose 'bristly black person and shagged breast quite open and rarely purified by any ablutions, was wrapped in a foul linen nightgown, his bushy hair dishevelled. In these cynic weeds and in epicurean good humour did he dictate his politics, and in this school did the heir to the Crown learn his lessons.' That had been written in the days when Fox and the Prince had been in opposition, when the Lord Chancellor had sworn there would be no peace until both were lodged in the Tower; now that they led the government, their association was even more lamentable. Not content with this, Fox had positively encouraged the Prince —who, heaven knows, needed no encouragement—in every indiscretion from faro to Perdita Robinson.

It is a pity that George III and Charles Fox hardly ever met, except when they could not help it. Had they seen more of one another, the royal abhorrence might have been softened by Fox's extraordinary kindliness and charm. He might even have taken a view of the Perdita affair more favourable to Fox who, when the princely ardour waned, had taken the little lady off Florizel's hands and helped negotiate the necessary financial arrangements.

If George III loathed Fox, the dislike was fully reciprocated. Blind to the King's endearing private virtues and to the better side of his 'firmness characteristic of an Englishman', Fox saw in the King only a dull, obstinate bigot, of whom he spoke with habitual insolence. Though in other directions no hater, Fox found it 'intolerable that it should be in the power of one block-head to do so much mischief'; compared this amiable man to Satan; wrote, on the very day he kissed hands on taking office,

39

'Certainly things look very well, but he [George III] will die soon, and that will be best of all.'[11]

Of the Opposition leaders, the Earl of Shelburne was in the wings, awaiting his call to the Treasury when the King could achieve Fox's defeat. His was a complex character. A man of commanding figure and insinuating address, he was an expert in foreign affairs and finance, a disciple of Adam Smith. He had taken the trouble to study the American question, instead of merely striking attitudes about it; and was convinced that, with firmness, liberality and proper handling, America could have been kept within the Empire. He was a very able man, but had one overwhelming drawback—no one trusted him a yard. He had acquired the reputation, not wholly deserved, of an intriguer, and the nickname of 'Malagrida',* after a Jesuit who was judicially strangled and burnt for plotting against the King of Portugal. Even the King, who rated him far higher than any of the Coalition, called him 'the Jesuit of Berkeley Square'.[12]

The nation at large greatly preferred the rival Opposition leader, William Pitt, son of the Great Commoner. So did George III, despite the dangerous radicalism of this young man, who positively wished to broaden the franchise.

Pitt was tall and thin, stiff in his carriage, aloof in his manner, a trifle pompous for his age. The harsh, rigid lines on his face, his pride which was probably the result of shyness, repelled friendship as much as Charles Fox attracted it. He had tried gaming at Goosetrees Club, playing earnestly without getting dipped, but had given it up. He had been put up by Fox for Brooks's, but seldom entered the place even while he was in political sympathy with its members. *'Pretty Girl Indifferentissimus'*, his chastity was a joke among the *ton*. He was fond of field sports, but became more and more reluctant to drag himself away from his work. He had little general conversation, and in everyday social life was apt to

> Pass muffins in Committee of Supply,
> And buttered toast amend by adding 'dry'.

* The nickname was the occasion for one of Goldsmith's celebrated *faux pas*: 'I cannot understand why they call Your Lordship Malagrida, for Malagrida was really a very good sort of man.'

But a group of friends, including Henry Dundas, a tough Scottish professional politician, and Wilberforce, an earnest young reformer, found him stimulating at small gatherings. He never resorted to dinners, house-parties and the social side of party management; but was an adept at borough-mongering, and knew all the tricks of the political trade.

It would be almost impossible to find anyone more unlike his rival, Fox; but lest he be thought to have no human weakness, it must be added that he was addicted to the bottle. He had a prodigious capacity for port, which he not infrequently exceeded. The *Chronicle* depicted him entering the House, *plenus Bacchi*, and mumbling to Dundas:

> 'I cannot see the Speaker, Hal, can you?'
> 'Not see the Speaker? Damme, I see two!'

Disdaining riches, he lived and died a poor man, surrounded by friends to whom he had given jobs worth hundreds of thousands of pounds.

His industry, his accuracy, his application were formidable; but he had served too short an apprenticeship ever to acquire the basic knowledge of government: to the end of his life he was weak on detail, and he never gained that understanding of foreign affairs which Fox picked up as though by instinct, in such time as he could spare from his friends, his faro and his women. But Pitt had a profound conviction of the excellence of his own policies and was, consequently, quite unscrupulous in advancing them.

It was as a party politician and orator that Pitt shone. His big voice and sounding periods, his command of language, the flawless construction, neat logic and careful preparation of his speeches made them the antitheses of Fox's; while his occasional fierce sarcasm reminded the House that he was the son and political heir of 'the terrible Cornet of Horse'. He was, said Burke, not a chip of the old block, but the old block itself. Usually his face was ugly; but when speaking he was, said Fox, far from ugly.

Having quoted a hostile, but not unfair, judgement on Fox, one must do likewise for Pitt.

41

Pert without fire, without experience sage,
Young with more art than Shelburne gleaned from age;
Too proud from pilfer'd greatness to descend,
Too humble not to call Dundas his friend,
In solemn dignity and sullen state
The new Octavius rises to debate. . . .
Above the rest, majestically great,
Behold the Infant Atlas of the State,
The matchless miracle of modern days
In whom Britannia to the world displays
A sight to make surrounding nations stare,
A kingdom trusted to a schoolboy's care.

With all his blind spots, failings and acerbities, Pitt had dauntless political courage. He will, after all, go down in history as 'the pilot who weathered the storm'.

His only experience in office had been in Shelburne's Administration when, for a few months at the age of twenty-three, he had shown outstanding ability as Chancellor of the Exchequer. He had then twice been pressed, implored, by the King to form his own Ministry; but with extraordinary prudence and cold-blooded calculation of the odds against him, he had declined these splendid offers. Now he was awaiting a third call to greatness.[13]

The rivalry between Fox and Pitt, the Idle and the Industrious Apprentice, stimulated every lampoon-writer and epigrammatist in the county.

On Folly every fool his talent tries;
It takes some toil to imitate the wise.
Though few like Fox can speak, like Pitt can think,
Yet all like Fox can game, like Pitt can drink.[14]

Although their feud was among the most dramatic in English history, on matters of principle they agreed more often than not. They both wanted a wide extension of the franchise to new classes of voters and new industrial centres; and they were both baulked in this ambition by the dead-weight opposition of the majority of their borough-mongering colleagues. If Fox seemed to wish to curb, more than Pitt, the power of the Crown, this was mainly because he detested George III who invariably used that power against him:* if Pitt fought and intrigued to preserve royal power, it was because, for most of his political life, it kept him in office. Their royal master observed, 'Mr Pitt is sometimes in the wrong, Mr Fox often is—but when they both agree, they are sure to be so—What? What?' It was, in contemporary terms, on men, not measures, that they differed.[15]

With the minimum of help from the King in 'finding pasture enough for the beasts that they must feed', the Coalition might well be worried about their majority. But there was one rich and ever-widening seam of patronage which neither the King nor his Ministry had yet tapped; and to this, in the autumn of 1783, Fox directed his attention.

The affairs of the Honourable East India Company cried out for reform. Basically the trouble was that a trading corporation whose object was to exploit the riches of the East was unable to govern well, and indeed unwilling to govern at all, an expanding empire. They had failed even in their primary object, to make money, and had to ask Parliament for a loan of £900,000. The servants of the Honourable Company, however—those that survived the ravages of malaria, dysentery and too much to drink in a steaming climate—returned as nabobs whose fantastic wealth was already unbalancing the well-tried system of borough management by the landed interests. It was notorious that these fortunes were won by peculation, corruption and gross oppression of the natives within a system by which dissipated youths of the meanest natural parts, illiterate in their own and totally ignorant of any Indian language, ruled, remote and unsupervised, over whole provinces peopled by millions.

Fox, advised by Burke who had made a special study of the subject, proposed to transfer the whole government of the Company's possessions, including the patronage, from the Directors and Proprietors to a Board of seven Commissioners, nominated by the Ministry, who were to hold office for four years. After four years, the Commissioners would be chosen by the King.

* Fox's attitude to the political powers of the Prince, as Regent, was to be very different.

To modern eyes the proposal seems sensible. Public boards appointed more or less in this manner are constantly being entrusted by Parliament with wide powers. But it is safer to be wrong than to be right a couple of generations too soon.

The King never intended the Coalition to remain in office one hour longer than he must. But to shake off their hated rule he needed an issue on which he could plausibly dismiss them; all preparations made for a general election; and a Prime Minister who, in the face of a hostile majority in the Commons, very ably led, would make it clear that he would stay in office until that election, and that waverers might safely come over to him. Pitt had proved that he was the man; Mr Robinson* had had time to assess the sentiments, and price, of every gentleman in Parliament; Fox's India Bill provided the occasion, and the angry nabobs the funds, for an election.

The proposal to take over all the powers of the Honourable Company sounded the alarm-bell to every trading corporation in the country; while control of the vast and ever-increasing Indian patronage would establish Fox and the Prince of Wales for four crucial years as rivals to the King. Fox's Bill, admirable in principle, united in clamorous protest the King's Friends with the trading interests, traditionally radical, of the City of London.

Certainly the Company's affairs needed reform, and perhaps Fox's main object was to reform them. But he was not so innocent as to be unaware of the fact, apparent to everyone else, that the India Bill would so establish his power that, in four years' time, the King could do little to upset it. With the slightly puzzled acquiescence of Lord North, Fox and Burke were playing for high stakes; which they made clear by nominating as Commissioners seven steady friends.[16]

Both sides realized it was a crucial issue. Fox described the Bill as 'a vigorous and hazardous measure, on which all depended'. 'The die', wrote his friend, Colonel Fitzpatrick, 'is cast, and the Administration is to stand or fall on the issue of this question.' But Pitt, at twenty-three a cold-blooded professional politician, was a better judge of the odds.

* Secretary to the Treasury, the King's superb parliamentary manager.

The Bill [he wrote to a friend in the House of Lords] will be, one way or another, decisive for or against the Coalition. It is, I think, the boldest and most unconstitutional measure ever attempted, transferring at one stroke, in spite of all charters and compacts, the immense patronage of the East to Charles Fox, in or out of office. I think it will with difficulty, if at all, find its way through our House, and can never succeed in yours. The Ministry trust all on this one die, and will probably fail.[17]

Despite the tide of public opinion flowing strongly against it, the Bill passed all three readings in the Commons. There remained only the formidable obstacles of the King and the Peers.

So abhorrent did the King find the Coalition that he often contemplated abdication and had even drafted his abdication speech. He does not, however, seem to have realized at first the significance of the India Bill. Certainly to the Ministers he gave no sign of disapproval: 'the royal disinclination to the Bill was never intimated through the whole of its progress, but every expression held out a contrary idea'.[18]

Lord Temple, however, on 1 December warned the King that the Bill

is a plan to take more than half the royal power, and thereby to disable Your Majesty for the rest of your reign. The refusing* of the Bill, if it passes the House, is a violent means. The changing of Ministers might be liable to the same sort of construction. An easier way of changing Your Majesty's government might be by taking some opportunity of doing it when it shall have received more discountenance than heretofore. This is expected to happen in the Lords in a greater degree than can be hoped for in the Commons. But a sufficient degree of it may not occur in the Lords if those whose duty to Your Majesty would excite them to appear are not acquainted with your wishes, and that in a manner which would make it impossible to pretend a doubt of it.[19]

In short, Temple proposed that the King should mobilize against the Bill the backwood peers and all those dependent on royal patronage.

* i.e. the use of the veto, which most people (including the King) agreed was now obsolete.

45

Meanwhile Richard Atkinson, who was about to be elected a Director of the Honourable Company, was busy in another direction. It was his task, with Mr Robinson, who as Secretary to the Treasury would have been more properly employed in advising his political masters rather than their enemies, to persuade Pitt that he could safely form a government and face a general election.

On 3 December Atkinson wrote to Robinson, 'Everything stands ready for the blow if only a Certain Person has the courage to strike it.' Mr Jenkinson, one of the King's most faithful friends, assured Robinson two days later, 'The King sees the Bill in all the horrors you and I do.' The Certain Person, after further consultation with, probably, Pitt, struck the blow on 11 December, between the first and second reading in the House of Lords, writing on a card, 'His Majesty authorised Lord Temple to say that whoever voted for the India Bill was not only not his friend, but would be considered by him as an enemy; and if these words were not strong enough, Lord Temple might use whatever words he might deem stronger and more to the purpose.' Well might Jenkinson claim, 'This is a bold measure, but things are in the hands of men of resolution.'

By the 15th, 'The town was full of rumour of a change in administration.' For the backwood peers and the country gentlemen were rallying as though the Royal Standard had just been raised at Nottingham. Fitzpatrick saw the danger signs. 'The bishops waver, and the Thanes* fly from us!' Boreas's mercenaries deserted him by dozens.[20]

All this was very gratifying to Mr Atkinson, who on the 15th had a secret meeting with Pitt, Dundas and Robinson. Robinson had undertaken to supply Pitt with an up-to-date appreciation of the support he might expect, before and after a general election, if he formed a Ministry. This estimate,† prepared during the previous week and submitted to Pitt on 15 December, warned him of a hostile majority of between fifty and seventy in the present House of Commons; but assured him, after a properly conducted general election, of a safe margin of at least

* The Earl of Bute, prototype of the King's Friend, was nicknamed 'The Thane'; and the name stuck to his successors.
† Summarized in the Appendix.

130—secured mainly by management of the close boroughs and Scottish seats.[21]

To this Mr Robinson added 'a wild wide calculate of money wanted for seats, but which I always disapproved and thought very wrong'.* Intricate and detailed calculations of the price of every seat indicated that £193,500 would be needed for the general election. This sum far exceeded the resources of the Crown†; but it was well within the capacity of the Company and its nabobs.[22]

In the House of Lords the Prince voted against his father. But 'His Majesty's name has been used', complained Eden, 'without reserve or scruple, among the Bishops, the Lords of the Bed-chamber, the Scottish peers and some individuals open to that species of application.' So the Lords threw out the India Bill. The King heard the news at a meet of his staghounds. 'Thank God!' he exclaimed. 'It's all over. So that's the end of Mr Fox!'[23]

The Ministers did not resign, but waited to be dismissed by a curt note from the King. 'Lord North is by this required to send me the seals of his Department, and to acquaint Mr Fox to send the seals of his Department. Mr Frazer or Mr Nepean [Under-Secretaries of State] will be the proper channel of delivering them to me this night. I choose this method as an audience on such occasions must be unpleasant.'

When Nepean called at the Secretary of State's house, Lord North was, characteristically, in bed. 'If you will see me,' he called through the bedroom door, 'you must see Lady North too.' He then handed Nepean the keys of the cabinet where he kept the seals, rolled over and went to sleep. Fox did not at first take his defeat so philosophically. 'We are beat', he complained, 'by such treachery on the part of the King, and meanness on the

* Why did Mr Robinson think this very wrong? Probably because it indicated the entry, for the first time on a large scale, of big commercial interests and open bribery into parliamentary management. In the past, management had been mainly by patronage and family interest, gentle-manly methods compared to those about to be employed by the Honourable East India Company.

† Whose combined Secret Service, Special Service and Civil List expend-iture at this time averaged under £100,000, very little of which was avail-able for political purposes.

47

part of his friends. . . .' Two days later, however, he had recovered his good humour and, seeing Dundas on the Opposition bench, took his arm and said, with his fat, genial smile, 'What business have you on this? Go over to the Treasury bench.'[24]

Nobody knew whom the King would choose to succeed as Prime Minister; but all doubts were resolved on 19 December by a bland motion in the Commons for 'a new writ for the Borough of Appleby, in the room of the Right Honourable William Pitt who, since his election, has accepted the office of First Lord of the Treasury and Chancellor of the Exchequer.'

There was a moment's astonished silence, then an explosion of laughter from the Opposition benches. None of the Coalition believed that the new Ministry could last long after Christmas. It would be a mere 'mince-pie Administration', meaning to 'gain a few days' time, in order to make a capitulation, if it can be obtained. They are considered as a set of children playing at Ministers, and must be sent back to school.' The Foxites determined to use their massive majority in the present Parliament to crush the Ministry before it could seek temporary safety in a dissolution. Lord North declared, 'There is not a man in the House who does not believe that a Dissolution is at hand.' Fox, in his best denunciatory form, said, 'No one would say that the prerogative of Dissolution ought to be exercised merely to suit the convenience of an ambitious young man. And I here declare, that if a Dissolution does take place, I shall move a very serious inquiry into it, and bring the advisers of it to account.'[25]

Pitt, however (against the advice of the King and most of his colleagues), had no intention of seeking a dissolution. He needed time for the disadvantages of impecunious opposition to impress themselves on the mercenary troops of Boreas—time to approach all those gentlemen who, Mr Robinson indicated, 'with civility and proper management could be made steady friends'. Above all, he needed time to convince the King, by his stubborn resistance to Fox's majority, that he was the only acceptable Prime Minister. (Shelburne was waiting impatiently in the wings.)

The next few weeks were occupied with bitter and brilliant

arguments about the King's action. Fox, in one of his best speeches, said:

> It is not a question of whether His Majesty shall avail himself of such advice as no one readily avows, but who is answerable for such advice. . . . How, Sir, are the Ministers situated on this ground? Do they not come into power with a halter about their necks, by which the most contemptible wretch in the Kingdom may despatch them at pleasure? Yes, they hold offices, not at the option of the Sovereign, but of the very reptiles [i.e. Temple] who burrow under the throne; they act the part of puppets, and are answerable for all the folly and the ignorance, and the temerity or timidity, of some unknown juggler behind the scene. Boys without judgement, without knowledge of the world or the amiable decencies of a sound mind, may follow the headlong course of ambition, and vault into the seat while the reins of government are placed in other hands. But the Ministers who can now bear to act such a dishonourable part, and the country that suffers it, shall be mutual plagues and curses to one another.

To this Lord North added, 'I will not say that a peer has not a right to advise the Crown; but the moment he gives that advice he ought to take the Seals and become a Minister, that power and responsibility may go hand in hand.'[26]

The Opposition's censure on Temple's intrusion was passed by 153 to 80, a cruel blow to Pitt's new Ministry which was further shaken by the immediate defection of Temple, who resigned in a huff at not being accorded, for his services, 'some mark of the King's approbation'—such as, for instance, a dukedom. 'The confusion of the enemy', Fox exulted, 'is beyond description, and the triumph of our friends proportionable.' Mr Gibbon assumed that 'Billy's painted galley must soon sink under Charles's black collier.' But Pitt showed the stubborn courage he was to display in desperate circumstances fifteen years later, and the King felt that 'to one on the edge of the precipice, every ray of hope is pleasing. I therefore place confidence in Mr Pitt bringing forward some names to fill an arrangement, which if they cannot, they already know my determination [i.e. to abdicate].'[27]

49

Reading the speeches and arguments bandied back and forth about the unorthodox use of the King's prerogative, one cannot but feel that Fox was right in describing the King's plot as treachery to his own Ministers. 'I would have minded less', said Fox, 'an honest veto.' But the landed gentry and the growing commercial interests, in whom political power resided, regarded the Coalition with such suspicion and hostility that they applauded the King for routing it without examining too closely his methods. Fox, with a safe majority in the Commons, had at his disposal one weapon to which, if it were used, Pitt had no reply: he could refuse Supplies. But Pitt's brother-in-law, Lord Mahon, an ex-Wilkite on the extreme left of Radical politics, assured Pitt, 'They will not stop Supplies. It is the very thing they will not venture to do.' Mahon was right. Fox dared not, in the face of public opinion, take this extreme step.[28]

Through the first three months of 1784 Pitt and Fox entertained and exasperated the political world by their brilliant bickering. Fox, by implication, denied the right of veto by saying the King could exercise it only by the advice of his Ministers, and that the confidence of the House of Commons was enough to keep a Minister in power regardless of the royal wishes. Pitt insisted that the choice of Ministers rested solely with the King, not with the House of Commons. The 'country gentlemen', the 'independents', hankering as always for an end to faction and some form of broad-bottomed Administration, urged Pitt and Fox to combine. But Fox was determined not to treat with Pitt until he resigned; and Pitt 'would not consent to march out with a halter about my neck, and meanly beg to be re-admitted and considered as a volunteer in the service of the enemy'.[29]

Fox staked everything on his majority in the Commons, composed 'in part of men who had led the country to loss and disgrace in the American War; and in part of men who had promised to bring them to punishment for that misconduct'. Early in the year his majority actually increased, and Pitt, for once despondent, told the King, 'Sir, I'm mortified to see that my perseverance has been of no avail, and I must resign at last.'

'If so', said the King, 'I must resign too.'

The King was in a state of extreme agitation, constantly harping on abdication if Fox vanquished him. 'If in the end they succeed, my line is a clear one, to which I hope I have fortitude enough to submit', he wrote on 13 February. On 4 February, before a crucial debate in the Second Chamber, he trusted that

> the House of Lords will this day feel that the hour is come for which the wisdom of our ancestors established this respectable corps in the State. For if the two only remaining privileges of the Crown are infringed—that of negativing Bills which have passed both Houses of Parliament, and that of naming the Ministers to be employed—I cannot but feel that I can no longer be of any utility to this country, nor can I with honour continue in this island.[30]

But gradually the Coalition's majority was eroded away, as more and more of North's mercenaries realized they were on the losing side. At the same time, any Administration in being always appealed to a large section of country gentlemen. 'My system', wrote one of them in January, 'was generally to support the government. It is in the interest of a country gentleman that it should not be embarrassed nor made expensive.' Scores of honourable gentlemen who, holding such views, had automatically supported Lord North in office, now as automatically transferred their support to Pitt.[31]

The King felt the wind shift in his favour, writing to Pitt on 15 February, 'The House of Lords by a not less majority than 2 to 1 have declared in my favour; and my subjects at large, in a very much more considerable proportion, are not less decided.'[32] Every kind of commercial corporation sent in loyal addresses, and it 'rained gold boxes' as Pitt was given the freedom of one city after another. On 28 February he was presented with the Freedom of the City of London, and a scandalous riot occurred as he and Mahon drove home past Brooks's.

> Ah, why Mahon's disastrous fate record?
> Alas, how fear can change the fiercest lord!
> See the sad sequel to the Grocers' treat;
> Behold him dashing up St James's Street,

51

Pelted and scared by Brooks's hellish sprites
And vainly fluttering round the door of White's.[33]

Fox, accused of fermenting the riot, triumphantly cleared his character. 'I was in bed', he proclaimed, 'with Mrs Armistead, who is ready to substantiate the fact on oath.'

Fox harried Pitt with one attack after another, but steadily the Coalition's majority dropped. In December it had been over seventy; by 8 March it had fallen to one. Pitt exulted at the enemy 'on their backs'.[34] On 25 March the King dissolved Parliament.

The General Election of 1784 has often been hailed as a triumph of enlightened public opinion, mobilized by the virtuous Pitt, over the old eighteenth-century gods of nepotism, corruption and patronage. There is, as in most historical truisms, some truth in this, for public opinion was probably more active at this election than ever before. The rise of the County Associations which were local political parties in embryo; the relatively free and full reporting of parliamentary debates; the improvements in newspaper production, all helped to form public opinion, were all steps towards a modern political system.

Other historians, fascinated by the mechanics of eighteenth-century politics as exhibited by Mr Robinson's papers, have insisted that the election was won entirely by Mr Robinson's methods. His political appreciation, prepared for Pitt in December 1783, was a wonderful *tour de force*. He examined the probable alignment of every member of the House of Commons, estimating who were steady friends—more than hopeful—might be talked to—may be got with expense—open to future events—will require great attention and management. Nowhere did Mr Robinson show the smallest interest in a gentleman's political principles, in his opinion on the India Bill or the Royal Prerogative or in whether he called himself Whig or Tory. He expected a drop in the Opposition vote of between 108 and 116. In the event, 'Fox's Martyrs' numbered 47 by defection* before

* Including Administration men, Under-Secretaries and such, who, regarding themselves rather as Permanent Civil Servants, automatically transferred their support from the outgoing to the incoming Administration, and were expected to do so.

the election, and about 74 by defeat during the election, a total of about 121*—very close to Mr Robinson's estimate. But the expert was not always right: in some close boroughs his calculations failed: in some counties and open boroughs Pitt picked up an unexpected bonus, from popular support. The election seems to have been won mainly by Mr Robinson; but he was certainly assisted by public opinion; and both factors were stimulated by the massive financial intervention of the East India Company and other interested corporations.[35]

Whatever its cause, Pitt's crushing victory established him in power for a generation. Many of Fox's closest friends were beaten; and Fox himself carried Westminster only with the aid of the Duchess of Devonshire. This celebrated and not over-virtuous beauty, somewhat larger than life—'She cannot', observed Miss Sheridan, 'be called fat, but on the whole I think there is too much of her'—'when arguments failed, descended to entreaties, when entreaties failed, resorted to osculation'. 'I could light my pipe at your eyes!' exclaimed an Irish labourer, favoured with a salute which the Duke might reasonably have regarded as his own prerogative.[36]

Despite their general discomfiture, the Opposition celebrated Fox's personal success by a dinner at Carlton House, whence they proceeded to Mrs Crewe's ball. It was the sort of occasion on which the Prince of Wales showed up at his best. 'Here's Buff and Blue, and Mrs Crewe!' he called, raising his glass not for the first time that evening. 'Here's Buff and Blue, and all of you!' their fair hostess most happily replied.

After the election, Fox spent more and more time with Mrs Armistead, enjoying the quiet country life which appealed to the lazy side of his nature. When, on a stifling day in the House someone suggested they would be better employed lying on a lawn with a book, Fox murmured, 'But why a book? Why a book?' For long periods he ceased even to attend Parliament, excusing himself somewhat unconvincingly to Portland, 'It is not by our interference that we have the best chance of making them sick of their folly.'[37] He realized that, without some singular blunder by Pitt and the King, there was no prospect of upsetting this Ministry; and, reverting to the traditional politics

* Not, as has often been stated, 160.

53

of the age, he based his hopes not on success in Parliament, but on the reversionary factor; not on his own exertions, but on a Regency or a new reign which, in view of the state of the King's health earlier in 1784, did not seem a bad bet. Pitt had been compared during the election to 'a lad which hath five barley loaves and two small fishes; but what are they among so many?' It was the familiar difficulty of eighteenth-century Administrations, and Fox exploited it in the familiar manner,[38] his policy and hopes reduced to dependence on the Prince of Wales and the reversionary factor.

> Though matters at present go cross in the realm,
> You will one day be King, Sir, and I at the helm:
> Then Thurlow and Pitt from their state we shall fling;
> They may go below stairs, Sir, so we are the thing.
> In vain are harangues, I as well may be dumb,
> And let motions alone till our day, Sir, is come.
> But time's on our side, Sir, and now on the wing
> To make me a statesman, and you, Sir, the King.

The next four years were years of political stagnation, with conditions similar in many respects to those of the time of Walpole and George II. With Pitt's quietly efficient, economical government, the King's popularity rose steadily. He lived down the odium attending his inefficient persecution of Wilkes; he lived down the failure of his American policy; and by 1788 he was sometimes laughed at, but generally loved by his people.

No major political differences separated the rivals, Pitt and Fox. They held similar views on franchise reform; they equally abominated the Slave Trade; they co-operated in the persecution of Warren Hastings. In such a situation, the reversionary factor dominated politics, and political interest centred on the relations between the King, Pitt, Fox and the Prince of Wales.

In February 1784, there 'was in the whole kingdom no more violent Foxite' than the Prince.[39] To the Foxites this was not a matter for unmixed satisfaction; for His Royal Highness's political friendship carried with it obligations regarding His Royal Highness's finances and amours. In particular, Florizel expected his friends, as a pressure-group in Parliament, to obtain funds sufficient to maintain him in a manner becoming the First Gentleman of Europe. The money squeezed from the King in 1783 fell far short of his princely requirements. Within two years, he was £160,000 in debt, and the bums were in Carlton House. The King asked for his full accounts, and could only suggest that the Prince set aside £10,000 a year to pay off his debts. 'How can I', the Prince appealed to his friends, 'when my expenses are twice my income?'

Desperately, the Prince announced the dramatic intention of disposing of his establishment and 'travelling abroad on a plan of economy'. To this the King refused his consent unless the Prince would agree first to marry.[40]

It was decided, in order to bring the Prince to his senses, to subject him to the persuasive diplomacy of Sir James Harris.

'If Your Royal Highness will give me leave, I will propose to Mr Pitt to increase to £100,000 on two conditions. The one, that you will set aside £50,000; the other, that you will cease to be a man of party, and reconcile yourself to the King.'

'No, Harris, Pitt would never carry such a proposal: the King would not hear of it. The King hates me. He would turn out Pitt for entertaining such an idea. Besides, I can't abandon Charles and my friends.'

Harris pressed his point, until the Prince exclaimed with some irritation, 'My dear Harris, will you force me to repeat, *the King hates me*. Take and read all our correspondence for the last six months.'

Sir James did so, and it was certainly an eye-opener in filial relationship: 'I am hurt to a degree, Sir, in what I have read. But the Queen must have a reconciliation at heart!'

'Look ye, Harris, I can't bring myself to say I'm in the wrong when I'm in the right. The King has used me ill. I wish the public knew what you know now.'

Harris was not so sure of this. 'I should be sorry, indeed, Sir, if this was known beyond these walls. For I am much mistaken if the public would not pronounce a judgement widely different from what you think.'

He then approached a somewhat more delicate matter. 'May I suggest, Sir, the idea of your marrying? It would be most agreeable to the King, and most grateful to the nation.'

55

'I'll never marry! My resolution is taken. I've settled it with Frederick.* No! I'll never marry!'

'You *must* marry, Sir. You owe it to the country, to the King and yourself.'

'I owe *nothing* to the King', retorted the Prince passionately. 'Frederick will marry, and the Crown will descend to his children.'

The prospect horrified this wily diplomat. 'Till you are married, Sir, and have children, you will have no solid hold on the affections of the people. If you come to the throne a bachelor, and His Royal Highness the Duke of York has sons to succeed him, your situation will be more painful than it is at the moment. Our history furnishes strong examples of the truth of what I have to say.'[41]

The Prince of Wales seemed impressed with this, but was not yet ready for matrimony as the price of being extricated by Parliament from his financial difficulties. He was violently (it would be inaccurate to attribute depth to His Royal Highness's affections) in love with a widow, Maria Fitzherbert.

This lady, rather older than the Prince, not very pretty, not very bright, was universally admitted to be formidably respectable and of an amiable sweetness of disposition. She was certainly not the type which usually stimulated the Prince's ardour; but Florizel was so infatuated with her that, unable to succeed *sans cérémonie*, he was beseeching her to marry him—secretly, for his marriage without the King's permission would be illegal; and since Mrs Fitzherbert was a Roman Catholic there was not the slightest prospect of that permission being obtained.

Fox was appalled by the probable results of the Prince marrying 'Mrs Fitz' and having children. 'Were I Mrs Fitzherbert's father or brother, I would advise her to prefer any other species of connection with you to one leading to so much misery and mischief.' Knowing his man, Charles Fox added, 'a mock marriage, for it can be no other, is neither honourable for any of the parties nor, with respect to Your Royal Highness, even safe.'

The Prince hastened to reassure his dear Charles, 'Make

* Duke of York, the next heir to the throne.

yourself easy, my dear friend, there not only is, but never was, any grounds for those reports which of late years have been so malevolently circulated.'

Four days later, on 21 January 1785, his importunity overcame Maria's prudence, but not her virtue; and, without mentioning the matter to Fox, he secretly married her.

It could hardly be expected that the matter would long remain a secret. Nor did it. At the end of April 1787, an Opposition Member moved in the Commons for an Address requesting the King to rescue his heir from a very distressed situation. Fox pressed the Prince's case, and Pitt hinted that he had certain information which, 'in view of his profound respect for the illustrious family concerned', made him deprecate any debate on His Royal Highness's private affairs. Mr Rolle, the Member for Devonshire whose principal contribution to debate was his technique of coughing down Burke's interminable harangues, said that the constitution was threatened, '*both in Church and State*'. The cat was out of the bag. Fox rose ponderously to deny 'a monstrous calumny, a low, malicious falsehood, destitute of all foundation'. When challenged by Rolle, Fox insisted that he denied it in point of fact, as well as in law, the thing never having happened in any way: he spoke, he said, with direct authority. Pitt improved the occasion by murmuring the words of Othello, 'Villain, be sure thou prove my love a whore.'

In order to placate his wife who would be displeased at an announcement that she was living in sin, the Prince said to her, 'Only conceive, Maria, what Fox did yesterday! He went down to the House and denied that you and I are man and wife!'

Mrs Fitzherbert was outraged at this public slur on her reputation;* and the Prince, understandably agitated, was obliged to confess the awkward truth and appeal to a junior satellite to extricate him from this scrape. 'Charles has certainly gone too far, and you, my dear Grey, shall explain it.' Mr Grey prudently declined.

'Then', said the Prince, 'if no one else will, Sheridan must.'

Sheridan treated the House to some vague compliments to

* Of which she was very careful, refusing to receive Lady Tyrconnel, the Duke of York's female friend, 'as a lady whose character is contaminate'.

the lady's character; and there the matter was allowed, offici-
ally, to rest. But Mrs Fitzherbert never forgave Fox; and Fox,
assured of the marriage by an actual witness of the ceremony,
would not speak to the Prince for a year.*

However, Fox and his friends managed to persuade Pitt that
it would not be a good thing for the Prince to go bankrupt or
abroad: the King, with a very bad grace, granted him from the
Civil List a further £10,000 a year, together with £160,000 to
pay his debts and £20,000 for improvements to Carlton House.

It is not, therefore, surprising that, in November 1788, knowledge of the distressing nature of the royal malady produced a
first-rate political crisis; for everyone in politics knew that the
Prince of Wales 'would take the first opportunity of calling into
power those to whom he was indebted for the parliamentary
management of his private affairs, and his emancipation from
that state of inconvenience and distress in which his own
imprudence had involved him'.[42]

* They seem, however, to have been on friendly corresponding terms,
e.g. in July 1787: 'My own expenses since I came of age have been £120,000
p.a. .... I beg you will not think of going to Newmarket till you have heard
again from me.'

CHAPTER IV

The Royal Patient at Windsor

With the arrival at Windsor of the Prince of Wales and Captain Payne, Comptroller of his Household, the secret was out. In the absence of Charles Fox, his mantle had been assumed by Sheridan; and to the playwright Jack Payne sent, every few hours, bulletins which, passed eagerly round Brooks's and Devonshire House, produced there an agreeable exhilaration as the Prince's friends saw power within their grasp and an end to the long, penurious years of opposition.

In a letter written probably on 5 November, at half-past ten at night, Payne reported:

> I arrived here about three quarters of an hour after Pitt had left. . . . Pitt desired the largest delay in the declaration of the present calamity. The Duke of York, who is looking over me, bids me add that His Majesty's situation is every moment becoming worse. His pulse is weaker and weaker; and the doctors say it is impossible he will survive it long, if his situation does not take some *extraordinary* change in the next few hours.

Sir George Baker wrote that day:

> Having had some quiet sleep, His Majesty this morning was more composed. His appetite was perfectly good at breakfast, and he conversed with his family cheerfully and with little inconsistency. His pulse in the morning at 74. After breakfast he [illegible] with the Princess Royal. In the evening I found his pulse as before, alienation of mind and much more agitated than he had ever been.* The pulse was very quick. but he was never so quiet as to allow me to take the strokes.

* There was a good reason for this. See p. 61.

59

With the excuse that Sir George Baker was on the verge of a nervous breakdown (though he seems in fact to have been perfectly calm), the Prince had called in Dr Warren, who had a lucrative practice mainly among the great Whig houses. He was a fashionable general practitioner, especially popular with female patients to whom 'he recommended himself by assuring them that their health depended greatly on their spirits: he therefore seldom objected to dissipation in winter, and often found the water-drinking places they best liked absolutely necessary for them in summer'. Immoderately devoted to the Opposition, he insisted on reporting to the Prince, not to the Queen, which added to her distress.

The King, however, refused to see him, saying, 'You may come here as an acquaintance, but not as my physician. No man can serve two masters. You are the Prince of Wales's physician—you cannot be mine.'

Warren had, therefore, to be planted where he could hear what went on, relying for more particular information on his colleagues. Until he could gain access to his patient, his observations had little clinical value; but politically they were, to the Opposition, beyond price.

'Dr Warren', continued Payne, 'adds to me, he will answer for the King's never living to be declared a lunatic.'[1]

The Queen was in an agony of anxiety at his eyes 'which she could compare to nothing but black-currant jelly. The veins in his face were swelled, the sound of his voice was dreadful. He often spoke till he was exhausted and, the moment he could recover his breath, began again, while the foam ran out of his mouth.'

For the distressing symptoms reported to him, the robust intelligence of Dr Warren had suggested the heroic remedy of blistering the King's shaven pate in order to draw the noxious substances from the brain to the skin surface. This excruciating operation the Opposition saw fit to celebrate in verse:

> If blisters to the head applied
> Some little sense bestow,
> What pity 'tis they were not tried
> Some twenty years ago.

The responsibility for this torture, inflicted on his patient with the best of motives, may be laid on Dr Warren because it was done on 4 November, the day after he took charge of the case; and there is no mention of it in the diary of Sir George Baker, whom he had superseded. It is probable that the consequent agony was the cause of many of the King's subsequent actions, and certainly of his insomnia.[2]

A day or two before Sheridan had, with uncharacteristic prudence, 'possessed Payne of any sentiments that it will greatly advance Your Royal Highness's credit that the language of those who may be suspected of knowing Your Royal Highness's wishes and feelings should be of great moderation in disclaiming all party views'. It was, perhaps, with this warning in mind that Payne added:

I need not add how necessary it is that neither my name nor those I use should be quoted, even to many of our best friends, whose repetition might frustrate views they do not see. . . . A few hours must terminate our suspense. His Royal Highness would write to you himself—the agitation he is in will not permit it. Since this letter was begun, all articulation even seems to be at an end with the poor King; but for the two hours preceding, he was in a most determined frenzy. I am myself in so violent a state of agitation, that if I am intelligible to you 'tis more than I am to myself.

On 6 November, his agitation unabated, Payne wrote again to Sheridan:

The King last night about 12 o'clock, being then in a situation he could not have survived, by the effect of James's Powder,* had a profuse stool, after which he fell into a profound sleep. He awoke with all the gestures and ravings of the most confirmed maniac, and a new noise in imitation of the howling of a dog. . . . His theme has been all this day on the subject of religion, and of his being inspired, from which his physicians draw the worst consequences.[3]

From Jack Payne to Sheridan, from Sherry to Brooks's— within a couple of days the news was widespread through the

* A powerful antipyretic compound of antimony.

Opposition; and on 7 November the Duchess of Devonshire was informed, 'Nobody can get at the truth, but he is certainly dangerously ill. I believe the King is quite disordered in his mind. The humour* to which the whole family is subject has fallen upon his brain, and nothing will save him except an eruption upon his skin.'

It was, of course, impossible to keep the drama from the Press. On the 5th the Queen, uncharacteristically reading the principal Opposition paper, the *Morning Herald*, saw with speechless indignation a reference to 'some slight derangement'. Recovering her voice, she bade Miss Burney commit to the flames this outrageous journal, declared that the printer should be brought to account, and 'ruminated upon who should be employed to represent to the editor that he must answer at his peril for any further such treasonable paragraphs'. It was, of all people, Sheridan who was so employed, by the Prince at that, to 'go round, however late, and in my name declare to the editor of every paper that if they dare ever to insinuate even the most distant account of His Majesty's health, unless unauthorised to do so, I shall prosecute them with the utmost severity'. There is no record of His Royal Highness carrying out his fierce threat.[4]

'It appears', wrote William Grenville who, a supporter of the Government, was as depressed as the Opposition was elated, 'that Warren and Sir George Baker are unable to decide whether the disease is fatal. The other alternative is one towards which one cannot look without horror—a continuance of the present derangement of his faculties without any other effect upon his health. . . . The disease is confined almost entirely to the brain . . . water on the brain or ossification of the membrane . . . little reason to hope.'

'*Rex noster insanit*', wrote Dr Warren discreetly to a friend on the 8th. '*Nulla adsunt febris signa; nulla mortis venturae indicia.*'[5]

Just how mad was George III?

In their public pronouncements, the doctors spoke of fever: but in private, in the obscurity of a learned tongue, Warren denied that there was any fever. It is an important point, but one which, in the absence of records of the King's temperature

* A sort of skin disease.

—the clinical thermometer had not yet been invented—cannot now be determined.

Physicians diagnosed fever by the pulse-rate, the state of the tongue and the superficial warmth of the skin. These are not reliable symptoms. As it was recognized, even among laymen, that psychotic patients with fever have a better chance of recovery than those suffering from delirium without fever, the diagnosis of fever may have been intended by the physicians, consciously or subconsciously, to reassure themselves, the Royal Family and the public. Sir Gilbert Elliott was not deceived. 'The physicians talk of fever: but I am inclined to believe that they avail themselves of some occasional quickness of pulse to avoid the true name of his disorder, and also to avoid the declaration of a circumstance which would make his case much more hopeless—I mean that of delirium without fever.'

In modern terms the King's disorder was undoubtedly psychotic, of a manic-depressive type. Statistically it has been established that manic-depressives in middle age are characterized by 'pronounced peripheral development of the body cavities (head, breast and stomach) and a tendency to distribution of fat about the trunk with a more graceful construction of the motor apparatus (shoulders and extremities). The rough impression in well-developed cases is very distinctive: middle height, rounded figure, a soft broad face on a short massive neck sitting between the shoulders; the magnificent fat paunch protrudes from the deep vaulted chest which broadens out towards the lower part of the body.' It is a perfect description of King George III.

Psychotic attacks are commonly caused by an underlying conflict (such as between George III's natural character and that which he forced upon himself) exacerbated by violent frustrations, annoyances and emotions. The loss of the American colonies, the behaviour of his sons, even the impeachment of Warren Hastings, all agitated him to a degree dangerous to his precarious equilibrium. The death, in 1783, of his beloved child, Prince Octavius, was a grievous blow. Perhaps the horror of his eldest son's secret marriage to a Roman Catholic was almost as distressing as the loss of America, and there was nobody with whom he could discuss it. This was followed by his own violent attraction—no uncommon experience for middle-aged men with unamiable wives and large, troublesome families—for the beautiful, unattainable Lady Pembroke.

It seems probable that the strain on his constitution was increased by severe attacks of gastric influenza, before and after the tour to Cheltenham and Worcester. Certainly the royal household was in a positively toxic state that summer, busily passing on from one to another some very disagreeable virus infection.

A man of weaker character might have, subconsciously, dodged reality and sought refuge from these defeats, frustrations, disgraces and insoluble dilemmas in procrastination, self-deception, a lazy acceptance of the inevitable. But for George III there was no such easy way out. He was like a boxer who refuses to give way an inch to a larger and stronger antagonist, but stands his ground until he is battered senseless.

Thereafter all such symptoms as are confirmed by reliable witnesses—his loquacity, the sudden variation of his mood and spirits, quick changes between elation and depression, his psycho-sexual desires—are typical of a psychotic disorder of a manic-depressive type such as is nowadays treated by psychotherapy. One of his symptoms which surprised all who knew of it was that, during his illness, he ceased to interrupt his conversation with 'What? What?' and 'Hey? Hey?' 'It is extraordinary', wrote an observer, 'that his language is better and his conversation smarter, and that he is infinitely more graceful in his motions and much more active than he was at any period.' It was not, in fact, extraordinary: for manic-depressives are commonly free from self-consciousness, and therefore lose, during their disorder, their normal symptoms of nervousness or sense of insecurity. [6]

Reports of dramatic, not to say disgusting, symptoms must be heavily discounted. They date from the arrival at Windsor of the Prince of Wales, Captain Payne and Lord Lothian. Of Lothian, little need be said but that he was a toady of the Prince, later dismissed from his regiment for his conduct at this time. 'Think', wrote William Grenville, 'of the Prince of Wales introducing Lord Lothian into the King's room when it was darkened, in order that he might hear his ravings at a time when they were at their worst.' It is not an edifying thought; but in fairness to the Prince it must be said that Grenville's word is not above suspicion: he hated the Prince, and advised his brother, 'do not let this fact come from you: it is important that we should not seem to spread the knowledge of anything that can injure His Royal Highness's character in the public opinion'. The Prince himself certainly spied on his father, as was admitted by Sheridan's gay and gossipy sister Betsy, his ardent admirer:

> He went softly into the room and put his eye to the hole in a large screen that stood between the bed and the door. When he looked at the bed, the King happened to look up and immediately perceived the eye. The Prince withdrew at the instant, but the King called to one of the pages, 'I have seen my son.' They assured him he had not, however he persisted, and when he found they still denied it, gave no other answer but a most significant glance at the screen.

That Payne was the main source of the Opposition's information is clear from Sir George Elliott's letter of 8 November. 'The language of those with whom the Prince corresponds and who have seen Payne is that recovery is hopeless, but he may linger a few days.'[7]

How reliable a witness was Captain Jack Payne? The Duke of Richmond, who was fairly neutral in the disputes arising from the royal malady, dismissed him as a little monkey. George Selwyn, a shrewd if frivolous observer, described Payne and Lothian as 'confused and uncertain channels . . . no dependence on their veracity'.

It has been mentioned that Payne was devoted to the Prince, who had promised to make him a Lord of the Admiralty. This alone makes him a prejudiced witness, for the Prince was vitally interested in the King's insanity being widely known and believed incurable. Obviously the King was incapable at the moment of transacting business: if it was thought that he would soon recover, stop-gap arrangements would be made for the exercise of the functions of the Crown until his recovery; if, on the other hand, it was believed that he would be incapable of ruling for a long time or for ever, then a Regent must be appointed with full authority to exercise all the functions of the Crown; the reign of George IV and Fox would, in fact if not in name, immediately begin.

Furthermore Payne was involved in a dangerous intrigue to anticipate the grant to the Prince, by Parliament, of full regal powers. Lord Loughborough, the reversionary Lord Chancellor, a paladin of political prostitution who resembled a ship lying at single anchor, swinging round every time the tide ebbs and flows, read to the Prince the following advice:

> Upon the supposition of a state of disorder without possibility of recovery, or of a speedy extinction, the administration of government devolves on the Prince as of right. He is bound by every duty to assume it. The authority of Parliament will be interposed not to confer but to declare that right. The mode of proceeding which occurs to me is that in a very short time His Royal Highness should signify his intention to act by directing a meeting of the Privy Council where he should declare his intention to take upon himself the care of the State and order Parliament by a proclamation to meet early for the discussion of business. That done, he should direct the various Ministers to attend him with the public business of their offices. It is of vast importance that he should appear to act entirely of himself . . . not to consult, but to listen and direct.

Loughborough's denial, on 3 December, that he ever advocated the Prince's 'violently assuming his right without the privity of the two Houses of Parliament' is belied by these notes, written in his own hand.

The plot was for nothing less than a *coup d'état* carried out behind Parliament's back and presented to the two Houses as a *fait accompli* by the Regent who would then, by the normal methods, be able to secure the Houses' approval. Payne was in it up to his neck, and his neck it might have cost him, had the King been vindictive. He was writing from Windsor almost daily to Loughborough, as well as to Sheridan. On 7 November he reported, 'His Majesty is now so bad that I fear his dissolution is almost the best that can be hoped.' Two days later he wrote, 'The *last* stroke cannot be far off... the happiest possible termination to the present melancholy scene.... There should be no appearance of the *smallest intercourse* between this place [Windsor] and town as it might serve to inflame *some certain people*.... Was not William III desired to take charge of the government, and when the legislature of the country was thus completed in its three branches, it proceeded to ratify it by law?' To Sheridan he wrote, 'The Prince was very much pleased with my conversation with Lord Loughborough. I have been very much pleased with the Duke [of York]'s zeal.'

The Prince and Sheridan, themselves not markedly prudent, decided that Payne had gone much too far. 'The Prince', wrote Sheridan on 12 November, 'sent Payne to town this morning. I shall make an attempt at setting his head a little to rights, if possible, for he is growing worse and worse.... It is really intolerable, and I mean to speak very plainly to him.'[8]

Payne's evidence is, therefore, suspect because of his personal character and personal ambition.* Furthermore, it is all hearsay, the product of servants' gossip and tittle-tattle.

Truth [Payne himself wrote] is not easily got at in palaces, and so I find here, and time only slowly brings it to one's knowledge. One hears a little bit every day from somebody, that has been reserved with great costiveness and purposely forgotten.... Warren is the living principal in this business (for poor Baker is half-crazed himself) and is extremely attentive to the King's disorder. The various fluctuations of his ravings, as well as the general situation of his health, are accurately written down throughout the day.[10]

Unfortunately the journal of Dr Warren does not seem to have survived. The only first-hand medical reports are of two physicians who took a view of the royal malady very different from that attributed to him by Jack Payne.

* Captain T. W. Payne ('Jack' Payne) showed up better as a wit and a sailor than as a politician. When he was first introduced to the Prince of Wales, His Royal Highness said graciously, 'If I mistake not, you have been bred to the sea.' 'Oh, no, Sir', replied Jack Payne, 'the sea is bread to me, and damned hard bread, too.' Five years after taking a discreditable part in the Regency Crisis, Captain Payne fought his ship, the *Russell*, with skill and determination in the battle of the Glorious First of June.[9]

Withers, the *soi-disant* Page of the Presence, was almost certainly untruthful in many respects, and was a partisan of Pitt; but his stories, although sensational, and published in order to exploit the public interest, in no way tally with Payne's.

Colonel Robert Fulke Greville assumed the duties of equerry on 4 November, was in almost constant attendance on the King and kept a detailed journal of what he saw and heard. While Payne wrote of his sovereign raving, howling like a dog* and on the point of death, Greville recorded only loquacity, incoherence, insomnia, agitation and 'dwelling on religion. . . . Those around him frequently hinted that he was talking too much, and he often desisted upon the hint.'

On the same day Fanny Burney, all ears in a near-by room, could not hear a sound. As for Sir George Baker, his prosaic entries covering that period read:

> *Thursday, 6 Nov.* The delirium had continued throughout the night without sleep. The pulse this morning was at 120; but after bleeding it fell to 100. He has hardly any thirst and no appetite to his food.
> *Friday, 7 Nov.* Pulse at 86. The same alienation of mind. This morning his appetite for food returned.[11]

Captain Payne was, in short, a malicious liar, who put his singular talent for invention at the service of an unscrupulous and over-eager Opposition.

What *did* happen that night is that the King, believing she had deserted him, insisted on entering the Queen's room. Finding her in bed, he muttered, 'She is there', and seemed satisfied.

Miss Burney heard him next morning. 'I'm nervous, I'm not ill, but I'm nervous: if you would know what is the matter with me, I'm nervous. But I love you both very well, if you would tell the truth. Sir George has told me a lie—a white lie, he says, but I hate a white lie. If you would tell me a lie, let it be a black lie'—and so on, for hours on end.[12]

---

* This is commonly believed to be a symptom of all kinds of mania, and is therefore just what a layman would invent. It is, in fact, a symptom only of schizophrenia (split personality) which was certainly not the King's complaint.

The same evening the Prince of Wales, Duke of York, phy- sicians and equerries were sprawled uncomfortably on chairs and sofas in the ante-room when His Majesty suddenly ap- peared, mumbling, 'Frederick [the Duke of York] is my favourite, yes, Frederick is my friend. . . .' He is then alleged to have seized Sir George Baker, who made no effort to get his patient back to bed, held him against the wall and harangued him, 'You're mistaken in my condition: it's only nervousness, and you're nothing but an old woman!' Colonel Digby took the King's arm to lead him back to his room. 'I won't go! Who are you?' 'I'm Colonel Digby, Sir. Your Majesty has been very good to me often, and now I am going to be very good to you: for you must come to bed: it's necessary for your health.'[13]

The King looked at the Duke of York, muttered, 'Oh, my boy! My boy!' and went off like a lamb. But Payne reported him at that time as being '*so bad* that his dissolution is almost the best that can be hoped . . . violent heat, great chilliness'. As for Dr Warren, he confidently pronounced next day, 'The King's life is in danger. The seizures upon his brain are such that if he lives, his intellect will not be restored.'[14]

That day's entry, which makes no mention of this incident, is unfortunately the last in Sir George Baker's diary. For some five weeks, the only eyewitness account of the royal malady is that of a layman, Colonel Greville.

Unquestionable the King was, physically, a very ill man; and the brutal discomfort in which he lived would be enough to make any invalid worse. It was the coldest winter in living memory, but for some reason known only to his physicians, no fire was lit in his room: so icy was this apartment that no one remained there more than half an hour at a time—except, of course, the unhappy invalid. The combined genius of several doctors could devise no treatment other than James's Powders, violent purges and emetics counteracted by sedatives; and blistering the patient's head and legs in order to draw the humour from the brain up, or down, to the extremities. This operation was particularly painful to the King who, like many very fair people, had a sensitive skin; it was certainly a con- tributory cause of his insomnia and of paroxysms so violent that his attendants had to sit on him to hold him down. Not unnaturally, after sitting on their sovereign, his pages 'behaved with a degree of familiarity and insolence that often irritated and hurt him'.[15]

The King seems to have had a poor opinion of all his physicians, and to have now turned particularly against Sir George Baker who for nearly three weeks had coped single-handed with this very difficult case. 'You should talk to me', he told a visitor, 'for our poor friend there', he indicated Sir George, 'is too nervous at present.'

Withers relates that the King was sitting in an arm-chair by the fire:

> swaddled in fine linen like an Egyptian mummy. (Strait waist-coats are for the vulgar. If the sovereign be disposed to be a little outré in his deportment, he is pinioned in an envelopment of lawn.) Sir George came in and unfastened his arms to feel his pulse; whereupon the royal patient gave him a blow on the forehead which laid him on the floor, and then poured over him the contents of the chamber-pot. Standing over his physician, and reciting the rules of the 'Order of Cloacina',* His Majesty exhorted Sir George to maintain its honour and dignity. He then retired to his chair and said, 'Rise, Sir George, Knight of the most ancient, most puissant, and most honourable Order of Cloacina.' After which, he laughed himself to sleep.†[16]

Politicians soon realized the extraordinary difficulties resulting from the King's illness. If he lived, a Regency would probably be necessary, but could not be established, according to ministerial supporters, without an Act of Parliament; and how could an Act be valid without the King's consent? Naturally

* Cloacina was the Goddess of Privies, a subject of much lavatory humour.

† How are we to take this story? With a large pinch of salt. The incident must have occurred, if at all, before the arrival of Dr Willis, who introduced the strait-waistcoat at Kew: but before Willis's arrival, the King was not allowed a fire in his room. Sir Lucas Pepys swore that no form of coercion was used until Willis came. (See p. 94.) If the King was swathed like an Egyptian mummy, he could not have used his chamber-pot without help; and surely his attendant would not have left it unemptied beside him? However, tales like this would help the sales of Withers's book.

the Ministers' opinion was coloured by the knowledge that the Regent, who must obviously be the Prince of Wales, would dismiss them without hesitation. The Opposition were in a situation of acute embarrassment. They would not be human if they had not been elated at the prospect 'of a better and more honourable dependence than the Faro table, which had been so long the principle support of so many of them'; yet while Jack Payne and Dr Warren insisted that the King was dying, they could not in decency rejoice. About mid-November, however, it became clear that Payne's hopes had been too sanguine. The King was still very much alive, 'talking incessantly for many hours together, without any appearance of sense or reason, sometimes knowing the persons that are about him, at other times mistaking them'.[17]

The 12th November was a very trying day for the King's attendants. From eleven o'clock onwards he was rambling about

Eton College, of the boys rowing, etc., but everything he mentioned was in a great hurry and agitation. At length this extreme agitation caused a violent perspiration. . . . He was prevailed upon to drink some barley water. . . . At about 3 o'clock he became more violent and his talking was hurried and agitated to a great degree, and in consequence he put himself in a violent perspiration. At times his pulse rose to 130. . . . At 5 o'clock His Majesty became exceedingly turbulent, and made strong efforts to get out of bed. . . . He afterwards became more composed.

Colonel Greville sat up with His Majesty:

About 3 o'clock he had a violent struggle,* jerking very strongly with arms and legs but making no attempt to rise. Three quarters of an hour after this he became quite collected, during which the opportunity was taken of changing his sheets and blankets, at which he expressed much satisfaction. Immediately after this he talked of being shaved and proposed to clean his mouth. He did it as well as could be, washing his mouth and gargling his throat as well as ever. . . . He asked how many days he had been confined to bed, looked round at his attendants with attention, and smiled,

* Were his blisters very painful, perhaps?

71

and nodded to them frequently. He then desired he might change his linen. All this he did as well as could be. . . . He had been without sleep for twenty-nine hours. Most commonly when His Majesty sat up in bed he was more collected and sensible than in a recumbent posture.[18]

Greville's diary for 12 November has been quoted at length, because it shows the King at his worst during this part of his illness. On most days Greville records merely loquacity, insomnia and incoherence.

On the 15th the King felt better, and desired that the Eton boys should be given a holiday, the guns fired and the 'Dettingen Te Deum' sung to celebrate his recovery. He realized he was not normal, and remarked, 'I am getting into Mr Burke's eloquence, saying too much on little things.' He said he liked the Chancellor, Lord Thurlow, 'though he was in Opposition for a short time, but then it was only for a moment because he was grum, and he can be grum at times to this day.'

On the 16th the King, physically better, believed himself almost well and 'struggled hard for obedience. A warm bath having been proposed, His Majesty proposed terms if he took it; but his consent was at last obtained by management.' For fifteen minutes he sat in a tub of water kept at a temperature of 95°; he was then put to bed and read to. Hydrotherapy is still much used in psychotic cases; it was almost the only useful treatment introduced by the physicians in November. The King liked it, and asked for it to be repeated.

'The humour', reported the wiseacres, 'began to show itself in the legs, when the King's imprudence* drove it to the bowels: the medicine which they were then compelled to use repelled it to the brain. They are now endeavouring by warm baths to bring it down to the legs, which Nature had already pointed out as the best mode of discharge.' Sheridan's sister, Betsy, exasperated at the delay, observed on the 16th, 'The news is just the same, but certainly something will soon be settled, and according to our wishes.'

Lady Harcourt, in waiting at Windsor, wrote on the 18th to Lord Sydney:

* Too much Cheltenham water?

I saw just now Mr Keate, the surgeon, who sat up last night with the King. He says he slept for five hours quite quiet, awoke composed and talked for some time as usual and was quite pleased; but as he awoke more, he fell into the old way and so continued. But, says he, the King is certainly better; there is no doubt of it, and therefore there are great hopes of his getting right again; I believe we are too impatient and expect too speedy a cure. . . . I was pleased to hear Mr Keate say this, you know who he belongs to. . . . I have not seen the *Herald*, and don't know what it says, but I am sure the *Morning Chronicle* speaks good sense feelingly, whoever the writer is, I love him.[19]

On that day a new physician, Sir Lucas Pepys, was introduced, who prescribed woollen bootikins for the patient's raw and blistered feet. They were not a success, and were 'entirely removed by Dr Warren and the King forbad Sir Lucas Pepys to attend his present confinement'. On that day the King talked without ceasing for nineteen hours, interrupted only by hoarseness and a catch in the throat. Sir Lucas, however, took a better view than Warren of the King's condition, and assured Miss Burney that the royal patient would certainly recover, though not immediately.

On the 19th the King was well enough to animadvert on the shortcomings of his equerries. 'They lose', he complained, 'their whole time at the table, by drinking so much wine and sitting so long over the bottle, so that when I want them in the afternoon, they are never ready.' He then, quite in his old style, twitted Colonel Digby on a long-drawn and very decorous flirtation. 'And you are as bad as any of them: not that you stay so long at table or are so fond of wine; but you're just as late as the rest, for you're so fond of the company of learned ladies that you get to the tea-table with Miss Burney and there spend your whole time!'[20]

Ministerial supporters, in fairly restrained terms, gossiped about the royal symptoms. The Opposition, disappointed in their first hopes and primed by Jack Payne, observed no restraint.

73

Some of his attendants [wrote the Duchess of Devonshire on 20 November, without, it seems, any authority but Payne's] perceived it in May last, when they heard the King saying, 'The Prince of Wales is dead, so women may be honest.' The Courtiers all affect to be mad—Lord Fauconberg says the world saw him in a strait-waistcoat, and Lord Salisbury says the King has as much sense as he has. . . . The foreign ministers perceived it at a Levee, and on his return from thence he showed his backside to his attendants, saying he had not the gout. He pulled off Sir George Baker's wig and made him go upon his knees to look at the stars. He begins by beating the palms of his hands, then crying, and then howling. He got naked out of bed, but Digby threatened him back.* As Dr Warren had been the first who had been severe with him, he often says, 'Don't speak, for Dr Warren will hear you.'† [21]

It is certainly true that the King's eyesight worsened during his illness. In the early stages, he had complained to Baker of blurred vision and colour-blindness. After it, he had to change his spectacles. There may, therefore, be some basis of truth in the Duchess's next titbit of gossip, happily recorded on 21 November; but this, too, is not mentioned by Greville. 'The last time the King saw the Queen, he almost set her on fire by pushing the candle in her face to see if it was her.' The Duchess suggested that the King had taken quack medicines which disagreed with him; and that as a child, he had been suckled by a woman who went mad.

'At Cheltenham', she elaborated on 23 November, 'he ran a race with a horse. At Windsor, he told West the Painter he would teach him to mix his colours, and throwing some on the ground, mixed them with his foot. And he would sit with the young women who embroidered, pretending to play on his fiddle.'‡ [22]

The 21st was a pretty good day for the King. 'His conversations were more continued as to their subjects and less interrupted than before. He now waited for answers and replied with

* See p. 69 for a more factual account of this incident.
† Dr Warren's evidence before the Parliamentary Commission totally discredits this story.
‡ There is no evidence to confirm any of these tales.

coolness and precision.' Greville hinted that nothing was worse for him than agitation. The King listened with attention to his equerry's warning, and promised to try to be more quiet. The next day, he was very restless and loquacious, and issued a number of hurried and not very sensible orders. Greville in the evening read to him a few pages of the Duchess of Kingston's trial.* Afterwards he spoke collectedly of some of the delusions from which he had recovered: how he had thought there had been a deluge, and that he could see Hanover through Herschel's telescope. He went through his prayers very well. On the 23rd, however, he 'talked with great rapidity on strange subjects, and sorry was I to hear [wrote Colonel Greville] that these were not free from indecencies.'[23]

While 'Devon's Fair' was filling page after page of her diary with the unseemly products of her political spite, William Grenville had some pertinent observations on the gossip which titivated Opposition circles and shaped Opposition policy:

The Opposition have been taking inconceivable pains to spread the idea that the disorder is incurable. Nothing can exceed Warren's indiscretion on the subject. . . . So long as the Opposition considered the case as desperate, they were affecting a prodigious concern and reverence for the King's unhappy situation. Now that the people entertain hopes of his recovery, they are using the utmost industry to combat the idea—circulating all the particulars of everything which he says and does, and adding the most outrageous falsehoods.[24]

On the 22nd Pitt was at Windsor. 'From what he said, there is no doubt of the King's being much better: at the same time, the accounts of the physicians are gloomy.' Pessimistic as they were, however, neither Dr Warren nor his colleagues, even in the heat of party strife, told the kind of tales that the Opposition politicians were industriously fabricating.

There was apparent, in the last week of November, an improvement in the King's condition which the bishops, with their usual instinct for self-preservation, were the first to sense.

* For bigamy. The Duchess was the deplorable 'Miss Chudleigh', central figure of the most salacious scandal of the day.

Before this, the Archbishop of Canterbury had written to the Prince 'a very handsome letter expressive of his duty and offer of service'. But now, on the 25th, in a debate in the Lords on the situation, 'there were but seven bishops present, which is a proof that crows soon smell powder.' The improvement was given somewhat grudging acknowledgement at Devonshire House. 'The proofs given of his returning sense are that he knew Colonel Manners and made a pun saying, "That is *good* Manners"; that he is attentive at prayers and more cleanly in his person. Burke says, that it is a strange way for reason to revisit a man, in the shape of a pun.'

The Duchess might have found more solid grounds for disappointment in the robust logic of the King's remarks to Sir Lucas Pepys, whom he did not like.

'Who the Devil sent you?'

'The Prince, Your Majesty.'

'Well, the Prince may pay you, for I won't pay your postchaise.'[25]

With the realization that the King was not likely to die of his illness, came the knowledge that the Opposition, agitating for a Regency, were in for a tussle with Pitt, a tough and cunning adversary.

The situation displays in the utmost clarity the mechanics of eighteenth-century politics and, in particular, of the reversionary factor. At the prospect of the King's death or long illness, reversions rocketed in value while places under the present Ministry found no takers. In such circumstances, according to the rules of the game, desertions from the Ministry to the Opposition could now be expected. 'Rattism', prophesied Lord Sheffield on 22 November, 'will prevail, and I should not be surprised if [the present Parliament], looking towards the rising sun, should turn out the very Minister that made it.' Pitt's tactics were first to delay the Regency, then so to hedge the Regent with restrictions on his power of patronage, that reversionary stock would fall and present places seem more secure.[26]

It was a game for the experts, and the Opposition longed for the arrival of Fox as the Jews for their Messiah. Meanwhile, as

Fox's understudy, they must make do with Sheridan, an excellent playwright, one of the best orators in the House, a convivial pot-companion, whose constitution and fine intellect were impaired by an excess of wine, preferably other people's, and by a corrosive mixture of brandy, arquebusade* and eau-de-Cologne. Already, though he was only thirty-seven, his face 'exhibited eloquent proof of his intemperance'—as, indeed, did his political judgement. 'He cannot', wrote his friend and admirer, the Duchess of Devonshire, 'resist playing a sly game; he cannot resist the pleasure of acting alone; and this, added to his natural want of judgement, frequently made him commit his friends and himself.' He enjoyed, however, the Prince's confidence; and, prompted by the egregious Jack Payne, had committed the Prince's party to simultaneous and, one would have thought, mutually exclusive intrigues with the Lord Chancellor in being and the Lord Chancellor in reversion.

The latter, Lord Loughborough, dropped his project of a *coup d'état* and proffered advice which was both sounder constitutionally and more seemly in a Chief Justice of the Court of Common Pleas. While still maintaining that 'on the declared incapacity of His Majesty, a right attaches to the Prince of Wales to exercise the Royal Authority with all its functions', he no longer urged the Prince to act first and inform Parliament later; instead, Parliament should first declare His Majesty's incapacity, 'on which the law must take its course'. This now became the accepted Opposition doctrine.[27]

Lord Thurlow, Lord Chancellor in Pitt's Administration, was a burly, bushy-browed, blustering, blasphemous bully who had held this office, except for the four months of the Coalition government, for over ten years. He was, personally, on bad terms with Pitt, whom he described as 'utterly incapable' and whose liberal measures, inside and outside the Cabinet room, he stubbornly opposed. He liked to think of himself as a non-party man holding, therefore, a sort of prescriptive right to the Great Seal, as the personal representative of the King, in *any* Administration. Very early in November, Payne suggested that the Chancellor might take a good opportunity to break with his colleagues, should they propose restrictions on the Regency.

* A sort of surgical spirit used for wound-dressings.

Sheridan reported to the Prince on the 4th or 5th that he had seen Thurlow. On or about the 11th, Payne urged the Prince, who liked Thurlow 'probably on account of his table qualities', to write direct to him. A day or two later the Prince sent for the Chancellor, and with that tact and delicacy which was one of his most amiable characteristics, put out a feeler which could give no offence. 'I have desired Your Lordship's attendance, not only as *my father's* friend, but as my *own* friend. I beseech you, my lord, to give me your counsel.'

But Thurlow was too crafty to commit himself yet. Advising the Prince to 'lie on his oars and show no impatience', he evaded also Pitt's direct questions on what he meant to do; and in a debate in the Lords, though 'suspected of being rattistically inclined, he was as firm as a rock'. At the end of the month he visited the invalid who said, pathetically, 'You shall dine with me, but perhaps I shall not give you a good dinner— I have not so much power as I had.' The Chancellor broke down in a timely fit of hysterics, and November ended with this sensitive political weathercock still wavering.[28]

On the 20th Parliament met—there was no way, with the King incapable of business, of further proroguing it. Pitt proposed a fortnight's adjournment, to which both sides were glad to agree: his own friends in hope of some improvement in the King's state, the Opposition because Fox should soon be home, and they dreaded embarking on a dangerous voyage under the erratic joint-captaincy of the Prince and Sheridan.[29]

On that day also George Selwyn wrote, quite inaccurately,* 'Today is fixed to speak reason to one who has none. Dr Warren is to tell His Majesty that he is stark mad and must have a strait-waistcoat. I am glad I am not chosen to be the Rat who shall put the bell round the Cat's neck.' This was typical of the sort of gossip which was eagerly repeated even among friends of the Ministry. One of the King's amusements, it was said, was looking through the Court Calendar marking the names of those he intended to dismiss; prudently, a page burnt this embarrassing document. The King was said, untruly,† to have

* Coercion was not, in fact, applied for at least another fortnight.

† Dr Warren informed the Parliamentary Committee that the King 'never showed any intention to injure himself'.

feigned sleep in order to put the keeper off his guard, then rushed to the window to fling himself out. He spent hours reading his Bible and *Don Quixote*, and writing lucid, eloquent despatches to foreign courts. He lavished honours on pages, attendants and gentlemen of the bedchamber. He tried to get to the Queen's room and, finding the outer door made fast, burst into tears. 'Surely', he sobbed, 'they might have thought one door enough to stop me?' At other times he railed against the Queen, 'We've been married twenty-eight years and never separated a day until now; and now you abandon me in my misfortunes.' When, however, he was paid a visit by 'a lady he used particularly to esteem [presumably Lady Pembroke], the event too well confirmed the expediency of the Queen's remaining at a distance'. At the end of the month, he meticulously followed his usual practice of counting out accurately and wrapping in separate papers all his servants' wage-packets; but he then deplored the unhappy situation of London, under water for a fortnight; and declared his determination to rescue valuable manuscripts from the Queen's House.[30]

In one of his interminable soliloquies, he was reported to have said, 'I hate nobody, why should anyone hate me?—I beg pardon, I do hate the Marquis of Buckingham.' It was a curious comment, indicating perhaps a twinge of conscience, on the man who, as Lord Temple, had shown him how to escape from the abhorred Coalition. Of the late Lady Buckingham, however, his judgement was more charitable. 'A good woman, though a Roman Catholic. . . . If she were alive, and the marriage-vows were dissolved, I believe Lord Buckingham would renew his. . . . By the by', he added archly, 'I don't think many of my friends would do so.'[31]

These reports, although unconfirmed by Greville's or any other first-hand accounts, were repeated by people who on the whole were sympathetic to the King. There is probably some truth in them. Eye-witnesses only said that he became so emaciated that all mirrors were removed from his room; and he sorely tried his household by his incessant garrulity. For weeks he refused to be shaved, saying that he had always shaved himself and dreaded a razor in anyone else's hand: his beard became so long that the Court barber was then afraid of attacking it.

79

Eventually one of his household, Mr Papendiek, volunteered for the unenviable duty. The royal razor-maker visited Windsor to ensure that the instrument was well sharpened; and Papendiek shaved both cheeks in a two-hour sitting, while the King never stopped talking and the Queen, out of sight, anxiously watched. A few days later another successful operation cleared the mouth and throat.[32]

Not least of his attendants' troubles was that the doctors were afraid to exercise any authority over the King, who played off one against the other—no difficult task when they so often disagreed. On the 24th, for instance, the King ordered Dr Warren out of the room, 'telling him he had sent him a harsh order that day which Sir George Baker had got altered'. He tried to push Warren out and, restrained by the equerries, finally retired pale with anger and shaking with rage. Sir George Baker, complained Greville, was

> patient and undecided. Indeed the general conduct of the physicians has not been so decided or firm as the occasion of their attendance has required. They appear to shrink from responsibility and to this time they have not established their authority, though pressed by every attendant. Too much has been left to the chance of proper and correct conduct of those who happened to be near the King's person. . . . The task becomes more difficult from the intricacies of various controls and various interferences. . . . We ought not to be embarrassed by fluctuating decisions nor puzzled with a multitude of directions from other Quarters.* [33]

On the 25th the King, irritated by one of the pages, gave him 'a smart slap on the face'. Soon after, on going to bed, he 'called for the page, took him by the hand, and asked his pardon twenty times'. On the 28th two pages actually had to 'hold him in his bed and overpower his turbulence'. Two days later, when being put to bed, he 'pulled one of his pages by the hair and endeavoured to kick another'.[34]

The attendants were ordered to preserve strict silence in the King's presence, and to answer none of his questions for fear of

* Probably a reference to frequent and often contradictory instructions from the Prince of Wales, as well as from the physicians.

agitating him. Thus, when the King asked Withers* whether there had been a hunt that morning, the page merely bowed. The King repeated his question, and again Withers bowed.

'Give me my lemonade', said the King.

When Withers approached to take away the glass, he was seized by the collar and 'attacked with such vigour and alacrity' that he had to call for help. When help arrived, the King let him go.

'Have you found your tongue now?' His Majesty inquired.[35]

These accounts of the royal rages blossomed into tales, industriously circulated by the Opposition, of murderous and suicidal violence:

> The King [wrote the Duchess of Devonshire] has taken the Duke of York's regiment from him because he said the Duke of York had taken pokers and tongs from his room. . . . The King is as mad as ever, for he ordered a tie-wig and danced a minuet with Dr Reynolds. . . . The King tore two of his attendants almost to pieces, and is so ill he is held down by force. The Prince and the Duke of York came with this account. . . . The King engaged a page to pretend sleep, because he said he could then sleep; and immediately picked his pockets—it is supposed in search of keys to find money to bribe them to let him escape. I saw [she added significantly] Mr Payne.[36]

From the Duchess's dairy, it is clear that the Prince, the Duke of York and Jack Payne brought her outrageous stories, which went out from Devonshire House as from a sounding-board. Their friends drew the most hopeful conclusions:

> His physicians are agreed that his frenzy is incurable. . . . Every day seems to produce worse symptoms. . . . Pulse as low as 72. . . . His Majesty is no more likely to die than I am; but with regard to his intellect, there is no appearance of amendment, nor any prospect whatever of recovery. . . . The bulletin daily talks of fever, but fever he has not. The word fever is probably substituted for insanity. . . . The physicians have never made use of any compulsion to His Majesty. This gave someone occasion to

* This, like other tales of Withers, must be viewed with some scepticism.

say, it was clear they meant to put the strait-waistcoat on the Prince of Wales.* [37]

The Opposition insisted that the Prince was behaving with great propriety and gaining much credit by his conduct at Windsor. For obvious reasons, they said:

> it is the policy of those attached to the Administration to represent the King's state better than it is. They affect to believe that he will certainly recover; that he is so much better; and many stories to that purpose, seemingly well authenticated, are circulated, which it is known are not true. There is little doubt of its being the general real opinion of the physicians that there is as little probability of recovery as in any case of the kind that has come within their knowledge. [38]

Naturally Pitt's friends had other views. They said the Prince's conduct was very heartless. He showed no consideration for the Queen's feelings, insisted on talking politics with her, banged his stick on the floor, condemned all she had done, bowed and stamped out without kissing her hand. Dr Warren continued to report direct to the Prince, not to the Queen, who broke down sobbing, 'What will become of me? What will become of me?' The Prince 'took the palace government from the Queen's hands, in consequence of which there was no command whatsoever'. The King, in his ramblings, complained bitterly of his eldest son, fearing that his brothers were following his bad example. On 25 November Jack Payne noted that 'the Prince is to see the Chancellor tomorrow; the chief object in the visit is to show him the King, who has been worse these two days than ever, very turbulent and incoherent'. [39]

> Can what I have just heard, coming from an ex-Minister, be true? [wrote Sir William Lee, shocked, to General Harcourt]. That it is determined to establish a sole Regent and dissolve Parliament forthwith? I tremble for the consequences to that individual. Was I in that predicament, nothing would induce me to act without

* A reference to the restrictions on the Regency which Pitt was planning.

co-adjutors. Such self-denial would *create return of confidence*, the contrary makes him but the tool of others and exposes him to difficulties hard to surmount. Surely before such a step is taken, the House of Lords should depute some other physicians and some of their own body to *see* the King, not rest the measure solely upon those who have hitherto been employed? The extremest urgency of foreign affairs can alone justify such precipitant measures in my own opinion. It is said that the foreign ministers have talked of *it* for several months as coming on.

George Selwyn prophesied, 'The misfortune will add to the veneration the public has of late had for His Majesty.' He was right. There was a general dread of the consequences of the Prince's accession: the physicians received letters threatening violence if they could do no better. A mob stopped Sir George Baker's coach and asked the news. 'Bad', said he. 'The more shame to you!' howled they. Sir Lucas Pepys told Miss Burney that, if the King died, none of their lives would be safe. Dissenters and Jews prayed for the King's health before the Archbishops and Privy Council had agreed on the draft of an Anglican prayer which critics found 'lacking in warmth and animation'.

With his master's popularity, Pitt's rose also. 'Never did the Administration stand so high in the opinion of the moneyed and commercial world', who dreaded Cavendish or, far worse, Sheridan in charge of the nation's finances. Although his more timid and impecunious colleagues suggested, as the proper gambit in reversionary politics, a coalition with Fox, Pitt refused to consider this, preferring to 'take his blue bag and return to the Bar'.[40]

The Prince's summons to Charles Fox found him placidly enjoying the delights of Bologna with Mrs Armistead. He had not opened a newspaper for a month, except to glance at the news from Newmarket. Without a moment's delay, he extricated himself 'from the arms of fading beauty' and hastened to the great destiny which should be awaiting him.

Fox arrived home on 24 November, having driven 1,000 miles in nine days, a prodigious feat in badly-sprung Continental carriages. It was too much for a fat man of forty, and his friends were shocked to see him shattered and emaciated, sallow, his eyes swollen, stockings hanging loose on his shrunken calves. He was far from pleased at what he found.

Sheridan, in whose prudence and political acumen his best friends put little reliance, was, according to his proud sister, more esteemed by the Prince than any man in England—so much, indeed, that gossip named him as the next Prime Minister or (of all ludicrous incongruities) Chancellor of the Exchequer. He had taken refuge from his creditors at the house of Mrs Fitzherbert, which suggested the unwelcome probability of Mr Rolle returning to the charge. His 'silly vanity' had offended many of the party, especially the Duke of Portland, who had given ponderous warning that he would never sit in a Cabinet with the playwright.

Moreover, Fox had a horror of negotiations with Thurlow, a man whom he loathed, whose presence in the Cabinet would not only, he felt, be a betrayal of Lord Loughborough, but would put the kiss of death on the new Administration.

However, Thurlow had a series of secret meetings with the Opposition leaders, culminating, after a Cabinet meeting, in a long drinking session with the Prince, the Duke of York and Dr Warren who voted him 'a glorious jolly dog'. The Prince and Sheridan between them secretly committed their party to Thurlow, who seems, however, to have prudently evaded committing himself to them.

Not surprisingly, the secret leaked out. At the conclusion of a Cabinet meeting at Windsor, the Chancellor could not find his hat. Suddenly, to his evident confusion, a page came running with it and said loudly, 'My Lord, I found it in the closet of the Prince of Wales!' On another occasion Pitt, innocently asking if Thurlow had received a message, was told by the messenger, 'Yes, and Mr Fox was with him.' 'It is unquestionably true', wrote Grenville on 30 November, 'that he has seen Fox, and I believe he has also seen Sheridan repeatedly, and certainly the Prince of Wales: and of all these conversations he has never yet communicated one word to any other member of the Cabinet. . . . You will be at no loss to guess whence the Prince obtains his knowledge of the plans of the [restrictions on the] Regency.' A contemporary caricature shows Thurlow remarking, as he turns his coat inside-out, 'One side will do as well as another.'[41]

It was decided to move the King from Windsor. Kew would be more convenient for the physicians and Cabinet, and the King would be able to walk in the gardens without (as at Windsor) being overlooked from his subjects' upper windows. The King, however, disliked Kew, especially in winter, so his removal was an operation requiring some *finesse*. What was to be done if he refused to go? The physicians and Cabinet together discussed this delicate question, and agreed that every stratagem, short of force, should be used. The Queen, knowing his aversion to Kew, reluctantly consented.

It was agreed that he should not be moved until five in the evening, so as to avoid crowds along the route. The Queen and Princesses would set off in the morning, giving him a lead as though he were a nappy horse. The date fixed was 29 November. All preparations having been made, the King was cautiously informed of the plan. He objected, and refused to get out of bed.

It was decided to enlist the Prime Minister's support. 'Sir', said Mr Pitt with a cheerfulness he was far from feeling, ''tis a fine day. Won't you get up and set out for Kew, where the Queen has just gone?'

'No', said His Majesty, 'I won't. She has gone without my leave, and must return to beg my pardon.'

He resisted every persuasion, though craftily offering to make terms. He consented to go, but only in his own chaise, which he well knew had already gone with the Queen. Mr Pitt, baffled in his endeavours, left, and the King stayed in bed. At one o'clock Greville and General Harcourt told him that the carriage was waiting; but he was by no means disposed to listen. They urged him to get up, at which he became very angry, closed the bed-curtains and hid himself.

The palace was in the utmost confusion, with Princes, Ministers, equerries, pages, 'all conferring, whispering, plotting, caballing how to get the King off'. Through the bed-curtains, the King handed Greville a letter for delivery to the Officer Commanding the Welsh Fusiliers, then on Windsor duty. 'The anxiety with which His Majesty pressed us to forward this letter

85

induced me to suspect that his purpose was, that he should be assisted by military force.' Mr Pitt then wrote to the King, urging him to accept his physicians' advice. Harcourt and Greville tried again, at which the King 'drawing his curtains together with great force, again hid himself'. The physicians now implored him to get up and dress himself: the King however persisted in obstinate refusal. A firmer tone was then adopted, and he was plainly told that if he continued his refusal, he would be forced. On this he said he would get up if the physicians would go away. They retired, and Greville pressed him to dress, but on various excuses he delayed. The equerries told him he must not forget he had given his word to get up. General Harcourt seems to have added a promise, a deception which the King never forgot and never forgave, that if he went to Kew, he could join the Queen there. On this, His Majesty began to dress, but soon lay down again. Harcourt, taking up his watch, said that unless he finished his dressing soon, the physicians would certainly return to know the cause of the delay. Finding now that he was pressed on all sides, and that no further delays would be permitted, he jumped out of bed, said that he would finish his dressing and would soon be ready to go.

He kept his word. Emerging from the castle in his Windsor uniform, he stood for a moment on the carriage-step chatting with the postilions (whose names he remembered), asked some fussy questions about the horses and entered the coach. While the sentries, footmen and porters wept as though they would never see him again, he drove off, with an escort of cavalry. Colonel Digby galloped ahead to tell the Queen that at last he was on his way. A small crowd by the road took a melancholy leave of him: at which the King bowed with emotion and said, 'These good people are too fond of me. Why am I taken from the place I like best in the world?'

He cheered up during the drive; and on approaching Kew artfully allotted Greville and the other equerries various tasks on arrival so that, while they were busy, he could sneak off to the Queen's apartments. Getting out of his carriage, he spoke affably with the porter, strolled through the hall, then darted towards the room where he expected her to be. He showed great disappointment at finding the door locked, but was quickly ushered into his own apartments. He was very dissatisfied, and told Greville and Harcourt they had deceived him. He threatened to sit up and tire out his attendants. He remarked that he was very strong and active, and in proof of this he danced and hopped with surprising agility: the sight of such an exhibition in the dear King affected Colonel Greville painfully. Later he was foiled in a plan to rush out from his own apartment and reach that of the Queen. Greville does not confirm a story that he was allowed a glimpse of his children through a window, whence he had to be dragged despite pathetic protests. The night, not surprisingly, was an unpleasant one, especially as Kew House, planned and furnished as a summer residence, was cold and uncomfortable beyond all imagination. The floors of the rooms were uncarpeted; the passages were damp as well as dark and chilly; and only Colonel Digby's initiative procured sandbags to lay along the doors and windows to stop the freezing draughts.* The King occupied a large downstairs room with six huge windows and a 'new Water Closet'. At first he was allowed no fire. His bed, however, was of down feathers, which made his insomnia more bearable.[42]

The Prince of Wales, having 'remained a melancholy witness of the King's increasing malady as long as his feelings would allow',[43] returned with relief to town. Before doing so, he decided, with the help of the Duke of York, to remove to safekeeping the King's jewellery, cash and private papers. In this, his motives were impeccable: all these valuables were lying about in unlocked confusion, and he correctly handed them over to the Chancellor. The Queen, however, loving jewellery and knowing her eldest son, sprang to a conclusion which was on this occasion unjustified. Flying into an outrageous passion, she heaped abuse on her sons, whose reply was no less outspoken. Two ladies-in-waiting, witnesses to the scene, begged the Prince and the Duke not to speak of this unseemly quarrel, but of course they did. It was the start of a feud between the Prince and his mother that became the most unbecoming aspect of the Regency crisis.

* The privations of Kew were such that one page, Mr Fortnum, resigned to open a prosperous grocery business in Piccadilly.

87

'What a fine fellow my brother York is!' exclaimed the Prince, perhaps too elevated for complete discretion, a few days later. 'He never forsakes me! The other day, when we went to look for the King's money and jewels at Kew, as we opened the drawers, my mother grew angry. Says York to her, "Madam, I believe you are as much deranged as the King".'

Jack Payne, after cursing Pitt as 'William the Fourth and William the Conqueror', quipped 'Mr Pitt's chastity will protect the Queen.' It was a witticism which he was unwise enough to repeat in the presence of the Duchess of Gordon, who tore him to pieces. 'You little, insignificant, good-for-nothing upstart! You chattering puppy! How dare you name your royal master's mother in such style!'[44]

With Charles Fox's return, politics moved out of the dank thickets of backstairs intrigue. Everyone thought a Regency inevitable, and the Prince of Wales was the only possible Regent. The Ministry held that he could exercise no more powers than were given him by the two Houses of Parliament. The Opposition, on the other hand, maintained that the functions of the two Houses could be only declaratory, not legislative. Without a King, they were not a Parliament. Therefore, as soon as they had declared the King's incapacity, the Regent automatically assumed *all* the powers of the Crown. Then, and not until then, could Parliament, now complete, impose such restrictions on patronage as it thought fit. The difference may not seem to be very great: but in fact it was vital. 'I think', wrote Sir John Eden, a moderate Foxite, 'it will be contended to make him Regent immediately, and till the defect in the Kingdom is supplied, no restrictions can be made. When he becomes Regent, I think a majority to vote restrictions will not easily be found.'[45] Rattism, in short, would prevail; and with unlimited powers of patronage, the Prince would establish his friends in an impregnable position. The *Public Advertiser* put into the mouth of Fox:

> Let me but once possess the power
> Entire and unconfined,
> And we'll debate some future hour
> What part you wish to bind.

You cannot doubt that I'll resign
Whatever you desire.
An humble mind was ever mine,
And Peace I still inspire.

On terms like these I love to play
And thus at Brooks's borrow.
Lend me but all you have to day,
We'll sign the bond tomorrow.[46]

Pitt's game was to play for time, in the hope of some amendment in the King which would encourage Ministerial waverers; then, with his majority in Parliament, he could force through his plan of fettering the Regent with restrictions. He therefore arranged for the Privy Council to question the physicians. The main interest lay in the evidence of Dr Warren, who two days before had told the Duchess of Devonshire that the Bulletins were purposely made as obscure as possible; and that the King *might* recover, but personally he, Warren, did not think so. Now, to the Privy Council, Warren admitted that patients in the King's condition more often recovered than not; but he then added that he counted each relapse as a separate disease and recovery. 'So', as Charles Fox observed, 'taken seven madmen: six don't recover, but the seventh is mad seven times and recovers each time, the majority is in favour of the madmen who recover. . . .' Burke, who had hitherto kept fairly quiet in this crisis, was now most forward in cross-examination, and insisted on a categorical answer to his question, 'Can the King be cured?' The doctors said he could. But 'Warren was the most unwilling to subscribe to this opinion', and seemed much confused. After the meeting Lord Camden, a former Chancellor, observed, 'Dr Warren is a damned scoundrel, though I believe him to be a very able physician.'[47]

The next day, 4 December, a very full House of Commons met in an atmosphere of party animosity which had been markedly enhanced by the activities of the Prince of Wales. The Chancellor had advised him in November to lie low: 'Everything, Your Royal Highness, must flow to you of its course. You will only interrupt its course by eagerness to receive it.' The

Prince ignored this prudent counsel in favour of the more militant policy sponsored by Sheridan.

Before the end of the month he had 'presumed to address the Cabinet in terms that were thought a little royal. Some caution was thought necessary in wording the answer to avoid acknowledging any authority in him.' 'The general language of the Opposition was universal and immediate dismission' of the Ministry; and the Prince told the Duchess, he would 'utterly refuse any restrictions: they might do as they will'. The Chancellor, still perched uncomfortably on the fence, 'spoke in the highest terms of the Prince's knowledge'; but most of the Prince's friends were 'rather afraid of his premature ambition'.[48]

So violent was party feeling that, when Pitt said the King would probably recover, an Opposition Member leaped up and mimed the gestures of a lunatic cutting his own throat.

Pitt kept the Opposition guessing about his plans. One rumour was that the Queen would be made sole Regent, and had promised her son to abstain from politics. Horace Walpole heard that there would be a 'tripartite division of royalty between the Queen, Prince and Mr Pitt, which I call a *Trinity in Disunity*'. Others believed that 'great has been the struggle of Mr Pitt to effect a regency of eight persons, not a Regent. Having made the Prince his irreconciliable enemy by the attempt, he has given it up chiefly because the Chancellor would not support him, but would vote for the Prince.' Sir John Eden was nearest the mark in suggesting, 'the Minister wishes to defer the appointment of Regent, and to make it believed that the state of His Majesty does not require it, but I apprehend it is absolutely necessary. . . . It is said if the Prince of Wales is made Regent, he will make the Fitzherbert a duchess, and marry some princess for his consort.' The Prince and his friends insisted that the 'King had been mad for some months, but Pitt had concealed it for the purpose of governing without control'. Most were confident that Pitt would soon be returning to the Bar; but Sir Gilbert Elliott did not 'relish this triumphant sort of conversation before the battle is even fought: I remember that just such triumphs preceded our utter defeat four years ago.'[49] Despite such prudent warnings, Peter Pindar published his 'Epistle to a Falling Minister':

Drawn from a Garret by the Royal Sire,
Warmed like a viper by the friendly fire,
What hath thy gratitude sublimely done?
Fixed, like a snake, thy fang upon the son. . . .
To make snug, comfortable habitations
For thee and all thy pitiful relations* . . .

Yet what expect from thee, whose icy breast,
A stranger to their charm, the loves detest?
A Joseph, thou, against the sex to strive,
Dead to the charms that keep the world alive. . . .
Then may thy young, old, treacherous bosom feel
The rapid vengeance of some virtuous steel![50]

Pitt in the Commons, and Lord Camden in the Lords, on 4 December moved that the Houses take into consideration, in four days' time, the Report of the Privy Council's examination of the physicians. At the same time Pitt gave notice that he would move for a Committee to search for precedents. The Opposition were not content with the Privy Council's zeal in examination; and Pitt, on the 8th, grateful for anything which would waste a few days, agreed to the appointment of a Committee of twenty-one Members to examine the physicians again next day. With himself in the chair, Fox, Sheridan and Burke among those round the table, he could rely on the proceedings being protracted.[51]

At Kew, Colonel Greville was pained to record, 'the unfavourable symptoms of the King's disorder increased, and in his conversation oaths, which had never yet been heard from his lips, were blended not infrequently with indecencies'. On the 2nd the King 'even gave hints of being tired of his existence and entreated his pages to despatch him'. There was trouble next day when he demanded to go for a walk, which Pepys had imprudently promised the day before. After much discussion between equerries, physicians and the Queen, he was offered a walk of a quarter of an hour on the terrace.

* A reference to Pitt's elder brother, First Lord of the Admiralty, who, owing to his incorrigible unpunctuality, was known as 'The Late Lord Chatham'.

He was angry, and declared he would not stir out of his room unless he was allowed to walk ten miles. . . . It was clear that he entertained hopes of being able to slip away and giving us a run. He told one of the pages that his plan had been to put the bottle of Arquebusade Water in his pocket, and after throwing some of it in my eyes, to run off. A plan not ill-conceived, by heads of steadier reflection.

Altogether it was by far the King's worst day. 'He was mischievously jocose and burnt two wigs belonging to one of the pages.' At another time he was childishly playful, begging romps and making his pages wheel him about the room. Next day he refused to get up, and 'defended himself by gathering up his feet, and then darting them forward with violence against those who pressed upon him'. He was painfully conscious of his misfortune; and, sketching with tolerable accuracy plans and alterations to Kew House, drew a line firmly and straight, which he described as 'Pretty well, for a man who is mad'. All in all, the Duchess of Devonshire hardly exaggerated in writing on 3 December, 'The King is so mad that he pulled off the page's wig and made him fetch and carry it.'[52] It was high time for a competent doctor to take firm charge at Kew; and fortunately there was such a man.

CHAPTER V

Dr Willis and Sons

The wife of one of the equerries advised the Queen to send for the Rev. Dr Francis Willis, who had cured her mother of a mental illness. This gentleman, aged seventy-three, who was to become the object of bitter party controversy, managed to combine the duties (or, at least, the emoluments) of Rector of Wapping and physician-in-charge of his own private madhouse at Gretford, in Lincolnshire. He had taken up his particular branch of medicine after obtaining his degree of Bachelor of Medicine at Oxford when he was forty-two years old. He was, therefore, very well qualified by experience in treating the insane: it is possible, however, that his theoretical knowledge was more sketchy; for the University of Oxford sometimes gave medical degrees, in unusual cases, with undue liberality.[1]

It is difficult to obtain an unprejudiced picture of Willis. To Ministerial eyes he was honest, cheerful, courageous, blending in his countenance intelligence and placid self-possession—a country squarson who rode fifty miles in a day, shot partridges on Saturday and preached on Sunday, true to type, except that his parishioners were lunatics. Miss Burney found him 'fine, lively and independent . . . a man of ten thousand, honest, dauntless, light-hearted . . . not merely unacquainted with Court etiquette, but wholly, and most artlessly, unambitious to form any such acquaintance'.

The Opposition saw a very different, and somewhat blurred, image of 'Dr Duplicate', as they called him because of his two professions. In one week the Duchess of Devonshire described him as 'a clergyman who is used to the cure of madmen and treats them with kindness, even keeping a pack of hounds and allowing them to hunt and shoot'; 'a boastful, sanguine man, violently with the Administration'; and 'a fierce-looking man with a commanding eye, by which he manages his patients'.[2] Many thought him 'not much better than a mountebank, and not so far different from those that are confined in his house'.[3] In general the Opposition repeated that he ruled his patients by cruelty; and their bard, Peter Pindar, produced some fairly nauseating lines on the subject:

> Suppose we chaunt old Willis and his whip,
> At which the human hide revolts,
> Who bids, like grasshoppers, his pupils skip
> And breaks mad gentlemen like colts.[4]

Gossip, on both sides of the political fence, thrived on tales of the King being beaten, starved, chained to a staple. It was said that a German page, George Ernst, picked him up bodily in Kew Gardens, carried him indoors and flung him on a sofa, saying to his English attendants, 'There's your King for you!' But examined critically, these stories have very little substance. The Opposition blamed Willis for ill-treating the King; ministerial supporters said Willis stopped the ill-treatment. The recorder of the story of George Ernst says that this incident occurred at *Kew*, in *October, before* Willis arrived. But the King went to Kew on 29 November; and did not walk in the garden until 11 December, several days after Willis's arrival. Moreover, the gardens were in full view of the windows of the Queen's apartment, and Ernst would hardly have treated the King with disrespect, let alone violence, within sight of the Queen or the equerries. Also, Ernst was not, as was alleged, dismissed, but remained a Page of the Backstairs until 1801. Finally, one of the physicians, Sir Lucas Pepys, swore that before Willis's arrival, none of them dared use any form of coercion, because 'the smallest resistance would have called the whole country to his fancied rescue'.[5]

Willis's reputation as a mountebank rested, as will be seen hereafter, mainly on treating his patients as far as possible like normal human beings, not savage beasts. He was a great believer in the value of cleanliness, tidiness and work for the mentally deranged—a crude form of psycho-therapy; and visitors to Gretford were surprised to see ploughmen, gardeners, threshers, thatchers in black coats, white waistcoats, black silk stockings and breeches, their heads 'bien *poudrés, frisés et arrangés*', working away like anything while paying from five to

94

twenty-five guineas a week for their treatment. They all dined together, in some state; though occasionally Willis would frown at a patient who then hurried out of the dining room after committing some social solecism such as slyly snipping off a guest's pigtail. Newspaper gossip declared that Willis, ignoring social distinctions among his patients, gave them all numbers and badges.[6]* Above all, he talked with his patients, trying to draw them into intelligent conversation.

Yet at the same time, Willis was not afraid to enforce discipline. The chief control available was the strait-waistcoat; and this was used in circumstances which nowadays would have indicated the use of tranquillizing drugs. For instance, the King suffered terribly from the blisters on his legs, which went septic and suppurated: the pain was such that he thrashed about in bed and tore off the bandages. The waistcoat was, therefore, often applied, sometimes at his own request, to make him lie still and help him sleep.

At least Willis had a positive plan for treatment; whereas his colleagues, or rivals, had little plan other than purging, blistering and hoping for the best—or the worst, as the case might be.[7]

Furthermore, Dr Francis Willis—or, rather, his son and assistant, Dr John Willis,† who faithfully reflected his father's views—kept a detailed record‡ of treatment and events.[8] It is a great pity that there is no diary by a medical man covering the period between 7 November, when Sir George Baker's diary ends, and 16 December, when Dr John's begins. Like Sir George's, Dr John's diary reads as though it were wholly true, though perhaps not the whole truth. The fact that the diaries were obviously intended not for publication,§ but for their

* Whether or not this is true, the black and white uniform was probably intended to have the same effect.
† Hereafter, for clarity, called 'Dr John', as he was known in the King's household.
‡ In fact, two diaries were kept, a rough and a fair copy.
§ This is proved in Baker's case by the abrupt ending of the diary before the King was cured; and in Willis's case by the inclusion of frank details of the King's vagaries *after* Willis had declared him cured, the publication of which would certainly have damaged the diarist's reputation. Neither has yet been published.[9]

95

authors' information and record, increases their credibility. Between them, they provide a yardstick by which to judge other accounts of the King's illness, not only during the periods they covered but also, by comparison, during the period between them. They prove most of the stories, repeated by so many historians, to be grossly exaggerated, and many to be completely untrue.

The essentials which distinguished the Willises from the other physicians were that they were specialists in mental cases; that they staked their reputations on curing the King and had a positive plan of treatment; above all, in conspicuous contrast to Dr Warren, that they *wanted* to see him cured.

Dr Willis agreed to treat the King if he was allowed the same authority as over any other patient, and could bring in his son, Dr John, as his assistant, and his own experienced attendants.[10]

On one of his early bad days at Kew* the King, vexed at the Archbishop of Canterbury not coming to administer the Sacrament, and at the pages' evasive replies on this subject, suddenly got under the sofa, saying, 'As you deny me everything, I shall converse here with my Saviour, and no one will interrupt.' Mr Papendiek had to pick up His Majesty and carry him off to bed, where he fell into a deep sleep. Another day, he quarrelled with a page, Compton, who told him outright that his father, Frederick Prince of Wales,† had been void of principle and unreliable over money. 'All this', observed the King, with some justification, 'is rather too much to tell a sovereign, though it may be and no doubt is true.'[11]

There is no confirmation of these stories in Greville, but undoubtedly the King was very bad from 1 to 4 December. On the other hand, he made some sensible, pertinent and revealing comments on people who had, or had not, called to inquire after him. 'Has Lord Howard ridden down on his little white charger? Tell him not to trouble himself: I know he's not sincere: he was angry with me for not letting him marry Lady

* Mrs Papendiek says this happened on Christmas Day, but from internal evidence she must be wrong. It happened, if at all, *before* Willis's arrival.
† 'Poor Fred'. Compton was about right.

Effingham. I knew his family would not treat her or her daughter well.' Among the callers was Lord North, who had recently gone blind. 'He might have recollected me sooner', said the King. 'However he, poor fellow, has lost his sight, and I, my mind. He meant well to the Americans—just to punish them with a few bloody noses, and then make bows for the future happiness of both countries. But want of principle got into the army, want of energy and skill in the First Lord of the Admiralty [the Earl of Sandwich], and want of unanimity at home. We lost America. Tell him not to call again. I shall never see him.'[12]

On 5 December, according to Greville, Willis was introduced to the King, who excitedly complained about the other physicians. Then he said, 'Sir, your dress and appearance bespeak you of the Church. Do you belong to it?'

'I did formerly', replied Willis, 'but lately I have attended chiefly to physics.'

'I am sorry for it', said the King with emotion. 'You have quitted a profession I have always loved, and you have embraced one I most heartily detest. Alter your line of life, ask what preferment you wish and make me your friend—I recommend you Worcester.' He then begged Willis to take Dr Warren under his care as one of his patients and remove him to Lincolnshire.[13]

The arrival of Dr Willis, a known mental specialist, preyed on his mind. He told a page that he could never show his face again in England, but would retire to Hanover.

In the evening Willis again called and, finding the King still making agitated complaints about Warren and the other doctors, tried to calm him down. The King grew more and more excited, called on his attendants for help and tried to push Willis out.

Dr Willis remained firm, and reproved him in determined language, telling him he must control himself or otherwise he would put him in a strait-waistcoat. On this hint Dr Willis went out and returned with one in his hand. It was in a paper, and he now held it under his arm. The King eyed it attentively and, alarmed at the doctor's firmness, began to submit. . . . On Dr Willis wishing him good night and recommending composure and moderation, he retired.

97

[Greville was] much struck with the proper manner and the imposing style of the authoritative language which Dr Willis held on this occasion. It was necessary to have this struggle. He seized the opportunity with judgement and conducted himself with wonderful management and force. As the King's voice rose, attempting mastery, Willis raised his and its tone was strong and decided. As the King softened his, that of Dr Willis dropped to softening unison. . . . The King found stronger powers in Dr Willis . . ., gave way and now returned to somewhat of composure. . . . This seems to have been the first solid step leading to permanent recovery.[14]

Colonel Greville now took ten days' well-earned leave.

Mrs Papendiek's account of the meeting of Willis and the King is not that of an eyewitness, and was written many years later, by a person whose memory was often at fault. It may, however, relate a conversation which took place on another occasion. According to this lady, Pitt introduced Willis.

'Sir, we have found a gentleman who has made the illness of which Your Majesty is labouring his study for some years, and we doubt not he can render comfort, and alleviate many of the inconveniences Your Majesty suffers.'

The King asked eagerly, 'Will he let me shave myself, cut my nails and have a knife at breakfast and dinner; and treat me as his sovereign, not command me as his subject?'

'Sir', said Willis, 'I am a plain man, not used to Courts; but I honour and respect my King. I know my duty, and have always endeavoured to do it strictly. Bred to the Church, religion has been my guide, and to do all the good I can is my constant maxim and earnest desire.'[15]

No sentiments could be more agreeable to the King, who thereupon desired to shave himself. He had not been shaved for two or three weeks, and pleaded great 'uneasiness and distress' at the razor going over his lips and throat—which was not surprising seeing that the barber had, at the last shaving, been almost equally nervous. 'It is necessary', Willis explained later, 'for a physician to be able to judge, at the moment, whether he can confide in the professions of a patient.'

So although the physicians had previously agreed 'to put

98

everything out of his way that could do him any mischief', Papendiek was now told to bring a razor, well sharpened, which Willis himself handed to the King and, fixing him with a stern eye, said, 'I'm sure Your Majesty is too good a Christian, and has too much sense of what you owe to your people, to attempt self-destruction.' The operation, under the surveillance of Dr Willis, was performed very creditably, considering the King had never properly learned how to use a razor. Later, he was allowed a penknife to trim his nails. There is no evidence but Warren's that Willis said next day, 'I shudder at what I have done.' But Willis himself admitted that the concession was a mistake, 'for His Majesty imagined, thence, that he might have liberty to do other things'.[16]

The meeting between the King and Dr Willis, the shaving, the nail-cutting, all gave rise to the most violent controversy, with Ministerial and Opposition sympathizers giving quite different accounts of the same event. Lord Ailesbury, for instance, reported, 'Willis had a struggle at first with the King, but fairly subdued him. The King asked, "By what authority do you come?" "By the authority of the Privy Council, and Your Majesty's subjects in general." "Then the game is up", said the King, "for I have received not a check, but a check-mate." '[17]

The Duchess of Devonshire wrote:

When Dr Willis went in, the King opposed him, but at last was so much subdued by the sight of the strait-waistcoat that he was permitted to shave himself and cut his nails. The truth is, that the King is very bad, but Dr Willis has frightened him. He is violently with the Administration, and Sheridan has been tonight with Warren, who answers for it that Willis's account will tomorrow coincide with theirs [i.e. with the Ministry's]. The King wanted Sir George Baker to have the waistcoat on, and calls Warren Sir Richard Rascal.[18]

But William Grenville was pleased to report on the 7th, 'Dr Willis has already acquired a complete ascendancy over him, which is the point for which he is particularly famous.'[19]

However well or ill the King was, Willis at once attributed his condition to too much work, too much exercise, too little food and drink, insomnia and anxiety. He promised to effect a complete cure, though he would not say how long this might take.[20]

Meanwhile, for five days he used no coercion, but 'endeavoured to persuade and explain what method must be made use of, if there was not a ready compliance'. Certainly an important part of his treatment was to encourage His Majesty to carry on rational conversation, which often showed the patient very wide awake. One day, early in their friendship, the King good-humouredly questioned the propriety of Dr Willis being at once a physician and a clergyman.

'Sir', Willis replied, 'Our Saviour went about the world healing the sick.'

'Yes, but He didn't get seven hundred a year for it, hey?'[21]

It could hardly be expected that the distinguished London practitioner who had been, in a manner of speaking, treating His Majesty for over a month, should welcome the appointment, without his being consulted, of an obscure country doctor, a clergyman at that, whom the Privy Council had invested with overriding authority. Warren bitterly resented it; and applied himself to thwarting and disparaging Willis in every way. The confidence, not to say conceit, of the new broom had the unfortunate effect of strengthening Dr Warren's profound conviction that the King was quite mad, and always would be.

It was, however, in private that Warren expressed his real opinion. To the Parliamentary Committee he said that, as most people similarly afflicted did eventually recover, there was a probability that His Majesty would recover. He could give no idea of how long the illness would last, nor of its causes: he saw no signs of convalescence. He was not a mental specialist, but in twenty-eight years of general practice, had seen many cases of lunacy. 'There are no symptoms', said Dr Warren, 'but the single one of want of understanding.' In general his evidence betrayed a total ignorance of the fundamentals of psychiatry, and of the existence of different types and degrees of mental disorder.[22]

The other doctors more or less agreed with Warren, though Willis committed himself more strongly:

I have great hopes of His Majesty's recovery. If it were any other person but His Majesty, I should scarce entertain a doubt: but when His Majesty reflects upon an illness of this kind, it may depress his spirits and retard his cure more than a common person. . . . I have had an average of thirty mental patients a year for twenty-eight years. Nine out of ten have recovered if put under my care within three months. . . . In my experience, six to eight weeks is the shortest time for recovery, eighteen months the longest: the average is about five months*. . . . I cannot say that I yet see any signs of convalescence, but there are signs leading to it. His Majesty's irritation has, in a great measure, subsided. . . . I attribute His Majesty's illness to weighty business, severe exercise, too great abstemiousness and little rest . . . perhaps when the mind was upon the stretch with very weighty affairs.

Dr Willis's description of the King's alternating moods, of 'violence and acuteness' followed by 'lowness of spirits and despair', is a sound analysis of the symptoms of manic-depressive psychosis; and indicates a thorough knowledge of the subject.

Under cross-examination by Burke, Willis somewhat weakened his evidence by admitting, 'If a person has been brought twice under my care, and twice cured, I reckon two cures, as I should of a fever.'

Dr Willis's sturdy optimism was just what Pitt needed. It shook Fox, who admitted that his evidence has 'knocked up all our hopes'. It annoyed the Duchess, who wrote, 'The King had a bad night. Dr Willis permitted him to write to the Queen and receive her answer, which drove him quite mad so as to knock his head against a wall, etc.† Burke says the Queen has but one virtue, and one vice. The virtue, decorum; the vice, avarice. . . . The fact, I believe, is that the King is entirely subdued by Dr Willis, who knows how to manage mad people.'[23]

Above all, Willis strengthened waverers and checked 'rattism'.

* His estimate of the time necessary for a cure is confirmed by modern experience. Few modern mental specialists would, however, believe that he cured nine out of ten patients.

† Dr Warren informed the Parliamentary Committee that the King 'never showed any intention to injure himself'.

Since Dr Willis has been called in, [wrote the Archbishop of Canterbury] our hope has been more firm and constant, and at this moment stands very high. He says the symptoms are greatly abated, the irritation of nerves very greatly subdued, the violence gone. A sense of the necessity of acquiescing in the advice he gives now induces the patient to submit to that advice, to eat what is ordered, to be more silent, to go to bed early, to court sleep. Sleep is obtained without opiates.[24]

They talk [wrote George Selwyn on 8 December] much more of his relapse than of his not recovering. Let him only recover, and we will take our chance of the relapse, and in the meantime repair all the mischief that will be done by those who are going to storm our town. . . . Willis says the King, when disordered, is able to exert uncommon force. . . . They are now searching for precedents of relapses, and every man at Brooks's has made a comfortable collection.[25]

The Chancellor himself was impressed. Before Willis's arrival he had told Sheridan, 'I am a man of no party, and to a man of your discernment, that is saying enough.' But only the day after Willis came, the Duchess sadly recorded, 'The Chancellor is now supposed by some to be against us and side with Pitt. The Armed Neutrality* are for us.'[26]

Pitt and Dundas pressed Thurlow for his intentions. The Chancellor evaded their questions, and neatly changed the subject to his rival, Loughborough, rumours of whose plan for a *coup d'état* had leaked out, presumably through Sheridan, who was the soul of indiscretion. Thurlow advised with ferocious jocularity:

If he voices his doctrine in the House, the natural mode of proceeding will be to have his words taken down by the Clerk and, if they are not satisfactorily explained by his lordship, to send him to the Tower. . . . Seriously speaking, 'tis not necessary to proceed to so violent a measure. A Resolution would suffice, on the repug-

* The remains of the Shelburne and North groups, including sometimes the Duke of Richmond.

nance to the Constitution of the executive power devolving on anyone, during the casual incapacity of the sovereign, without the consent and authority of Parliament.

In the House of Lords, however, although he was Chairman of the Lords' Committee examining the physicians, the Chancellor said not a word during the whole examination.[27]

On the 10th occurred the first of many debates[28] on the crisis. Pitt presented the Report on the examination of the physicians and, playing rather too obviously for time, blandly proposed a Committee to search for precedents.

This was too much for Charles Fox, who sprang to his feet and excitedly denounced this transparent manoeuvre. 'Why are we to search for precedents? It is notorious that there are none! Here we have an Heir Apparent of full age and capacity to exercise the royal power. He has as clear, as express a right to assume the reins of Government as in the case of His Majesty's death.'

At these words, Pitt slapped his thigh and exclaimed, 'I'll un-Whig the gentleman for the rest of his life!'

Fox hastened to qualify his imprudent words by adding, 'His Royal Highness should not himself judge when to exercise it: the two Houses of Parliament should pronounce when.' But it was too late: the damage was done.

Clearly the Opposition's best plan would have been to accept the Regency at once, without argument, with whatever restrictions Pitt imposed upon it. Pitt would then have been turned out; Fox would be in a position, with the help of the Regent, to choose his own time for a dissolution of Parliament and a general election which, despite the restrictions of the Regent's patronage, they would have an excellent chance of winning. The new Parliament would then have abolished the restrictions and Fox would have been firmly in the saddle—until the King recovered; and who could say when that would be? But Fox was not on form. He was still suffering from the exhaustion of his drive from Bologna and from dysentery contracted *en route*. Thus weak and distracted, he discarded his highest trumps and, advancing a rash claim, presented his antagonist with the very thing Pitt wanted, a fascinating question of constitutional theory and principle which Parliament could debate for weeks without reaching any conclusion.

Pitt took up the point at once. 'I maintain, from every precedent and every page in our history, that the assertion of such a right, either in the Prince of Wales or in any other individual, is nothing less than treason to our Constitution.' Then he, in turn, went too far, adding, 'The Prince of Wales has no more right to the Regency than any other subject of the realm.'

His last observation seemed to many of his hearers as indiscreet as Fox's: but since its effect was simply to give the Opposition a good debating-point, and for Pitt every day spent debating was a day gained, the indiscretion, if such it was, served well his main purpose.

The rest of the day was occupied largely by Fox and Pitt qualifying their somewhat unfortunate claims, and trying to efface the impression they had made. Fox said, 'I spoke merely as a Private Member of Parliament, wholly unauthorised by His Royal Highness or any other person.' He denied that he had ever said the Prince should *assume* his right. 'Mr Pitt has admitted that the Prince of Wales has an "irresistible claim" to the Regency: there is no difference between this and an "inherent right". Whatever doubts may exist on this point, none can arise on the propriety of investing him with the sole administration of the Government, together with the unlimited exercise of all the royal functions, powers and prerogatives.'

Pitt, however, had no intention of being diverted from the pursuit of the elusive hare which Fox had so imprudently started.

Let us ascertain, in the first instance, our own rights. The matter must be settled on constitutional principles. No part of the royal authority can vest in the Heir Apparent as a matter of right; though as a matter of discretion and expediency it is highly desirable that whatever portion of it shall be exercised should be conferred on the Prince of Wales. Whatever authority is thought necessary for carrying on the public business ought to be conferred. On the other hand all authority which is not necessary ought to be withheld.

After Burke had called Pitt 'one of the Prince's competitors', and 'the Prince opposite', Sheridan, with inconceivable folly, enraged Members by threatening them with 'the danger of provoking the Prince to assert his right to the Regency'. The House then adjourned to 15 December.

In the Lords, the Opposition case was put by Loughborough. Parliament, he said, could only provide for the exercise of the royal authority on the extinction of the royal line, leaving no heir; or on a total subversion of government by a breach of the implied contract between King and subjects such as had occurred in 1688. Otherwise, the regal authority must pass direct to the heir, the Prince of Wales. The two Houses by themselves could not make even a Turnpike Act, so how could they make a Regent?

Interest, however, centred on the political agility of the Chancellor, who adroitly avoided expressing any opinion. Loughborough's argument, he said, with whatever force it might come from a magistrate so eminent, to himself was new. He then retired behind a smoke-screen of compliments to the Prince of Wales, praising Loughborough for not resting any part of his argument 'on the private virtues of that illustrious personage who should always have his applause when the expression of it would not be an impertinence'.

These debates gave ample scope for the political gossips. The supporters of the Ministry gloated, 'Fox advanced the most extraordinary doctrines'; 'only think of Fox's want of judgement, to bring himself into such a scrape'; 'Fox's declaration has been of great service to us. Is it not wonderful that such great talents should be conducted with so little judgement?'[29]

The more sanguine members of the Opposition claimed that 'Pitt is playing the game without temper or judgement. His declaration that the Prince of Wales had no better right to the Regency than any other subject, gives as much offence and alarm as Fox's assertion that he was of right entitled to it.' But on the whole it was 'all hurrah and triumph at White's', and corresponding gloom at Brooks's, where everyone realized Fox had blundered. 'I suppose', muttered Sheridan sourly, 'he has some little right, has he not?' Sheridan and his colleagues 'resolved to go through with Fox's principle of right, but in

their hearts don't quite agree, and are sorry it's come on.'
Sheridan actually reproached Charles Fox, who airily replied,
'It's better always to take the bull by the horns.' 'Yes', retorted
Sheridan, 'but you needn't have drove him into the room that
you might take him by the horns.'

Mrs Thrale,* on the outer fringe of politics, thought that:

> Fox, Burke, Sheridan and all the Opposition people want an
> unlimited Regent. How unconstitutional! How dreadful! Pitt, I
> think, wants a settled republic: how unconstitutional is that too,
> but far less dangerous. Pitt is honest, the others are not: *he* is
> ambitious only, they are avaricious. The Prince's character makes
> his elevation to power extremely perilous to the State; his connec-
> tion with a Catholic lady increases our peril. How unfortunate
> that he should be so wicked![30]

Hers was a fairly common opinion.

The Chancellor's refusal to commit himself was a great
inconvenience to Pitt and Fox, and also to those gentlemen
who required guidance on whether it was safer to rat or to remain steady. Besides these, the Armed Neutrality of thirty in
the Commons and twenty in the Lords were also waiting for
his lead to show them which party was more likely to reward
their merits.[31]

On the 13th Fox, with the utmost distaste, asked Loughborough to surrender to Thurlow his reversionary interest in the
Chancellorship.

> I have swallowed a pill [he wrote to Sheridan]—a most bitter one
> it was—and have written to Lord Loughborough, whose answer
> of course must be consent. What is to be done next? Should the
> Prince himself, you or I, or Warren† be the person to speak to
> the Chancellor? The objection to the last is, that he must probably
> wait for an opportunity, and that no time is to be lost. Pray tell
> me what is to be done: I am convinced, after all, the negotiation

* She was a friend and patient of Sir Lucas Pepys, who was nearly as
hopeful of the case as Willis.

† An interesting indication of how deeply Dr Warren was committed to
the Opposition.

will not succeed, and I am not sure that I am sorry for it. I do not remember ever feeling so uneasy about any political thing I ever did in my life.[32]

Nothing but ill health could have induced Fox to write such a letter to a man of whose judgement he had the lowest opinion. In the event, it was Sheridan who carried Fox's offer to the Chancellor. But he was too late: Thurlow had already been convinced by Willis that the King would soon recover.

Sheridan thinks the application late rather, as the Chancellor has pledged himself to support the limitations. Sheridan says he left him with the impression of his being a great rogue—he tried to sound Sheridan on a plan of undermining Fox. He told Sheridan one limitation would be, the Household to be continued under the Queen for six months; nor could this, he said, signify the Queen and Prince being so well together. He owned the Queen was a termagant. He said, if the Prince refused the Regency,* they must have Lord Justices.

Sheridan said, 'But what may become of your head, when he is King?'

'You may hang the Chancellor', replied Thurlow, 'but you can't alter the law.'

Sheridan is now rather for accepting, with the limitations remaining for six months. Charles Fox very much against it—great embarrassment.[33]

As for Loughborough, he was outraged at being shelved, and in an angry letter to Fox, suggested that Thurlow simply wished to 'find the key of the backstairs' and rule the King and Ministry himself, through his influence with the Queen.[34]

The whole question of limitations on the Regency had been vastly complicated by Willis's optimism and Warren's assumption that the King would not recover. Everyone realized, though nobody dared say so, that if the Prince of Wales became Regent with full powers over his father's household, including the physicians, his first act would be to replace Dr Willis, who had staked his professional reputation on curing the King, by Dr

* i.e. with limitations.

107

Warren, whose reputation depended on the King being incurable. Since the Prince's friends would be dismissed the instant the King recovered, it seemed improbable, in these circumstances, that the King would *ever* be declared sane. So the Privy Council decided to put the government of the household and physicians under the Queen, not under the Regent. Thurlow, in an apologia which he later wrote to explain his equivocal actions, put the point with brutal clarity:

> My first care was that the King should not be in the care of the Regent's Ministers and that no obstacle should be thrown in the way of his recovery. As I foresaw that objections would be raised to any symptoms of his recovery, I took the mode of proof out of their power: but still, with a Parliament at their back, what might they not do to prevent his recovery! They might so intimidate the Queen's Council that they would be afraid to declare the King convalescent. . . . And if I had stood out, as I should have done, at all hazards in the King's support, an impeachment would probably have been my reward.

The essence of the Regency crisis was not whether the King could recover, but whether he would ever be allowed to recover.

Many people shared the Chancellor's suspicions, but few dared admit them in public, and none in Parliament. Mrs Thrale, however, who loathed the Prince of Wales, did not hesitate to express even more sinister apprehensions.

> Our Opposition people catch greedily at the notion of his being a confirmed lunatic—no wonder! They will despatch him, I suppose, and say he did it himself. . . . Madness is in itself no incurable disease; half one's acquaintances have been as mad as our poor King can be, and do vastly well again. . . . And why must the King be precluded recovery? *Because he is the King*: and has people about him ready to ease his shoulders of the trouble, I trust. That's all! Poor man! How distressful is his situation! And in how much danger is his life![35]

Rumours of the Privy Council's plan, which Thurlow had betrayed to Sheridan, spread quickly through the Opposition;

GEORGE III
After Sir William Beechey

GEORGE, PRINCE OF WALES

WILLIAM PITT
After Karl Hickel

CHARLES JAMES FOX
From the portrait
by Karl Hickel

'*ANTIENT MUSIC*'

From the cartoon (1787) by Gillray

The King and Queen are under the canopy; Pitt (*extreme left*) leads the music. The coalition of a fox with the features of Fox and a chamber pot with the features of North is pursued by hounds. The concert is being given by a Handel choir of many leading figures of the time.

WINDSOR CASTLE

KEW HOUSE

DR FRANCIS WILLIS
From the pastel by John Russell

DR JOHN WILLIS
From the pastel by John Russell

SIR GEORGE BAKER
From the portrait by Ozias Humphry

DR RICHARD WARREN
From a portrait after Gainsborough

'FILIAL PIETY'

From the cartoon (1788) by Rowlandson

The drunken Prince of Wales bursts into the King's bedroom.

'BLUE AND BUF LOYALTY'

From the cartoon (1788) by Rowlandson

Dr Francis Willis (*extreme left and right*) and Sheridan

FANNY BURNEY
From the portrait by E. F. Burney

BETSY SHERIDAN

COLONEL GREVILLE
After Ozias Humphry

and the Queen, for the first time in twenty-eight years, found herself a factor of political importance. On the 7th she had assured the Prince that she had no political ambition; but within a week, prompted perhaps by Pitt and reassured by Willis, she began to see herself as the main obstacle to her son's domination. Soon she was spoken of in Brooks's, Carlton House and Devonshire House, as the political partner of Pitt. 'Many', wrote Sir John Eden, 'think the Minister means the restrictions on the Regency to be such that the Prince must decline it, and that he will appoint the Queen Regent, and continue to govern in her name.'[36]

As for Willis, who was busy destroying all their hopes, no man could be more odious to the Opposition: he could do nothing without being traduced and misrepresented, especially by the Duchess of Devonshire. 'The King much better, walked 2 miles in his garden, and asked young Willis [Dr John] to walk with him—this represented as a proof of sense, but is in fact, as Warren said, a proof of mad cunning, as he hates the father, to get the son over to him—he asked young Willis to kick his father out of the room. The King played at draughts, which the sanguine courtiers call playing at chess.' On the 14th the Duchess saw Dr Warren. 'He blames Dr Willis's imprudence who let the Queen come to the King last night. He was tolerable at first, but got quite wild—proposed marriage between a keeper and Mme Schwellenburg.* The Queen fainted, and the King had the waistcoat on for the first time.'[37] It is interesting to compare this with other accounts.

In his evidence before a Parliamentary Committee, even Warren's story was less picturesque. On 12 December the King in Kew Gardens saw his children. He displayed 'considerable emotion, which was accompanied by acts demonstrating that emotion'. Notwithstanding this, on the 13th Dr Willis introduced 'that Person whose great and amiable qualities we all know must necessarily make her the dearest and tenderest object of His Majesty's thoughts'. After a short interview, His Majesty showed great irritation; strict coercion was applied for the

---

* Keeper of the Robes, a formidable old dragon, the cross Fanny Burney had to bear.

first time, and blisters. Dr Warren spoke to Dr Willis 'with some degree of sharpness'.[38]

Lord Ailesbury recorded:

> At seeing the Queen, the King was much agitated: but declared it made him very happy, and he would do all he could to recover, which he was indifferent about before. He was exceedingly affectionate to the Queen. Dr Willis said, 'You are not attending to your backgammon.'
>
> 'How can I', said the King, 'when the person I love most in the world is in the room with me?'
>
> He had a bad night, and wore the strait-waistcoat from 4 p.m. to 9 a.m.[39]

Here is Willis's story, as told to the Parliamentary Committee. There were good consequences from the King seeing the little Princesses at a window during his first walk on the 12th.

> Such occurrences can scarce be too frequent, as it comforts the patient to think that he is with his family and that they are affectionate to him. The irritation occasioned by a patient seeing his friends is entirely over-balanced by the softening into tears which ever leads to amendment. I led in Princess Amelia myself. His Majesty showed the greatest mark of parental affection I ever saw. The other physicians protested, but I told them I was sent to make use of my own discretion, and they could not think themselves proper judges of it. That, or the next, evening he had a quarter-hour interview with the Queen. The King persuaded Princess Amelia to fetch the Queen. Coercion was used that night for the first time. It was the blisters, not seeing the Queen, that gave him a bad night. The blisters were settled at a consultation with the other physicians. I was told they had not irritated him before, at Windsor.[40]

Yet another account says merely that the King held and kissed the Queen's hand for half an hour, and the little princess sat on his lap. Sir George Baker, in the official bulletin, wrote, 'After having seen the Queen and Princess Amelia, His Majesty has passed a very unquiet night and continues this morning

very much agitated.' Lady Harcourt, referring to this contro-
versial occasion, wrote some days later:

> We are mad with all the doctors except Sir Lucas Pepys. Dr
> Warren dines every day at Carlton or York House, says the King
> has not spoke one word of sense since his illness. Sir George Baker
> says it would be happy to hear it was *all over*, for that he never
> can recover.* They are outrageous with Dr Willis for many things,
> particularly for letting the Queen see the King, which I don't
> believe did him any harm, on the contrary good in many respects,
> why should not Sir G.B. be honest enough to impute the King
> having bad nights to the blisters drawing on his legs? Was not
> that as likely to disturb him as having seen the Queen? I could talk
> about this for ever, but I believe the less said about it the better,
> especially *from me.* . . . I beg you will mention to Lord Ailesbury
> and Lord Brudenell that it was taken notice of they were not in
> the House of Lords. It would be kind to give their attendance now
> constantly in case business should arise. Honest men must get the
> better in the end of villainy.[41]

Meanwhile both sides prepared for an encounter on the 15th.
Pitt, wrote Betsy Sheridan angrily, 'is determined to fight every
inch of the ground, and gains time and gives trouble to others
though there is not the smallest probability of his holding out
long.' The Prince, stimulated by Sheridan's company until four
in the morning, personally canvassed the Peers, and appealed to
Lord Lonsdale, an ornament of the Armed Neutrality, 'to discountenance any proposition that may be brought forward to
insult and arraign my character and conduct. In that light I
regard Mr Pitt's determination to press for a discussion on a
claim I have not preferred.'

Handbills were circulated, 'Fox for the Prince's Prerogative';
and Mr Rolle threatened further to muddy the waters of discussion by introducing his pet subject of Mrs Fitzherbert.

* I am inclined to think that the statement attributed to Baker has some
connection with a letter attributed to him which he strongly denied writing.
(See pp. 140–1.) Lady Harcourt was writing to Lord Sydney, one of the Secretaries of State: Baker's letter was supposed to have been written to Lady
Sydney.

In the Lords the Opposition tried to evade a discussion on the Prince's claim of right, but Lord Camden, taking his cue from Pitt, insisted on devoting to it as much time as possible. 'The rights of the two Houses, having been questioned', he declared unctuously, 'cannot be left undecided.' The Duke of York, on behalf of his brother, tried to dissociate himself from Fox's indiscretion, disavowing any claim not derived from the Will of the People. 'The Prince', he said, 'has preferred no such claim.' (This was quite true: the claim had been preferred by others, for him.)[42]

The main interest, however, was Thurlow's recantation. With tears pouring down his face, he refused ever to desert his beloved King, who had conferred on him so many favours 'which whenever I forget, may God forget me!' This moving display of loyalty did not have the desired effect on those members of the Lower House who heard it. 'God forget you!' exclaimed Wilkes. 'He'll see you damned first!' Burke suggested that to be forgotten was the best thing that could happen to the Lord Chancellor; and Pitt was heard to mutter, 'Oh, the rascal!' But on the country at large, ignorant of his intricate manoeuvres, Thurlow's speech made a great impression, and his fidelity was commemorated in innumerable portraits, snuff-boxes, pocket-books. No doubt he carried to Pitt all the secrets which the Opposition had been so imprudent as to entrust to him—just as he had disclosed to the Prince the secrets of the Ministry.[43] Charles Fox, however, 'was very happy that the Chancellor has declared against us. There are great suspicions of the Queen taking a strong part.'

Though still a sick man, Fox was sustained by his optimism, writing that day:

We shall have several hard fights in the House of Commons this week and next, in some of which I feel we shall be beat; but whether we are or not, I think it certain that in about a fortnight we shall come in. If we carry our questions, we shall come in in a more creditable and triumphant way, but at any rate the Prince must be Regent, and of consequence the Ministry must be changed. The manner in which the Prince has behaved through the whole has been the most steady, the most friendly and the handsomest that can be conceived. You know, when he sets his mind to a thing, he can do it well, and in this instance he has done it most thoroughly. The Duke of York, who is steadiness itself, seems as warmly our friend as the Prince himself. In short, with regard to the Prince, everything is easy and pleasant, much beyond what I could form any idea of. In regard to other things, I am rather afraid they will get up some cry against the Prince for grasping, as they call it, at too much power: but I am sure I cannot in conscience advise him to give up anything which is really necessary to his government; or indeed to claim anything else as Regent but the full power of a King to which he is certainly entitled. The King himself (notwithstanding the reports you may possibly hear) is certainly worse, and perfectly mad. I believe the chance of recovery is very small indeed, but I do not think there is any possibility of his dying.[44]

Neither Fox nor any other of these heroes of Whig mythology gave a moment's thought to the difficulty of governing without a parliamentary majority, or of obtaining such a majority in the face of a hostile public opinion. The Regent, they assumed, must provide a majority for them, as his father had provided it for their rivals.

The odds in Brooks's that night were evens on the outcome of the struggle: and next day, Pitt was markedly embarrassed by the offer of £100,000 from the City, to make him independent of fortune after his dismissal, which 'no consideration on earth would induce him to accept'.[45] Unshaken in his determination to procrastinate to the last, he insisted on reverting to the Prince's claim of right.[46]

I readily acknowledge the most eminent qualities of the present Heir Apparent. But it has been asserted that he possesses a title as indisputable as he would have had by the natural demise of the King, because the present suspension is a civil death. Can we then consider His Majesty's indisposition, which is not an uncommon case* and in general only temporary, as a civil death? I am persuaded that we can not. . . . The lofty terms in which that claim of right was originally made have, I admit, been since somewhat

* A revealing observation. See pp. 9–10, and Mrs Thrale's letter on p. 108.

lowered. It has likewise been declared that no intention exists of enforcing that right: but words cannot afford a guarantee that such attempts may not be resumed or asserted.

Fox challenged Pitt to put the motion, 'Whereas the Prince of Wales has never claimed any right to the Regency, it becomes necessary to declare that he has no right, and we therefore declare His Royal Highness sole Regent.'

He knows he dare not risk it. He would not be supported by twenty members. He appears to have been so long in possession of power, that he cannot endure to part with it. He is determined to cripple his successors. If a foreigner were to ask if the monarchy of Great Britain is hereditary or elective, he must be told, when the King is in good health, it is hereditary: but when he is ill, it is elective.

Pitt, said Fox, would never have proposed the limitations had he not known himself unworthy of the Prince's confidence.

Poor North, blind, was led to the Opposition benches; and Pitt then moved three Resolutions:

1. That the King was unable to attend public business.
2. That it was the right and duty of the two Houses of Parliament to make good the defect of the royal authority.
3. That the Peers and Commons should determine the means by which the royal assent should be given, on behalf of the King, to such Bills as might be passed by the two Houses. He suggested that the Chancellor might vicariously indicate royal assent by affixing to them the Great Seal.

The vital question of restrictions on the Regency, which was on everyone's mind, Pitt did not mention.

At some time that evening, Pitt had a note from Dr Willis saying the King was better and would certainly recover. This he read out, after the debate, at White's. Betsy Sheridan states, probably incorrectly, that he also read it out before the division in the House. Whether or not this turned the scales, 'the messieurs at Brooks's were much mistaken', for when Lord North moved, to close the debate, 'that the Chairman now

114

leave the Chair', he was defeated by 268 votes to 204, a very full House. The armed neutrality, however, voted against Pitt and many of his friends ratted.*

'Fox's declaration', wrote Lord Sheffield next day, 'seems to have done more harm than I imagined, and Pitt's mountebank speeches suit the nonsense of many. Pitt means to govern, or obstruct through a majority in the Lords.'

Willis's letter enraged the Opposition and embarrassed many of his friends, though George Selwyn cheerfully called him the King's rat-catcher. Stories against him redoubled.

Willis has done all sorts of real mountebank things, which have frequently done harm. The last experiment was of letting the King see one of the Princesses and the Queen. He caught up Princess Emily and swore no power on earth would ever separate them. The girl was terrified. So was the Queen. [The King has said], 'You know a man who has been in a strait-waistcoat can never wear the Crown again.'[47]

On the 16th Greville returned, and resumed his account of the King's illness. On the same day, Dr John Willis started his diary.[48] So from the 16th we have two detailed accounts of the royal malady, written from two quite different viewpoints. Greville seems to have been devoid of political ambition or even opinions: he simply wanted the King to get well, and hardly cared what happened in the meanwhile. Worn out, perhaps, with the intolerable strain of the past few weeks, during which he was continually called upon to control and thwart his master, his whole vision and diary is filled with his difficulties and the King's day-to-day aberrations. He had neither the experience of mental ailment, nor the objective judgement to see, through the frustrations and disappointments of the King's fluctuating condition, a steady overall improvement.

His political position was peculiar in that, while utterly loyal to the King, he disliked the Queen, distrusted Pitt, and re-

* Compare these figures with the analysis of the House six months before, which gave the Ministry 280 votes, the Opposition 155, neutrals and independents 122. See p. 28.

mained on amicable terms with the Prince of Wales. With the Opposition case he seems to have had much sympathy; and he had friendly social contact with the Opposition leaders through their celebrated hostess, Mrs Crewe, and the Duke of Portland, who were both his relations. He viewed the prospect of a Regency without dismay.

There is a vital difference between Greville's diary before he went on leave and his diary on his return. From 6 November 'a regular and constant watch' was kept over the King, by the equerries and pages: one of the equerries had always to be either in the King's room, or in his ante-room: they were in charge of the pages, who were in personal attendance on the King. Greville bore the brunt of this honourable, though exhausting duty, for he was the King's favourite equerry. From 20 November to the end of the month he was with the King for several hours every day. The early part of his diary is, therefore, that of an eyewitness, or at least of a man in authority over eyewitnesses such as pages.[49] After Willis's arrival, however, Greville saw the King rarely, and only when specifically invited by Willis. Page after page of the latter part of his journal betrays his chagrin at being relieved of responsibility and thrust into the background. His diary is that of an honest man, devoted to the King, but seldom an eyewitness of the events he relates, and consumed with jealousy of the Willises. Furthermore, he was by nature inclined to pessimism.

Dr Francis Willis (and his qualities were reproduced, somewhat diluted, in his son, Dr John) was an optimist. He was very experienced in this sort of case, neither frightened nor shocked by symptoms which alarmed a layman. A strong party man, he knew perfectly well that the Regent would, if he could, dismiss him within an hour, replacing him with Dr Warren. This he believed, not without reason, would be fatal to the King's hope of recovery. Although he was too good a physician deliberately to distort the truth, no doubt his political views and his optimism coloured his son's diary. He saw no reason to relate all the clinical facts to the Royal Family, least of all to the Prince of Wales who was avid to hear and, indeed, industriously invented them. When all is said, Dr Willis was, in the end, vindicated by success.

Dr John and Greville differed not so much in the *facts* they recorded, as in their interpretation of the facts. Greville probably told the truth in so far as he could judge it from the gossip he heard: Dr John told the truth, but probably not the whole truth.

It was arranged by the Privy Council that Willis should be in charge of the King's person and domestic arrangements, working within the limits of a general policy agreed with his colleagues. Sir Lucas Pepys, Dr Gisborne and Dr Reynolds attended in rotation from 4 p.m. to 11 a.m., when Sir George Baker and Dr Warren arrived. They then all saw the King; and agreed (or disagreed) on the daily bulletin and the treatment for the next twenty-four hours. Two surgeons, two apothecaries, three of Willis's own men and the pages were also in attendance.[50] No responsibility was given the equerries, who were regarded as mere hangers on. Although in theory Willis could do nothing which had not been agreed with his colleagues, he and his son were always present while they were not, which in fact gave him far more weight. This, of course, they resented; and they all tended to side with Warren until the amendment in the King's condition became obvious to the most stubbornly blind eye.

On the morning of 16 December, for instance, Willis wanted to publish in the daily bulletin that the King had had a good night with six hours' sleep. The others, however, elicited from the pages that it was not continuous sleep, but three interrupted periods. 'You see, Dr Willis,' said Pepys complacently, 'you can't make it a good night without splicing.'[51]

Relations between the doctors were also complicated by the anomalous position of Dr John. Baker, Warren and the rest treated him merely as his father's assistant; which galled him since he was himself a qualified physician, a graduate of Oxford and Edinburgh, with fourteen years' specialist experience of mental disease. 'I was a physician of equal responsibility', he complained in his diary on the 16th, 'but here wholly unnoticed, and why?' When Dr Willis upheld his son's professional standing, Warren said 'in a pshaw kind of dictatorial style, "No more of it, doctor, no more of it! You never can set it right, as long as you live." '[52]

117

In the eyes of his colleagues, Willis could do nothing right. For instance, on the 18th Dr Warren found His Majesty reading *King Lear* which, not unnaturally, he thought unsuitable. Jumping to conclusions, he 'expressed great objection to Dr Willis', and reported it to the Prince of Wales. In fact Willis was not to blame, for it never occurred to him that Colman's works, which the King had innocently requested from the Library, included a potted version of *Lear*. However, no great harm was done, the King merely observing, 'Thank Heaven, I have no Regan, no Goneril—but all Cordelias, all Cordelias!'[53]

A terrific row occurred over Willis's reports to the Prime Minister. Dr Warren, by his own account, was informed by the Prince that Willis had written at midnight a grossly optimistic letter which Pitt read out at White's at five in the morning. He told Willis that as the King was very bad that night, and under coercion, he regarded it simply as a political letter.

'It's surprising', said Warren, 'that a man could stoop to writing a political letter.' Then, taking Willis's hand, he added, 'I'm extremely sorry for what has passed. I always had a good opinion of you; but now I've entirely changed my opinion, and shall have a bad one as long as I live.'

Willis retorted, 'My letter, when I wrote it, was true. I look upon it not as false. The King continued through the day sometimes irritable, in general in good humour—made great complaints of his blisters.'

The Duchess wrote a characteristic version of the encounter: 'The express was to have found Pitt at the House, for Willis is a great Pittite, and thought it would influence the division. . . . Warren said Willis disgraced his former character as a clergyman, and his present one as a physician, by becoming a political note-writer.' Betsy Sheridan heard that 'Warren, in a great passion, almost called the other a villian and other words of the same import.'

The truth of the matter was, that the King had had a good afternoon on the 16th, but a bad night, mainly because of the blisters which had been applied with Warren's and Baker's concurrence. Pitt produced, for inspection by the Parliamentary Committee,* all his recent correspondence; but no letter was

* On 7 January.

found written that day later than the afternoon: and Dr John recorded in his diary, 'It so happens the letter was written by me, John Willis, at half past 4.' This does not, of course, mean that it was not intended to influence the division in the House: probably it was; but it was an honest estimate of the King's condition and prospects at the time it was written; and Dr Warren had to apologize to Dr Willis.

The Queen intervened with cold animosity in the physicians' feuds. When the Princess Royal had a fever and sore throat, she would not let Sir George Baker attend her, saying that he could never expect favour after his recent performance. 'The others', prophesied Betsy Sheridan, 'will probably all be dismissed in their turn as, being questioned on oath, they could only answer according to their consciences.'[54]

Colonel Greville on his return from leave found 'strong symptoms of jealousies among the Medical Corps and much bustle extended to other parts of the establishment'. Dr Willis had given the sick-room arrangements a good shake-up, introduced some of his own male nurses, and in particular had issued orders that no one enter His Majesty's room without his, or Dr John's, permission. Such reforms could hardly meet with his colleagues' approval, and there was a brisk quarrel on the 16th when a page refused Dr Warren admission because His Majesty was asleep.

'But I must go in', Warren insisted. 'You know I am a spy upon you all.'

It was an unfortunate remark, which he probably meant as a joke: but to Willis's men it was no joke, and it became the subject of an unbecoming wrangle before the Parliamentary Committee.

'How is the King?' Warren then asked.

'Very bad', said the page.

'What sort of a night has His Majesty passed?'

'A terrible one.'

Dr Willis then arrived, and Warren protested, 'I don't choose to take my opinion from pages' reports.'

'You may open the door', conceded Willis graciously. ('It was', Warren afterwards complained, 'a circumstance that I do not recollect ever having happened to me before, someone else generally opening the door for me.')

The King was in a strait-waistcoat and, according to Warren, greeted him, 'I have been very ill indeed, Dr Warren, and I have put myself into this waistcoat; but it is uneasy to me. Will you take it off?'

Dr Warren, 'perceiving that in the King's exhausted condition this indulgence was safe', replied, 'Most willingly do I obey you, Sire.'

Dr Willis agreed, 'His Majesty will rise soon, and then we shall be able to do without coercion.'

That is Dr Warren's account of the incident. Dr John wrote in his diary, 'Dr Warren released him. It appeared to be done at a moment when he was not capable of promising or adhering to any promise of honour. He jumped up and down in bed till he tore off his blisters. Dr Warren said it was all a trick in His Majesty.'[55]

Dr Willis, however, 'laid great stress on the effect of the blisters applied to His Majesty's legs by Sir Lucas Pepys's prescription, to which he imputed much of the excessive uneasiness he had experienced and much of his late violence.' He said the King's bad nights were occasioned by the great pain of the blisters, and reproached his colleagues for not warning him that the King was particularly sensitive to this treatment.

An attendant intervened and said that last night, when the King called, he came in slippers. 'Now you come like a man of sense', said the King. 'I could have hanged Hawkins* one night. I called him up because the blisters gave excruciating pain; and he, instead of instantly coming to relieve me, delayed looking for his shoes.' Moreover the Queen told Willis that His Majesty was singularly sensitive to blisters, and twenty-five years ago, from the pain of one applied to his back, 'got out of bed, lay on the floor and rolled about like a madman'.[56]

Willis accused Warren of disturbing the King's rest by going into his room when he knew he was asleep. Pepys patched up the quarrel, and persuaded Willis to 'deny malicious reports that Dr Warren had violently awakened His Majesty'. But

---

* A surgeon, sometimes in attendance.

Willis only did so with the mental reservation that Warren had disturbed the King when about to go to sleep.

During the period of these unedifying squabbles, the King's conversation rambled over many subjects:

> He was good humoured, sociable, inclined to mimicry. He spoke much of the use of the lunge in training horses. 'It is an essential part of *manège*. . . . I prefer horses under 15 hands. . . . I love hunting, but I'm afraid of leaping, and even on a road I think of my neck and my family. A King should not ride bold. . . . I don't like Burke, he is flowery and dishonest. I dislike the whole party; but the one I like least, thank God, is at Rome*. . . . The English Constitution is the finest in the world: if it has a fault, it is that of not being fit for a King. . . . I always hated an ambitious man. I hate a minion, too. . . . I wish my son were more steady. The people like me, because they are afraid to trust my son. He has behaved like a boy. He has disinherited himself by marriage. I can't and never could bear Roman Catholics.'[57]

The bulletin described him as 'much disturbed' in the morning. However, he was well enough that evening to play backgammon; and on the 18th, Willis 'had not the least doubt of His Majesty's complete recovery'. But the *Morning Herald*, the principal Opposition paper, made a point of remarking, on the 22nd, 'Dr Willis has had a patient under his care for nine years whose malady is exactly similar to that of our present sovereign.'†[58]

On the 19th the blisters were particularly painful. The King became 'more touchy, and symptoms of returning crossness appeared'. But he was delighted with the arrival from Windsor of his little spaniel, Flora. Greville watched, without being seen, the King being put to bed by Willis's nurses.

> The present control established over His Majesty was new to me, but he appeared now to be accustomed to it himself. Dr Willis's men fomented his legs, preparatory to their being dressed. Whenever His Majesty put his hands out of bed, one of Dr Willis's men

---

* Charles Fox, who had, in fact, returned from Italy.

† The word 'present' is significant.

took hold of it and, putting it back again, covered it with the cloths, which did not even interrupt his conversation, so habituated was he now to this new system. . . . I begin to think Dr Willis is rather too incautious a man for his present responsible situation. He is certainly unguarded and imprudent, and too much so for a man who leans strongly to a political party. . . . He attacks Mr Fox and the Opposition with as much zeal as any partisan I know.

Dr Willis quoted with zest a remark he had heard, that Charles Fox had the flux because for some time he had eaten nothing but his own words. [59]

In the West End, the Opposition's attack was directed mainly against the Queen, now 'so dreadfully reduced that her stays would wrap twice over'. 'She is', wrote one of the Prince's friends, 'playing the very devil, and is at the bottom of the Cabals and intrigues against the Prince. One principal engine of the intriguers is the opinion that the King's recovery is to be expected with certainty and very speedily. Dr Willis was brought for that purpose, he being a noted shot with the longbow, besides being a quack.'

Peter Pindar addressed Pitt as 'dear as a Diamond* to the best of Queens'; and the Queen as:

> Oh Lady, whose great wisdom thinketh fit
> To spread thy petticoat o'er William Pitt.

A monstrous insinuation in the *Morning Herald* of 20 December, three days after the Queen had begged her son to keep her name out of the Press, was generally believed to have been inspired by the Prince himself. 'We can assure the public that some very extraordinary motives for the conduct of a CERTAIN LADY will be laid before them, unless she recedes from her present plan; and though the Love of DIAMONDS* may be forgiven on the score of female frailty, there are things which cannot be excused.'

---

* References to the Queen's passion for jewellery; also, perhaps, to 'Diamond Pitt', the Prime Minister's nabob great-grandfather. She received from Warren Hastings a present of diamonds which gained some notoriety.

Even in the public eye, the Prince was hardly presenting a becoming example of filial solicitude. He was bosky at the Opera, and seen reeling into political meetings at Carlton House. 'There is nothing I detest more', he said loudly at a Court function, pointing at his mother, 'than a face open and smiling, with a heart false and wicked.'[60]

Night after night he was drinking at Brooks's (where the members laid bets* on the date of the Regency and referred to a certain Court card as The Lunatic) and mimicking his father's supposed gestures and ravings. Charles Fox was alarmed by his conduct, and on the 19th indicated a preference for the Duke of York. He quickly corrected himself, 'Oh, I'm the most prudent man alive, I'll never mention it again!' On the 20th, however, the date of the scurrilous paragraph in the *Morning Herald*, 'while pulling up his stock and shaving before a whole roomful, he said, "The Duke of York for my money!" '

Most people, the Duchess admitted, thought it 'wrong of the Prince and the Duke of York to canvas so much'. Such equivocal activity was best left to their junior satellites, two of whom were with Betsy Sheridan all day 'preparing an Address to come from different parts of the country to counteract Mr Pitt'.[61]

The Prince had a good deal to annoy him, for on 17 December he had what he described as an impertinent letter from Pitt. 'The Prince very hurt. The Duke of York very stout, and talks of civil war.' The Prince was, moreover, bothered not only with his brother's unhelpful contributions to the debate, but with divided counsels in his own party. 'Sheridan', wrote the Duchess of Devonshire on the 19th, 'is for accepting the limitations, and then get rid of them. Fox and the Duke of Portland against, but he thinks they will come round. Dr Warren told me the Chancellor could not decide, he wished he would—had seen the King, in good humour but quite mad.'[62]

On the political stage, Fox was ill on the 19th so Pitt gladly agreed to an adjournment. Sir John Eden 'would not be surprised, according to the surprising luck that always attends our Minister, if Charles Fox should fall a martyr to his exertions, for he is far from well. The Minister talks of despatch, but does not

* Though stated in contemporary memoirs, this is not confirmed by the Club Betting Book.

press it. We believe he wishes delay, to take advantage of the Chapter of Accidents. It will probably appear to you that both parties have acted too warmly.'[63]

There was a long, desultory debate on Pitt's second Resolution, that it was the right and duty of the two Houses to supply the defect in the royal authority. After Fox had been neatly compared to Falstaff at the time of Henry IV's last illness, with the implied comparison of the present Prince of Wales to Prince Hal, the resolution passed without a division.

The third Resolution*, on how a vicarious Royal Assent could be indicated on Bills which had passed both Houses, was the 'citadel of the Ministry, within which Pitt meditated to capitulate on terms'. The Opposition, wishing to force him to unconditional surrender, moved to 'address the Prince of Wales to take upon him the Administration during His Majesty's indisposition'. Thus, they claimed, the Third Estate would be supplied, and only when that step was taken should the Houses present to the Regent the limitations on his power: of his acquiescence, there could not be the slightest doubt.

Pitt, however, voiced the strongest doubts: 'Who can answer for his not using the royal negative, when the limitations are presented to him for consent?' The Cabinet had therefore decided to counterfeit the Third Estate by empowering the Chancellor to put the Great Seal to Bills which had passed the two Houses.[64]

It was an ingenious dodge, obviously far less constitutional then merely allowing the Prince to assume the office of Regent, but neatly checking the Opposition's plan. It was attacked in one of the most extravagant speeches of Edmund Burke.

This cadaverous, bespectacled Irishman, now nearly sixty, to later generations was famed mainly as an orator. His contemporaries, however, had no time for his interminable, turgid and cantankerous harangues, full of complicated imagery and recondite quotations.

Too deep for his hearers, he went on refining,
And thought of convincing while they thought of dining.

* See p. 114.

The sound of his brogue, it was said, emptied the House like the dinner-bell.

He was a man of intelligence and sincerity, generous and humane, who for twenty years had tried to fit out his party with a policy and a coherent doctrine. But, like most Irishmen, he had no vestige of humour; and was further handicapped by a complete inability to see an opponent's point of view, or even to appreciate that an opponent might have a point of view. His friends claimed that he was

> Though equal to all things, for all things unfit;
> Too nice for a statesman, too proud for a wit;
> For a patriot too cool, for a drudge, disobedient,
> And too fond of the Right to prefer the Expedient.

But his profound conviction that Edmund Burke was always right, while his adversaries were not only wrong, but dishonest, corrupt and immoral made him unnecessarily offensive in debate, which did his cause more harm than good.

> 'Tis often said that, upon Irish ground,
> No poisonous snake has ever yet been found.
> Revealed the secret stands of Nature's work—
> She saved her venom, to create a Burke.

Having battled for most of his career in penurious and frustrating opposition, he saw in the royal malady the prospect of a belated fall of manna from Heaven. But now it seemed as though the infamous Pitt might defraud the Opposition of their long-awaited opportunity; and disappointment brought out the worst in this warm-hearted, talented man.

'Folly personified, shaking his cap and bells under the laurels of genius', he launched a tirade against Pitt's plan for the use of the Great Seal.

A composition of wax and copper is to represent the Sovereign. ... I disclaim all allegiance to a King so formed. I will never bow down before Priapus. It is intended to set up a man with black brows and a large wig [Lord Chancellor Thurlow]: he is the fit person: trust none of the Royal Family: he will be a kind of scarecrow to the two Houses. I approve not of robbery, house-breaking, highway robbery or any other: yet each of them is more excusable than law forgery.

It was a time when 'double-talk' pervaded every debate,[65] and men keenly appreciated the irony of Charles Fox, who had spent the last ten years in enmity with the Crown, now championing every jot and tittle of the Royal Prerogative: while the rights of Parliament were upheld by Pitt, who had been hoisted into power through an underhand abuse of that Prerogative. Now Burke, whose whole political career had been devoted to reducing the power of the Crown, pleaded with extravagant emotion, 'If the unfortunate monarch whom we all lament could know of the proposition now agitated, he would cry out with Macbeth

> Upon my head they placed a fruitless crown,
> And put a barren sceptre in my gripe,
> Thence to be wrenched with an unlineal hand,
> No son of mine succeeding.

' "Restore me", he would add, "to my former state. Let me not behold a black-browed phantom seated on my throne." '

On the subject of restrictions on the Regent's power of making peers, with extraordinary folly he suggested more peerages and sinecures for the 'great Whig families'. When the irritated House, which thought the great Whig families had quite enough already, roared its disapproval, Burke turned fiercely on them, 'I know a pack of hounds that would eclipse you in senseless vociferation!'

It was in its way a brilliant performance, but scarcely helpful to the Prince's cause: and he 'finished his wild speech in a manner next to madness'.

Pitt closed for the Ministry, speaking (for almost the first time in the long debate) with remarkable frankness. 'The Regent may fill the other House with peers while we are actually deliberating whether the power shall, or shall not, be limited.' He carried his Resolution by 251 votes to 178.

Up till Christmas, the Opposition (other than Charles Fox) still had faint hopes that the Chancellor would come to terms with them. But on Christmas Day Thurlow told Fox that the negotiations were at an end. Fox was delighted, writing to Loughborough:

It was much the pleasantest occasion I have had with him for many years. Upon the business of our interview he was perfectly open and explicit, and dismissed the subject as soon as possible with great good humour, in order to talk on general ones in our old manner. He was in a talkative vein, and France, Spain, Hastings, Demosthenes and Cicero were all talked over as if between two friends who had neither political contention nor enmity.

On 26 December, Pitt's three Resolutions were carried to the Lords. The Opposition moved to 'address the Prince of Wales to take upon himself the executive government as sole Regent': but Lord Camden insisted on wasting time by debating Fox's imprudent claim of right, 'since men's minds must be set at right upon that subject'.

The Marquess of Lansdowne (better known as the Earl of Shelburne), although still resentful of Pitt 'vaulting into his vacant office' in 1783, supported the Ministry. 'The Crown, my Lords, is not a discardable property, like a pig-stye, but held in trust for millions, which Parliament can mould, shape or alter.' His encomiums on the Prince of Wales were capable of more than one interpretation.

Let us suppose, my Lords, that the present Heir Apparent, instead of residing at Windsor and exhibiting a model of tender regard towards his sovereign, instead of doing the honours of his country towards foreigners and raising the national character for polished manners, had been caballing away his time in the capital. Let us suppose he had been intriguing with the army and navy, cultivating his interest with foreign courts, or raising money to carry on his ambitious projects, thus attempting to enforce his claim and to maintain his right by undue means. Would not every man in the kingdom wish that the two Houses of Parliament should exclude him from exercising the powers of Regent?

The Opposition lost their motion, largely because nearly all the Bishops and Lords of the Bedchamber were by now convinced that the King would recover.

On 30 December Pitt sent the Prince (wrote Betsy Sheridan*) 'an impertinent letter, and in an impertinent manner'. It was, complained His Royal Highness, 'a letter with such restrictions as no dictator could possibly, I think, have been barefaced enough to have brought forward'. He begged Loughborough to 'come to Charles's as soon as you possibly can, to take these matters into consideration'. Pitt's letter was, in fact, respectfully worded, but delivered in a somewhat casual manner by a common messenger to the hall porter at Carlton House. Pitt firmly and unequivocally offered to the Prince of Wales the Regency with certain restrictions agreed by the Cabinet, on the assumption that the King would soon be cured. These restrictions were:

1. The Regent's power shall not extend to the creating of any peer but of the royal issue having attained the age of twenty-one.
2. The Regent shall not make any grant, salary or pension, reversion or annuity for life or any other term other than during His Majesty's pleasure, except such offices as are required by law to be granted for life.
3. The Regent shall have no power over the real or personal property of the Crown.
4. The guardianship of the King, and the government of the King's household, shall be entrusted to the Queen.[66]

The first two restrictions were, of course, designed to prevent the Prince of Wales and Fox obtaining, by the massive use of patronage, a permanent majority in Parliament. The weakness of Pitt's position was that, if the King's illness were prolonged, the Regent, dissolving Parliament, might have enough residuary patronage to secure the election of a friendly House of Commons, and persuade enough peers to vote for the withdrawal of the restrictions. The third restriction was dictated by common knowledge of His Royal Highness's financial position and the

* In Betsy Sheridan's *Journal* her comments on this letter are obviously misdated.

frailty of his promises. The last was designed, frankly, to prevent the Regent replacing those doctors who hoped they could, and wanted to, cure his father, by those who had given up hope and did not so wish.

The Prince held agitated conferences with Fox, Burke, Sheridan and Loughborough to draft a reply. 'Saw Sheri at night', wrote the Duchess on New Year's Day, 1789. 'He came here though he ought to have been writing the Prince's letter. Burke had wrote one, he said, all fire and tow, Lord Loughborough one, all snow and ice—and he was to make one out of both. It will probably go tomorrow.' Wrapped in a fine pelisse given him by the Prince, Sheridan was again at Devonshire House until late on 1 January, to complete his draft of the Prince's letter and got the final version copied by his wife. Next morning, he went on to Charles Fox, who was living at Mrs Armistead's 'to avoid the bore of seeing people who are told he is out of town': and found, pinned up on the chimneypiece, his own note promising to be there by nine o'clock the previous evening. There was a brisk row, and Sheridan could give no better excuse for his procrastination than 'I'm as God made me.' Both sulked all next day, but made it up on the 4th.

Whoever was responsible for it (perhaps mainly Sheridan), the Prince's reply was an able document. He saw the restrictions as a project for 'producing weakness, disorder and disunity in the government: dividing the Royal Family from each other; separating Court from State; disconnecting the power to command service from the power of animating it by reward; allotting to the Regent all the invidious duties of government without the means of softening them by any act of grace, favour or benignity.'

'Nothing', it seemed to Betsy, 'can be better than what he says on this occasion. The most perfect moderation blended with a strong sense of the unworthy manner in which he is treated by the Minister. . . . The King continues the same. Their new word "comfortable" means nothing more than his not being outrageous.'

However, 'in compassion to the unsettled state of the nation', and afraid that, if he refused Pitt's terms, the Queen might be offered the Regency, His Royal Highness, under protest, accepted. 'They are thinking of a way', the Duchess had written on the 31st, 'to make the Prince's answer, which is to be a noble one, made public.' A leak was duly arranged, and the text of this confidential document was soon common knowledge.[67]

The Cabinet, after some debate on the propriety of answering the Prince's letter, eventually drafted a reply. It would never, they declared, have occurred to them to propose that plan 'if they had thought it would appear in that light in which they had the mortification to observe it is considered by Your Royal Highness, but they felt bound to adhere to these principles in the propositions to be offered to the consideration of Parliament.' In shorter and less stately language, they stuck to their guns.

Thurlow himself took this missive to Carlton House and, finding the Prince with Fox, asked, 'Does Your Royal Highness require an answer to your letter, or not?'

'No', said the Prince.

'As it has been written', suggested Charles Fox, 'we might as well look at it.'[68]

So Thurlow handed it over. Naturally it did nothing to appease the Prince, who at a dinner given by his brother, had expressed passionate resentment against Pitt and the Queen:

> I saw Pitt only once at Kew. Some person told me that he and the Duke of Richmond had come. My mind being fully occupied by the sad state of things, I forgot they were there until I was told they had been waiting two hours. The Duke was most obsequious, bowed incessantly. Pitt was very stately and stared at me with unforgiving haughtiness. . . . I must also lament a sad change in Her Majesty: after I'd taken charge of the King's jewellery, she positively charged me with taking advantage of the King's weak state to get possession of his treasures!

The Duke of York, never particularly discreet after dinner, was equally angry and outspoken about the string of lies obtruded on the public by Dr Willis:

> I give my word that not one of His Majesty's children are allowed to approach him. The Queen, wrought upon by insidious arts, is

130

resolved to abet the daring attempt to supersede my brother's just pretensions and help his enemies. Dr Warren has assured me that His Majesty's mind is only subdued, his sanity in no way restored. The Queen has confidence only in Thurlow, who has learned a lesson in duplicity from Pitt. Oh, how miserable do I feel at being obliged to appeal to the public! At the necessity of exposing facts over which every symptom of filial affection urges my brother and me to throw a veil! Nothing, gentlemen, would induce us to do so, but a sense of what we owe to the public![69]

On the whole, the public remained unimpressed with the Prince's concern. But their complaints were not entirely without substance. During the last fortnight, in which carefully non-committal bulletins had been reporting 'a quiet night', 'a disturbed night', the King 'calm' or 'in a comfortable way', His Majesty had been at times pretty bad.

On the 20th, Dr John admitted in his diary, the King grew turbulent towards morning, and had to have the waistcoat. At nine o'clock he was moaning 'in a wild, monotonous, delirious way, "Oh Emily [Princess Amelia], why won't you save your father? I hate all the physicians, but most the Willises; they beat me like a madman.* Digby, Greville, you are honest fellows, come to relieve me! Take off this cursed waist-coat!" '

His pulse ran from 112 to 120, and a dose of bark was necessary to reduce his fever and made him sweat. Even after he was allowed up, he was irritable and easily offended. This is all recorded in Dr John's diary, and is probably all true, but it may not be the whole truth.[70]

Greville added that the King had to be further controlled by tying him down to his bed. 'However persuaded I had been of the necessity of obtaining positive submission, I have not been prepared for these harsher processes. I do not question that these have now been adopted on a practice sanctioned by

* They certainly did not. Dr John never mentions in his diary any beating. If he or his father had beaten the King without daring to admit it, he would surely not have recorded this raving. Nor does Greville mention any beating, and he would certainly have heard of it if it had occurred.

confirmed experience. I can but grieve, and hope for the best.'*

Greville gives more details about the King's morning delirium, when the Queen 'was in no favour, he called Mr Pitt a rascal and Mr Fox his friend'. His pulse-rate, says Greville, went up to 140. 'I cannot think it kindness to His Majesty or his family to disperse accounts more favourable than his unhappy disorder in fact can warrant.' The bulletin simply reported, non-committally, that the King 'had a bad night, and is much disturbed'.[71]

Next day, the 21st, Greville heard the King was at first irritable and inclined to dispute; later he became more calm, but still too talkative. In the evening he was a little worse, until Dr Willis 'recommended him to be more calm, or he would talk himself into a strait-waistcoat'. Dr John found him 'good-humoured and forgiving what had passed the day before'. The King said, rather dancing, 'I'm so well, I could dance.' Dr John said, 'I hope, sir, it will be a quiet day, and that Your Majesty will be steady and dignified.'

'I hate dignity in private life', retorted the King. 'I always talk too fast, and I'm naturally passionate, like yesterday: but my pride makes me hide from the public things that hurt me.'

The Chancellor came, and Dr John asked him, 'If Mr Pitt sends for my opinion, am I not at full liberty to give it?'

'Certainly', said Thurlow, 'so long as it is your opinion, without political views.'

The bulletin reported his mind 'much as it has been for some days past'.[72]

The 22nd was by all accounts a good day. 'Dr Willis', remarked Greville, 'said he thought he now saw a road which led him to the way home, but this allusion he did not explain.' The worst Greville heard was that the King 'continued a little ticklish and was obliged to be managed very attentively'. Dr John referred to 'good humour, good dinner and two games of backgammon with Dr Willis'. As an instance of how these two

---

* The story of the King being tied to his bed is probably an exaggeration. Greville does not claim to have seen it. The Duchess reports it as having happened a week later when, according to both Dr John and Greville, the King was much better.

honest men took different views of the same circumstances, their comments that day on the King's blisters are instructive. Dr John records with satisfaction the first regular discharge from the blisters. Greville distinctly implies that the blisters are the Willises' excuse for any of their patients' aberrations.[73]

Next day, the 23rd, however, Greville admitted that the blisters were 'in a state of considerable discharge. . . . In the disturbance of the night, the dressings had been torn off and the blisters in consequence rubbed. Whatever may have caused the late irritations, it is not unlikely that the blisters in such state, threatening a sore and under such usage, may have increased them greatly.' It was decided that the same surgeon should dress his blisters each day, so that it was done always in the same manner. 'This regulation', Greville perceived, 'stirred somewhat of jealousy among the parties.' The King was riotously inclined most of the day and, though good humoured, had to be kept under coercion.

Dr John, too, found it a trying day. 'Ungovernable through night. Constrained at 5. Tongue whitish. Pulse 108. Under constraint most of the day. High spirits, jocose and pertinent.'

Dr John gave him some apples. 'Now I like you', said the King.

'What!' replied Dr John. 'By the time you have eaten them, you will dislike me.'

'Very well! And if I do, it is like the rest of the world, who like no longer than it serves their own interest.'

He was put to bed in the waistcoat, and complained of the arms being too tight, so Dr John loosened them. He then asked to be released. Dr John said, 'How far can I trust to your honour to be quiet, if I release you?'

'I will try all I can to be quiet', replied the King, 'which is all a man can do.'

It was admitted in the daily bulletin that he 'had very little sleep, having had the strait waistcoat the whole night'. He slept and sweated well that night, and his pulse rate fell to 96. During the day he talked well, mainly of Garrick and Johnson, and was more sensible than Dr John had yet seen him.[74]

Not so the physicians, whose quarrels occupied most of Christmas Eve and Christmas Day. Several reports were issued daily: a published bulletin, and 'more particular reports' sent to the Queen, Prince of Wales, Pitt and Thurlow. There seems to have been a general agreement among the physicians to give the public as little information as possible: but about the private reports there were angry disputes, and Willis refused to sign a letter to the Prince of Wales which mentioned the strait-waistcoat. Of course he gave as his reason a wish to spare the Prince's feelings; but his real reason was, obviously, that everything he told the Prince was immediately broadcast.[75]

There was not a day in which Greville did not hear of the physicians' squabbles.

Nothing, in my opinion, can be more prejudicial to His Majesty's situation. . . . Still I do not see how they are to cease when one party is supported and attended to here, and the other party is not seen or questioned on events. It is now about three weeks since Dr Willis has been at Kew, and I have reason to know that Dr Reynolds as well as some other attendant physicians have not once been asked their opinion of the actual state of His Majesty from any distinguished authority since his arrival. Such proceeding may well give rise to misunderstandings, misinterpretations, if not to misinformation.

According to the Duchess, the Queen positively forbade the physicians to have any contact with the Prince, or to answer any of his questions. If so, they disobeyed her.

The Christmas Day bulletin said that the King had had a good night, and was quiet in the morning. But Greville heard from the attendant apothecary, Mr Dundas, that at the time he was reported quiet, he was as deranged as possible, believing that his pillow was the infant Prince Octavius who had died in 1783. Greville thought the King's health in a more precarious situation than it had yet been. The blisters were terribly painful; and one of Willis's men told Greville he had never seen the King so bad.[76]

On Boxing Day the King was tired, but calm. He got up with the waistcoat on under his gown, in case it should be needed; but it was not tightened, so he was at liberty. He lay on the sofa all day, very composed but ashamed of the waistcoat; tried on some new spectacles; and wrote a very correct and accurate order to the opticians for two more pairs.

The Queen caused trouble by insisting on the bulletin being altered from 'His Majesty was yesterday disturbed' to 'His Majesty was yesterday less calm.' Willis told the Queen that the King did not wish to see any physician but himself and his son, and that the others had agreed. So far, however, from agreeing was Sir George Baker, that he implied Dr Willis had invented the King's request.

Dr Willis also sent a verbal message to the Chancellor that he had 'never known the King so well as today', at which Greville was 'a little surprised'. However, the patient played a good game of backgammon, and went to bed composed.

'On the whole', thought Greville, 'this has certainly been a good day.' Dr Warren said, 'Although His Majesty may speak six or seven rational sentences, I won't allow him better: for if he's insane, he's insane.' 'But surely', noted Dr John, 'degrees are as allowable here as in fever?'[77]

The 27th brought further improvement, which was reported even by the Duchess of Devonshire; and on the 28th the bulletin reported the King better in every respect. '*Mais n'en croyez rien*', advised Betsy Sheridan.

He 'agreed to be shaved in hopes of seeing the Queen, and cried very heartily, and so it was allowed for almost one hour'. Dr John 'twice told Warren it was better not to disturb the King, but gained neither answer nor attention'.[78]

This visit by the Queen was the occasion for much gossip and argument. Their conversation took place in German of which the Willises, the only witnesses to the interview, did not understand a word. The ante-room was crammed with Greville, five pages and two of Willis's men, who could not hear what was said, 'though at times it appeared to us as if he was crying'. When, after nearly an hour, the Queen came out, she 'seemed to make an effort to look up and by her countenance to show she was not overcome'. Willis told Greville that the visit was a great success, that the King 'sat down by her while he spoke to her and often kissed her hand and cried frequently'. Later, however, Greville heard through the palace grape-vine, that the King had assured one of the pages that he had told the

Queen that 'he did not like her, that he preferred another, that she was mad and had been so these three years, that he would not on any account admit her to his bed till the year 1793 for reasons he then improperly explained. . . .' Dr Willis denied all this. Greville wished, however, he had not heard the King, on the Queen's leaving his apartment, refer to 'Esther'.

Undoubtedly something happened at the interview that Dr John never recorded. Probably this concerned Lady Pembroke, the King's old flame, then living near Kew. In the latter part of his illness the King often referred to the Queen as Vashti, Lady Pembroke as Esther and himself as Ahasuerus—in reference to the story in the Book of Esther of King Ahasuerus banishing his Queen, Vashti, because she would not come when he sent for her, and replacing her with a fair young virgin, Esther. Lady Pembroke remained untouched by the slightest scandal; and if she knew of the King's embarrassing infatuation, she ignored it.

The Opposition had an efficient spy in Kew House, for only two days later the Duchess of Devonshire noted, 'The Queen talked to the King in German, and he called himself Ahasuerus, and Queen Vashti and Lady Pembroke Esther—he told the Queen he could not lie with her until the year 1793 and said he would make Lady Pembroke Marchioness of Kingston.'[79]

On the 29th, wrote Dr John, the King was 'a little restless, and slightly confined. By choice lay quietly in that state till 2 o'clock. . . . The opinion of the other physicians seems to turn entirely on the numbers that have been cured or not, like a gambler's on the doctrine of chances, without the least knowledge or experience of the present case*. . . . Pulse 82–136, commonly 92.'[80]

On the 30th he was again confined for a while, and for the rest of the day was at liberty, but had on the waistcoat, ready for use, under his gown. He was in a good humour, and told Dr Willis, 'You're honest at bottom, yet impertinent to advise me. I'm vexed because I require it, but you're a fool to give it, when you see how it irritates.' He was costive, until dosed, and suffered from piles.[81]

He was under coercion most of the next day, but eventually

* i.e. of the present complaint. 'Case' was the word often used then for illness or complaint, e.g. 'His case is fever.'

released by Dr John 'upon honour and terms'. He talked much of Parliament, which he said was wasting its time in meeting, because no Act could be passed without him. Dr Willis agreed, reluctantly, to Warren and Pepys seeing him, provided they did not change the treatment. Playing backgammon, the King asked Willis many pertinent questions about his methods, fees and patients; he also spoke well about music. 'On the whole', wrote Greville, 'this has been a remarkable day.' Taking an overall view of Greville's diary, without being obsessed by day to day fluctuations, one can see an improvement in the King's condition over the last ten days of the year, especially when the blisters ceased to hurt him.

The bulletin issued on New Year's Day was the most favourable that had yet appeared. Dr Willis gave to Pitt and the Hanoverian Minister 'the most flattering accounts', and even declared that the King 'was at this moment as capable of transacting any business of state, as ever he had been in his life'. 'I own I was not a little suprised at Dr Willis hazarding . . . such very strong assertions. . . . I did know that the time was not yet come for us to be too sure. . . . If Dr Willis will blend the politician with the physician, he must expect the usual rubs of party, and becomes their fair game.'

In the evening Greville saw His Majesty without himself being seen, and was distressed to hear the King talking of Lady Pembroke and singing 'I made love to Kate', a popular ballad of arch impropriety. His manner was more familiar than when he was quite himself: on the whole, however, Greville found him certainly better; and at picquet with Mr Hawkins, the surgeon, the King got credit for 'throwing out his cards tolerably well'.[82]

The Willises on New Year's Day found the King 'much better'; but Warren refused to admit it. 'Whatever is bad', Dr John recorded in disgust, 'Dr Warren looks upon as decisive. Whatever is good, goes for nothing. If he speaks as he thinks, he is ignorant. If the contrary, God forgive him. I hold degrees here, as in other complaints. . . . The Lord Chancellor paid great compliments to our zeal and damned the other physicians.'

This was the regular theme of the Willis's complaints against

137

Warren, that he would not admit any amendment until the cure was complete. As he told Willis, 'While any insanity remains, I cannot see that there is any material alteration. If a man is perfectly reasonable for twenty-three hours, and deranged during the other hour, I consider him in the same light as if he had no lucid intervals.'

Dr Willis disagreed, 'holding degrees here, as in other complaints'; and his younger son, Robert, improved the occasion by an epigram.

That the sick, ere they're well, must be better, I thought,
'Twas agreed would hold true to the letter.
But Warren, reversing the maxim, has taught
That the sick must be well to grow better.[83]

On 2 January was another reverberating row. It started with the daily bulletin, the draft of which, prepared by Warren, said, 'His Majesty has had a good night and is calm this morning.'

Willis wanted this improved. First, he insisted that it was a *very* good night. Baker and Warren objected, and there was a wrangle. Finally Sir George said, 'I never knew any instance when, in matters of no importance, one physician did not yield to two. However, I will have no dispute with you. I will allow it to be a *very* good night.'

Next, Willis wanted to improve the latter part of the bulletin. 'A Certain Great Person [the Queen]', he warned Warren, 'will not suffer it to go so; and it must fall on you. Why should we send up what will only be sent down to be altered?'

Again the others gave way to him, and the draft was sent to the Queen, 'His Majesty has had a very good night, and in the morning is as he was yesterday.' The Queen, however, did not like even this, and changed it to 'and in the morning continues to mend'. This was too much for Warren, and another warm altercation produced 'and in the morning is in a comfortable way'.[84]

The Opposition's version of this incident is more highly coloured. 'The Queen wanted Warren to sign the bulletin that the King was better when he found him in exactly the same state of madness, only good humoured. Warren was stout, and the Queen pressed him to say what the King had said that was mad. Warren hung off, and the Queen exclaimed indignantly, "I suppose it was *indecent!*" ' 'She sent Lady Harcourt and Lady Charlotte Finch, whom Warren told the expressions were too gross, but that the King had said Dr Willis slept every night with the Queen.' Burke called Lady Harcourt and Lady Charlotte Finch, Keepers of the King's Ribaldry; and the story of Dr Willis's *bonnes fortunes* much amused the town.

'One cannot say the doctors disagree', wrote a friend of Fox. 'They are all on the same side but Willis, of whom you will not be long at a loss what opinion to entertain.'

As for Dr Warren, he advised the Prince (not entirely without justification) to learn a new glossary if he would understand properly the daily bulletins: 'calm' meant 'not absolutely raving', and 'rather disturbed' signified 'an outrageous frenzy'.[85]

Greville, who played picquet with the King on the 2nd, noticed that whenever Dr Willis was out of the room, the King rambled wildly on various subjects. But as soon as Willis returned, he 'turned more to the subject, played his cards better and talked more cautiously. I perceived he played a part occasionally with Dr Willis, and not ill.' Addressing himself in a low voice to Greville and Pepys, the King remarked with a wink, 'The doctor is a great rascal. Trickery in love and physics, you know, is all fair.' Later, in the most affecting manner, he took off his coat and showed them, underneath it, the strait-waistcoat with the long sleeves and strings hanging loose. Then he tucked these in until they might be needed.

On the 3rd the King was pretty well, but talked too much, until one of Willis's men checked him by showing him the waistcoat. Next day he was quick and ticklish to manage. The bulletin was 'despatched without objection which it well might, as it was more favourable than perhaps it ought to have been'.

Mr Best, Secretary to the Hanoverian Minister, came to make inquiries and asked what sort of a bulletin there would be.

Dr John answered, 'I doubt but an indifferent one. It does not deserve a good one.'

When the bulletin appeared, Greville whispered to Best, 'You know now how to read our bulletins.'

'With management, the day rubbed on without a crash.' The King read Latin for a while; and in the evening Dr Reynolds read to him, 'but it was not easy yet to fix him long to a subject'.*

Dr Reynolds cannot have a fair opportunity of judging accurately of the King while Dr Willis is in the room. There is somewhat of a trick in his management. The Willises have established such control over him, that the King himself manages in some degree his conversation when before him. Dr Willis always interposes and stops him when he is beginning to talk wildly or inconsistently, and thus turns his ideas.[86]

Willis complained to Greville that the page, Ernst,† had behaved badly. His manner to the King was rude and threatening, and the King seemed to stand in awe of him; Ernst had also behaved in a 'saucy and improper manner' to the Willises.

Greville, however, felt no obligation to pull the Willises' chestnuts out of the fire. 'Sir', he replied stiffly, 'as an equerry my powers are very limited, and I never exceed them. I've no authority at all outside the Stable Department, and I cannot interfere. I've never thought Ernst's manner pleasing. However, I'll talk to him if the occasion arises.'

Ernst hotly defended himself against 'false accounts'; and his relations with Willis were so bad that one suspects that he was the Opposition's spy at Kew.[87]

Sir George Baker seems again to have been the victim of some malicious gossip.‡ He complained to the Prince who wrote:

My dear Sir George,

I have made it my business to sift so far as I possible [sic] can this report that made you so uneasy this morning, and I find it originates from a letter supposed to be written by you to Lady

* It never had been, even when he was well.
† See p. 94.
‡ See p. 111.

140

Sydney. I write to you as the most immediate way of communication. I am

Sincerely yours

G.P.

P.S. Lady Sydney is supposed to have shown the letter to Mr Selwyn, who copied the words.

Nothing could be more alarming to Baker than the thought of George Selwyn exercising his wit on the subject. Promptly he wrote to Lord Sydney,* 'Copies and extracts of a letter are circulated, which I am said to have written to Lady Sydney respecting the present state of His Majesty. As no such letter has been written by me, I hope your Lordship will give me your authority publickly to contradict a report which is injurious to my reputation.'

We know nothing more of this curious incident: but it indicates that Baker had his enemies, and that stories to his discredit must be accepted with reserve.[88]

On the 5th Willis invited Greville into the King's apartment, obviously to show him off at his best, playing picquet first with Pepys, then with Hawkins. When the King talked too loud and fast, Dr Willis, by merely appearing, quietened him.

On 6 January a third Willis arrived, Thomas, John's younger brother, a Prebend of Lincoln. He read the King psalms, a prayer and a sermon, which seemed to have a good effect though Greville feared that it might produce a relapse into the religious mania that has been a symptom at Windsor.

So far, however, was His Majesty from religious mania that one day he interrupted divine service with loud, cheerful hunting cries.

The Chaplain looked at Sir George Baker, and Sir George looked at the Chaplain, and then . . . *risum teneatis amici* . . . they laughed. And the King laughed, and we all laughed; and Sir George said the prayers had done his Majesty a vast deal of good; and Doctor Duplicate† said the same; and that the King might eat his

* The Secretary of State to whom were addressed all the bulletins regarding the King's illness.

† Although nobody but Withers relates this story, it may well be true.

potatoes with a knife and fork, for he was a great deal better; and he hoped his Majesty, *in process of time*, would be able to go abroad—*with somebody to take care of him.*[90]

Dr Willis was, indeed, talking of taking the King out for a drive, if it could be managed. Unquestionably His Majesty, whatever minor relapses he might have, was getting better.

CHAPTER VI

In the Balance

The unbecoming squabbles at Kew reflected those in the outside world. Captain Sidney Smith* observed on 30 December:

> Dr Willis has every reason to hope for a perfect recovery. The opposition physicians say everything they can to invalidate the daily testimonies of the others. It is very certain that the Queen is very dissatisfied with Sir George Baker and Dr Warren, and very well satisfied with the change of treatment introduced by Dr Willis which, from the most violent and harsh, is now the most gentle possible consistent with the firmness necessary in such cases. The poor Queen is wore to a skeleton.[1]

Skeleton or no, she complained to the Chancellor of Warren in terms of passionate resentment, and swore she would never speak to him again. But Thurlow read her a lecture on manners, and two days later she was tolerably civil.[2]

The Prince gave dinner after dinner for peers and MPs, dealing out, like a pack of cards, the reversions of regiments, bishoprics, titles and colonial governorships.[3]

The Press commented without reticence or delicacy on every aspect of the situation. 'What!' exclaimed *The Times*, 'Not give us the power of having new places—new pensions! Sad tidings, these, for men who have waited so long in expectancy. No certain stipend for Mrs Armistead, Mrs Benwell, Mrs Windsor and other virtuous matrons belonging to the immaculate party!'

The Opposition made frantic efforts to buy up the London newspapers, and just before Christmas Sheridan mentioned at Devonshire House that 'The *Morning Post* could be got over.' On 2 January the Prince of Wales, who already subsidized

* Later the hero of Acre.

143

The Oracle, bought from Tattersall control of the *Morning Post* for £1,000 down and £350 a year. The transaction earned him a good deal of ridicule, for his agent in the deal was Mr Weltjie, an immensely corpulent German who had been a figure of fun in London as a pastrycook, and remained so in his subsequent metamorphoses as keeper of a gingerbread-stall in Leicester Fields, owner of a gaming club in St James's, and Clerk of the Prince's Cellar. 'Would it not become you', inquired *The Times*, which was soon to be refreshed with a Treasury subsidy, 'to confine your studies to the stewpan? Have you not purchased a leading share in the *Morning Post* with a view to making it subservient to the P——'s friend?'*[4]

The Opposition ladies wore Regency Caps, from seven and a half guineas, described by fashion writers as 'a mountain of tumbled gauze, with three large feathers in front, tied together with a knot of ribbons on which was printed in gold letters, *Honi soit qui mal y pense, de la Régence.*' Marked embarrassment was caused at a Devonshire House reception by a flunkey announcing Loughborough as the Lord Chancellor.[5]

The Earl of Pembroke, husband of the King's 'Esther', heard from his brother, 'Public business has occasioned more party violence, more personal animosity and rancour, than I have ever before experienced. . . . I imagine that in about a week the Prince of Wales will form a new government and dismiss the present, loaded as it is with the goodwill of the public.'[6]

But Lord Herbert was wrong, for on 5 January, after an adjournment due to the death of the Speaker, an injudicious inspiration of Charles Fox resulted in the Opposition proposing yet another examination of the physicians.

No doubt Fox calculated that Warren and Baker would prove the King incurable, and it only required thirty rats in the Commons, and fifteen in the Lords, to deprive Pitt of his majority and withdraw all the restrictions. But Fox was surely

---

* Through most of the period of the King's illness, the Government subsidized the *Morning Chronicle*, the *Diary*, the *London Evening Post*, the *St James's Chronicle*, the *Public Ledger*, the *Whitehall Evening Post* and *The World*. The resources of the Treasury gave it, of course, a great advantage over the Opposition which could only count on the *Morning Herald*, the *Morning Post*, and *The Oracle*. *The Times* won its Treasury subsidy later in the year.

wrong. If he had pressed for an immediate Regency, with whatever restrictions, 'Fox and Burke would have had an audience of persons always favourably disposed towards the Treasury Bench, while Pitt would have experienced the chill of departed power.' In such circumstances, Fox could probably have got the restrictions withdrawn; with luck, the knowledge that his despised son had been made Regent, might render the King's madness permanent. There was even a chance that, having been formally declared a lunatic, the King might not wish to resume power: indeed he himself later said, 'If the Regency had been established, I should not have come forward to overthrow it.'[7]

The debate furnished Burke with the occasion for another display of intemperance and bad taste:

> There are no signs of convalescence. The possibility of a cure diminishes as the disorder lengthens. The House must pay due attention to the report of the physicians' examination, before they cut and carve the government as they would cut up a carrion carcase for hounds. Are you going to build a weak and miserable machinery of government on a foundation of fraud, falsehood and calumny? The keeper of one madhouse ought to be set against the keeper of another, and by their collision we shall know the truth.

Pitt hinted that Burke's belief in Dr Warren might be influenced by wishful thinking. 'A foul aspersion!' screamed Burke. Fox, with more self-command, merely said he had not the least doubt of the hopelessness of His Majesty's case.

However, the debate was really unnecessary, for Pitt was perfectly willing to postpone the issue for several days while the physicians were re-examined.[8]

The first to be questioned, on 7 January, was Sir Lucas Pepys, who was rather more inclined than the others to agree with Willis. He could not say that he had observed any signs of approaching convalescence; but 'His Majesty is more easily controlled, and therefore advancing towards recovery. As control is the principal means used for recovery, I consider patients submitting to it more readily as a mark of some sort of ground being got.'

'What do you mean by easier subjection to control?'

'I mean a slighter degree of intimidation.'

'Can Sir Lucas Pepys speak with more certainty than at the last examination when you say His Majesty will recover?'

'Yes, I think I can.'

Willis declared he had such high hopes 'that if a patient of the same disposition were in my house, I should not have the least doubt of his recovery'.

'Can Dr Willis see any signs of approaching convalescence?'

'Yes. A fortnight ago the King would take up books and could not read a line of them: he will now read several pages together and make, in my opinion, very good remarks upon the subject. I think, in the main, His Majesty does everything in a more rational way than he did, and some things exceeding rational. . . . He is still exceedingly irritable, but not so irritable as he was, nor does the irritation continue one tenth so long.'

Of the bulletins, Willis said, 'I latterly scarce read them over, but signed to avoid trouble, thinking His Majesty better than the certificates implied.'

The Opposition pressed Willis and Pepys with many questions about coercion, without eliciting the sort of dramatic information they wanted. Warren's evidence they found far more satisfactory. He saw no signs of convalescence, and viewed Willis's expertise with a robust scepticism which they found very reassuring:

> Specialists, provided their parts and intellectual powers are equal to the business, will become more expert than other physicians. Otherwise they will deserve no preference but for the convenience they provide for the patients. . . . I have heard from some attendants that His Majesty is *not* in a state of amendment. There is *no* return of reason. Dr Willis has written to the Prince declaring progress I could not discover.

Then followed Dr Warren's version of the story of Willis's letter to Pitt, and of the Queen's interferences in the drafting of the Bulletin; and Warren expatiated at some length at Willis's imprudence in giving the King a copy of *King Lear*, and in letting him have a razor and penknife. 'Dr Willis admitted later that he shuddered at what he did.'

'On nine out of ten cures', asked Burke, 'would not Dr Warren require more evidence than the assertions of the man pretending to have performed such cures?'

'I certainly should.'

With the first day's examination,[9] the Duchess of Devonshire was pretty well satisfied. 'Sir Lucas Pepys tried to make the King better, but failed. Willis's examination favourable to us.' Willis told Greville that he had been 'very closely pressed by Mr Burke and Mr Sheridan—that he was angry with them, and with Mr Sheridan particularly. Mr Fox seemed to have gained on him by the more liberal manner in which he had examined him. He said none could behave more like a gentleman than Mr Fox had done towards him on that occasion, and that he had put the questions with great delicacy.'[10]

Meanwhile the King had had a good day, spending most of the morning reading Pope's *Essay on Man* with a fair degree of concentration. Greville was pained to be shown by one of Willis's men a promissory note signed by the King for a £50 annuity; but this act of minor generosity does not really seem a very alarming symptom.[11]

The next day's examination centred mainly on the drafting of the bulletins and the Queen's interference in this. Even Sir Lucas Pepys said that the reports showed His Majesty in the most favourable light; but he added that, until the examination by the Privy Council in early December, 'every account was purposefully framed so as to give the public no sort of information'—an answer which recoiled on the questioner, for that was before Willis's arrival.

'Do not specialists used to using discipline and coercion obtain a considerable degree of dominion over their patient?'

'Certainly.'

Sir George Baker admitted that the only medicine given by Willis, except with the consent of the other physicians, was one pill of calomel, which 'had the common effect of purges and no other'. Willis's system of coercion made the King more manageable, but 'I am not sure that anything has been done towards convalescence.' If Willis's prohibition against entering the

King's room is obeyed, 'no other medical gentleman can give any information on His Majesty'.

Dr Reynolds also said that the Willises were making the King more manageable, but not curing him.

'The Committee going strongly for us', wrote the Duchess of Devonshire, 'and great and important evidence coming out about the Queen.'[12]

Greville recorded, with some asperity, an interview with the Queen, 'the first honour of the kind I have had since my [eight weeks'] attendance on His Majesty. It was to see if I could set to rights Her Majesty's stop-watch, which had got into irregular striking. . . . Throughout the day, His Majesty continued in high spirits, but altogether calm.' Willis wanted to say in the bulletin, 'the King is better than ever', but Reynolds and Warren refused. However, Willis told the Prince so.[13]

On the 9th, Willis was recalled by the Committee. He insisted, with the experience of twenty-eight years' specialist practice, that the King's chances of a complete recovery were much better. Amendment had been delayed by the blisters, to which he had agreed only on his colleagues' assurances that at Windsor they had not upset the King: on the contrary, they produced great irritation, and had a bad effect on the whole system. He was confirmed by the good results of quiet and a tonic bark, with two calomel pills and a cathartic draught to prepare His Majesty for the bark.

Burke asked, 'What other medicine do you give His Majesty?'

'*Gum Quiacum*', replied Willis.

'*Gum Quackum*, I believe', snapped Burke.

But Willis got his own back when Burke asked him to describe the symptoms of incurable mental derangement. 'I will tell *you*', replied Willis with strong emphasis. Stabbing his finger at Burke and fixing on the Irishman his piercing eyes, Willis gave these symptoms a personal application which was very plain, and irritated Sheridan who, 'in a great rage, laid about him on friend and foe'.

Warren's evidence was again most agreeable to these gentlemen:

When Dr Willis or his son are present, His Majesty is under great awe; when they are absent, he talks and acts quite differently. I have never seen him read more than a line and a half at a time. His manner of reading is a strong proof of the existence of his malady. I see no symptoms of convalescence. Sleep has produced no amendment: nor has control and coercion. Before Dr Willis arrived, we tried to restore His Majesty to bodily health. Bark was the only tonic used. Blisters applied to the legs produced much pain, and increased the need for coercion.*[14]

The King had another quiet day on the 9th, and talked much of an outing in Richmond Park on which his heart was set. His political judgement, however, was unsound, for he spoke of making Lord North, blind and discredited, Speaker of the House of Commons. Sir George Baker refused to accept Dr John's assurance that the King had had a quiet night, and insisted on making inquiries from the pages.[15]

Next day, Willis testified before the Committee to a 'prodigious difference in His Majesty's condition. I do not think he has one symptom that marks an incurable. . . . Certainly I have much more influence and control over His Majesty than the other physicians; and people visiting the King without me tend to irritate him. The Chancellor directed me to put up a paper warning visitors not to enter His Majesty's room.'

'Has the King ever conversed with you on a subject which he has read? And how long after?'

'Very often, and sometimes several hours later, for His Majesty never forgets what he reads.'

'When did Dr Willis last employ coercion?'

'Coercion has not been used for a week, and in the previous fortnight much less frequently than before.'

There was so much wrangling among the members of the Committee that Willis, dozing in the ante-room, awoke suddenly and thought he was at Gretford with his patients breaking loose. 'What the devil are you making that noise for?' he shouted, in a somewhat unclerical tone.

Willis's evidence, and the firm manner in which he gave it,

* A most significant admission.

made a great impression, and induced many of the rats to change their minds. 'Nothing but treachery going forward', lamented the Duchess next day.[16]

The King, however, had a relapse over the week-end of the 10th and 11th. On Saturday the waistcoat, which had been left off for several days, was put on again, but as a warning only, not tightened up. His chief aberration that day was an inability to stick to the subject under discussion; but that had always been one of the royal failings. He had a very bad night, and 'recourse was obliged to be had to the waistcoat'. This was followed by a turbulent day. Warren and Pepys prescribed a tranquillizing drug, but Dr John would not give him this as he became quiet and fell asleep. This naturally produced one of those physicians' quarrels which so often enlivened the dull routine of Kew House. Agreement on treatment might have been easier had the doctors been able to agree even on their patient's pulse-rate: Dr John acidly recorded, 'Pulse 96 I say— 106 said Dr Warren—more said Sir Lucas Pepys.'

The Queen was determined to take the King for a drive in Richmond Park, and told Greville to make sure the horses were frost-shod. As it was snowing hard, and the King had had a bad night, Greville was astonished at the idea; to which Pepys and Warren strongly objected. Willis maintained that the King, having been promised his airing, must have it. 'Is his mind made of iron?' asked Dr John. 'It's proper to give him hope, and very necessary that promises should, where there is no good reason against it, be fulfilled.' However, the Willises were over-ruled and the King, rather sulky, reverted later in the day to his lamentable obsession about Lady Pembroke. He also stormed at Thomas Willis, insisting that he was born not to be dictated to, but to command. It was a disappointing day, though Greville took comfort from the report that the King, for the first time in three months, dozed for an hour in his chair after dinner. On the 12th, however, his pulse-rate rose to 120, and his observations on Lady Pembroke were so embarrassing that his promised outing was cancelled. He asked for access to the library, but Greville was 'sure he could foretell the consequence of such indulgence. He will tumble the books about without being able to give the attention of many minutes to read any. He will no longer remain satisfied with his present apartments, he will always be trying to come out to ours.'[17]

(Not the least convincing proof of the King's amendment is the impatience the faithful Greville now began to display towards his remaining vagaries.)

The King could hardly have picked a worse time for a relapse. Baker on the 12th told the Committee that he talked rationally for only about a minute, and then 'went into a state of total alienation'.

'How many patients have you kept under your sole care after three months' treatment?'

'Twenty, I believe.'

'How many of these were cured?'

'Not one. When the disorder degenerates into a state of fatuity, there is no hope of cure.'

Dr Warren's evidence that day concerned mainly his relations with Willis. 'I was always considered as the first physician, and therefore thought myself particularly responsible. I spoke to Dr Willis with some degree of authority, and to Dr Willis's three attendants in such a manner as to let them know their conduct would be strictly observed. My being First Physician led me to talk to Dr Willis about everything I heard of.' After this, the Committee was not surprised to hear that 'it sometimes led to disputes'.

To the Chancellor's private inquiry if the King would get better, Warren snapped back, 'I'll be damned if he does, and there you have it in your own words.'[18]

On the 13th and 14th His Majesty's thoughts were indeed fixed with concentration; but their sole object was Lady Pembroke. He wrote a series of cards for the doctors such as:

Sir Richard Warren Bart, First Physician
to the King.
Oh dear Eliza, ever love thy Prince
*Who had rather suffer death than leave thee.**

* Greville says this happened on the 13th, Dr John on the 14th—a curious discrepancy.

Dr Willis said, 'We had better burn these foolish cards', and his son seconded him.

'I could wish to burn them', said Warren, 'but in these trickle times it is better not.' Later, however, he said, 'Dr John, I've burned those cards.'

While playing picquet, His Majesty called Lady Pembroke the Queen of Hearts and, holding the King of that suit, exclaimed with rapture, 'Oh, if the Queen of Hearts would fall to the King!' It so happened that Willis was obliged to play the Queen, and His Majesty commented indecorously on his good fortune.

It was an obsession which not uncommonly overtakes respectable married gentlemen in their fifties; but it was, at this particular juncture in the affairs of the King and Mr Pitt, singularly untimely. To Dr Warren's credit, news of it did not leak out—at least not to Devonshire House.

In the evening the King calmed down and talked much of Lord North who was, he said, the man he loved most in all the world. 'I was once very angry with him, but since his misfortune, I've felt only compassion.' Later, when North called to inquire after him, the King said this did him more good than all the physicians.

Naturally the Opposition made the most of the rumours which seeped out from Kew.

My last account of the King [wrote Lord Sheffield on the 14th] is that he has had but five hours' sleep in three days and nights, and that he has been extremely furious. On Monday [12 January] Willis had ordered the carriage to take him out, because he had promised an airing the day before and never broke his promise. However Warren and Pepys thought Willis's promise of less consequence than the King's life and kept him at home; and this happened when the weather was eminently bad: I do not remember so hard a frost. . . . It is to be hoped that the vile attempts to make him appear better will cease when the business of the Regency is settled. The Queen was lately told by Warren that, instead of being better as to his disorder, he is rather worse than he was at Windsor.[19]

152

To this extraordinary opinion Warren stubbornly adhered for another fortnight.

Reading the report of the last two days' examination, filled with the physicians' unseemly wrangles on the King's shaving, the King's outings, the King's pulse, tongue, likes and dislikes, one gets the impression of Willis being driven into a corner by skilful cross-examination. However, he made some telling points:

> The Chancellor told me I should consult the other physicians as much as I could, but that I was to follow my own line and do as I had been used to do with patients at home. . . . Yesterday His Majesty took hold of my hand and complained of my having left him so much last week. . . . He is more afflicted with gusts of passion on any trifling contradiction unless I or my son are present. This I attribute to His Majesty being more sensible of himself and his situation. He cannot bear to be contradicted by the pages, and has gusts of passion at things they do in an unbecoming manner to which they had become used when His Majesty was not well.[20]

Generally it was conceded that the Opposition tactics had been a mistake, and that Dr Willis had come well through his ordeal. Not so Dr Warren.

> How ill [wrote Mrs Thrale] has Dr Warren managed his responses! Such manifest contradictions did I never see before. One moment he says the King has not steadiness enough to read more than a line and a half at a time, and in the next breath laments that Willis gave him *King Lear* to *amuse* him, and that His Majesty's observations upon the play affected him greatly. Some of these positions *must* be false. I never saw Warren or Willis in my life, and have no high opinion of the first *out* of his profession: *in* it such eminence as he has ever obtained, cannot be merited.

The Chancellor, who of all men should be able to judge the effect of evidence under cross-examination, spoke to Dr John 'in the most contemptible light of the proceedings of the Committee'; and the Duchess lamented 'great private treachery'.

On the whole, the attempt by Burke and Sheridan, in the Committee, to prove collusion between Willis and the Queen was viewed by the public with disfavour.[21]

On the 13th Pitt brought to the Bar of the House the Report of the Physicians' examination. Burke immediately moved for its re-commitment. 'Why have not the surgeons, apothecaries and other attendants been summoned?' He harangued the House on the 'omission or concealment of many circumstances necessary for forming a just estimate of the possibility of a cure. . . . His Majesty's life is not safe in Dr Willis's hands. I do not mean to impute his intentions—'tis of his rashness that I complain.' Pitt, thankful for ten days' reprieve, replied drily, 'The House will not think the Inquiry has been improperly narrowed when the bulk of the Report is duly considered': and the Opposition, intimidated by 400 folio pages, did not venture to divide.[22]

Three days later,[23] introducing the proposed restrictions on the Regency, Pitt said the Report added nothing to what was known, and did not alter the situation. All the physicians had agreed that the chances of a cure were the same as in December, except Willis and Pepys who thought them much better. 'The House must remember it is not placing a King on the throne, for the throne is full.'

Restrictions on the creation of peers and the grant of offices and reversions were accepted with surprisingly little argument: and hardly anyone disputed the prudence of removing His Majesty's personal property from His Royal Highness's reach. The main argument was on vesting in the Queen, assisted by an advisory council, the management of the King's household.

Here Pitt was fighting in a cramped position. The real necessity for this restriction was to prevent the Regent dismissing Dr Willis and leaving Dr Warren in charge, so that the King would never be certified as sane. But this he could not say. He could only plead, rather lamely, 'the painful emotions of the King, on emerging from his trance, to find all around him changed'.

As a matter of tactics, Fox and Burke entrusted the opening of the Opposition case to a highly respected country gentleman, who felt it was time his talents and integrity were rewarded by

a peerage. Mr Powis asked, 'Has the Heir Apparent acted un-
becomingly during his father's illness? Has he attempted by
cabal and intrigue to wrest from the King his sceptre? Has he
been guilty of treason? May not the Queen, too, have bad
advisers? I consider these resolutions likely to arm the mother
against her son.' It was an effective speech, because the only
answer to it was one which could not with propriety, or indeed
safety, be given.

Mr Pulteney, a backbencher of equal or even higher repute,
whose strange foible it was always to dress in ancient, thread-
bare clothes, answered him—also, of course, without mentioning the vital matter of the physicians:

> What! Cannot they govern without having the nomination of
> every butcher and baker in the royal household? . . . I will never
> admit the probability of a cabal being formed in the House of
> Peers hostile to the Regent's government. If, indeed, another
> measure as unconstitutional as the East India Bill should again be
> introduced, I readily allow that the Bedchamber Lords may form
> a powerful obstacle to its progress.

Charles Fox charged the Ministers with 'insinuating the
scandalous idea that a division can take place between a
mother and her son. I cannot utter in language of adequate
indignation my abhorrence of such a plan.' He asked angrily
how long the restrictions should last.

Pitt gave a vague undertaking to support the removal of the
restrictions, should the King's recovery be delayed. Pressed by
Sheridan to set a time-limit for the restrictions, and to describe
more precisely the Queen's proposed Council, he would only
say, 'Parliament will always have the power of removing the
restrictions. . . . It will be only a Council of Advice, of no degree
of control. The great officers of state, with some dignified
prelates, are intended to compose it.'

More by what was not said than by what was said in this
insipid debate, the Ministry carried its resolutions; the House
was adjourned for a week; and Charles Fox retired to Bath,
partly to recoup his health before undertaking the arduous
labours of office, partly to evade an embarrassing exchange

with Mr Rolle on the propriety of appointing a Regent who had married a Roman Catholic. *The Times*, doggedly pursuing a joke with six weeks' lead, said Fox's stomach was disordered from eating his own words.[24]

In the Lords, for the Opposition, the Bishop of Llandaff made a speech 'which would unquestionably have secured him an English mitre of the most solid description, and probably have translated him to Durham or Winchester, if the Regency had been consummated. The King's recovery chained him down for life to an obscure Welsh diocese.' His colleagues of the Bench, however, and the Bedchamber Lords put more faith in Willis than in Warren, and here, too, the Ministry carried it.[25]

Pitt's power having been incontestably proved, the struggle in Parliament lapsed. In the Press, however, and in private houses and correspondence, it continued unabated. The Queen, pointed out the *Morning Herald*, would have no less than 400 Household places at her disposal, and would be advised by a Council chosen by Pitt. How could the Regent shift such a massive obstruction? 'The daily bulletin', reported the same paper next day, 'is turned to stock-jobbing purposes by designing persons in "Change Alley". ' It thoughtfully continued with a detailed description of a lunatic cutting his keeper's throat.[26]

There were streams of deserters moving in both directions. The Duchess of Devonshire lamented 'great private treachery'; but Sir George Harris, whose supple diplomacy had extricated the Prince of Wales from one scrape after another, having been made Lord Malmesbury was 'violent in opposition when he had scarce got his scarlet robe on'. 'It is so certain now', wrote an Administration lady, 'where power will be lodged that many go over daily. The Rats, as they are called, are all on the watch.'[27]

Everyone realized that, 'though the Household may be established for the present moment, it may moulder and crumble away as soon as another Parliament may find it in their interest to undo what this has done.' The Archbishop of Canterbury, on the 16th, gave a fair summary of the situation as it appeared at the time to one with access to all current rumours and some of the facts, who could not quite make up his mind on which side of the fence to descend:[28]

The most dispassionate think that Willis's long experience gives him great advantage in judgement in this particular disorder, but that he is rather too sanguine in his hopes. On the other hand they think Warren unqualified by any experience to pronounce so decidedly unfavourable prognostics as to recovery. It is a strange subject for a party to exist on, and disgraceful to the country that it should be so; but so it is, and many pronounce Warren a party man, while Willis is supposed to delude himself by ambition.

Fox's illness seldom leaves him without severe attacks a week together. Their difficulties and quarrels are not likely to diminish. The jealousy in respect to Sheridan is not lessened by his actually being an inmate at Mrs Fitzherbert's, with his wife: they took refuge there on being driven out of their house by bailiffs. He [Sheridan] is on all hands understood to be the prime favourite; and to be so sensible of it as modestly to aspire to a Cabinet place, which is firmly resisted by the Duke of Portland who says they cannot both be in the same Cabinet. Sheridan would willingly submit to being Chancellor of the Exchequer; but it is thought things are not yet ripe enough for the Manager of Drury Lane to be Manager of the House of Commons. . . . The great embarrassment is that, the general run of the country being so with Mr Pitt, it is apprehended that a dissolution of Parliament will not mend matters. One cannot help thinking, however, with the knowledge one has of mankind, that a Regent once made will gain ground apace.

Betsy Sheridan had no doubts, writing on the 20th, 'All goes well and will be finally settled in ten days. The King still *worse*.' [29]

Although the Willises would not admit it, for some days after the examination of the physicians, the King had not been at his best.

The Queen was determined to get him out in his carriage, and on the morning of the 15th told Greville to get everything ready. Greville thought it most imprudent, and begged Willis to drop the whole plan. 'This is no trifling experiment, Dr Willis, and I hope the King will be composed and not expose himself on the trial.'

Willis said, 'The King wishes to go to Richmond Park, as the most private place within reach.'

'Doctor', said Greville, with fortunate insight, 'don't you see why the King wishes to go there? Haven't you discovered the drift of his wish?'

'Upon my word, Sir, I'm not in the secret.'

'The King', warned Greville, 'is certainly hoping to see Lady Pembroke there. When he comes near her house, he won't be well pleased with a refusal, and the chances are, he will become turbulent.'

Dr Willis went off to sound the King, whom he found dissatisfied with his dress.

'That one, Sir', said Willis, 'is good enough for an airing.'

'I must have my white breeches', the King insisted.

'Those blue breeches you have on, Sir, will do very well.'

'Ah!' retorted the King cunningly. 'You don't know where I'm going.' And then the whole plan came out, just as Greville had surmised.

The King was abusive and angry at being thwarted, and had to be restrained for an hour or two. After dinner, Dr John found him very difficult, 'struggling for power'. But in the evening he was better and, with old Willis and Dr John, who had a fine voice, sang 'Hark, the bonny Christchurch Bells' and other catches.[30]

Next morning, again noisy and turbulent, he had to be confined for three hours. Dr Willis came in for his full share of abuse; but, to Greville's amazement, allowed the Queen and Princesses to see him. The visit seems, against all probability, to have been a success: a completely independent witness told Greville that the Queen 'had mentioned to him the conversation which had passed and which had been quite proper'. But the rumour which Greville picked up from the pages was that the King had again reverted to the topic of Lady Pembroke, saying that the Queen had consented she should come to him.

Greville was taken in by Willis to see the King, whom he found by the fire feeding the Queen's little dog and fastening a blue ribbon round its neck. The King then suddenly became agitated and talked of hunting next day. To quieten him, he was given an emetic and 'puked very heartily'. He then knelt down and prayed God to 'restore him to his senses, or permit that he might die directly'.[31]

On Saturday, the 17th, there arrived Sir Joseph Banks, who had accompanied Captain Cook to Australia and then, in partnership with the King, imported the first flock of Merino sheep to England.* He was assured by Dr Willis that the King was 'charmingly, and as mild as milk', and spread the good news far and wide. The Queen spent an hour with the King and came out very cheerful. The three Willises, who were (as usual) the only witnesses of the interview, assured Greville that not one improper word had escaped.

When the King retired, his pulse was down to 74. Calm and in a good humour, he dozed over Gray's 'Elegy' before going to bed. Dr John wrote him down as 'better than ever before'; so did the pages, whose 'better acquaintance with the King's manner, and their correct characters', encouraged Greville to pay more attention to their report than to Willis's.[32]

The 18th January was observed as the Queen's birthday.† It was far from auspicious. The King had been worrying about this and insisting on having a new suit for the occasion. In the morning he was painfully disturbed. He struck one of Willis's men and threw a chair at another. The waistcoat had to be shown, but was not put on. In the evening, however, he was better. The Queen and Princesses sat with him and, with the Willises, sang catches.[33]

The next day was fine and sunny, the King went for a walk with the Willises in Kew Gardens. 'He made aim', wrote Dr John, 'for Richmond Gardens, which we put off by resolution.'

'Well', said the King, 'I find as Pope says, to enjoy is to obey.'

He walked cheerfully off to the Pagoda, which he wished to show Thomas Willis. 'We put him aside for want of a key. But His Majesty, discovering the key, struggled for it, and was offended, and from that moment walked with difficulty till at

---

* He had a link with the Willises in that his family also came from Lincoln, where his father had probably been at school with Dr Francis Willis.

† Though not, it appears from *Burke's Peerage*, her real birthday.

length he lay down and would walk no more. Two pages and our men carried him home and put him under coercion.'

Greville was astonished and shocked to see the King 'extended on his back and thus carried by some of the attendants'. The King, when yielding to *force majeure*, had said that it was pleasanter to be carried than to walk, and he liked it vastly.

The current gossip was that the King, walking in the gardens, spotted his

amiable and royal female relatives at an upper window. Regardless of anything but his own impulses, His Majesty threw his hat into the air and hurled his stick to an incredible distance. He then proceeded in a rapid movement towards the Pagoda, which he was very desirous to ascend. Being thwarted in this, he became sullen and desperate: so powerful was his resistance that it was three-quarters of an hour before Willis and four assistants could raise him.

There is nothing in Greville's or Dr John's diary to confirm the more colourful particulars here related.[34]

Next day, the King abused Dr Willis to Dr Warren, and the two doctors had a brisk quarrel about allowing him to be shaved. However, the operation was successfully performed; and His Majesty set out, arm-in-arm with the Willises, for the Botanical Gardens. He was very fractious and irritable in the evening, and confided in Sir Lucas Pepys that he would soon contrive to escape from Dr Willis. Dr Warren, meanwhile, less concerned with curing his patient than with proving him incurable, was writing to Dr Monro of Bedlam Asylum, 'Can you tell me without much trouble what you consider the symptom or symptoms of incurability?' Dr Monro replied, 'I should look upon that insanity as likely to prove incurable which comes on towards the middle stage of life without any known cause to which it is to be attributed unless it be a family complaint. The symptoms are great deprivation of sense: tending to fatuity: every tendency to that disposition is to be dreaded where the disorder is not abated by medicine or management: where there is a want of natural sleep.' However illuminating Dr Munro's reply, it was in answer to a question which should, one would have thought, have been asked several weeks ago, or not at all.[35]

For the next two days the King was cross and intractable, and on the 22nd Willis, having been personally abused, had recourse to the waistcoat. But on the 23rd he was better than for some time. He walked on the terrace in front of the house and called up to the Queen. Willis brought her to the window: the King begged her to come out, which she did, and walked with him for an hour. He was affectionate and composed, but harping on a plan to move to Windsor. Later he talked about arranging a joint Regency of the Archbishop of Canterbury, Lord Chancellor, President of the Council, Prince of Wales and Duke of York.[36]

He had a tiff on the 24th with one of Willis's men, cutting his cheek; and had to be confined to a specially made chair, fixed to the floor, 'which the poor King eyed with some degree of awe'. But next day, in a better humour, he displayed this chair to Dr Reynolds, calling it his Coronation Chair. At night, by his own request, he was 'put into a warm bath. Dr Willis did not disapprove, only desired that it might not be deeper than his middle when he sat down.'

He was, indeed, so well on the 25th that Miss Burney, in answer to a friend's inquiry, gaily wrote out a 'bulletin' herself:

> The King passed a very good night, and is perfectly composed and collected this morning.
>
> (Signed)   JOHN WILLIS
(Witnessed)   FRANCES BURNEY

The doctor lent his name very willingly, and with this bulletin her friend 'went and gladdened the hearts of every good subject of his acquaintance. These Willises are incomparable people.'

Next day, however, as though to punish her presumption, the patient was rambling, turbulent and abusive, complaining that no King but a King of England would be put in a strait-waistcoat. The bulletin went so far as to say, 'His Majesty was quiet yesterday, and is not quiet this morning.'[37]

It is strange that news of the King's relapse does not seem

to have reached Devonshire House; but Lord Pembroke, on the 21st, understood 'that there are scarce any hopes of the King returning to his senses; and I suppose ere this, the Prince of Wales is probably appointed Regent, which will give him the power of dissolving Parliament—a power he will, to be sure, use as soon as he has it'. On the 27th Lord Pembroke was convinced there would be no recovery.[38]

Fox, before going off to Bath, sent Portland his plan for the new Ministry. It contained no surprises: Portland was to figure-head the government as Prime Minister; Fox was to be one Secretary of State, Lord Stormont, the other; and Lord John Cavendish, Chancellor of the Exchequer. Lord Loughborough was to have, at last, the Woolsack; and Burke was to be rewarded for his services with the lucrative plum of Paymaster, though he would have far preferred a post with less lucre and more responsibility; Sheridan's modest political abilities were matched by the modest post of Treasurer of the Navy. Subsequent letters between Fox and the Duke discussed almost every post from Secretary of State to Grocer to the Prince, for Fox and the Prince meant to make a clean sweep.[39]

Pitt's Fabian tactics, conspicuously favoured by the Opposition's impatience, had been masterly. Already, it was acidly pointed out, 'the creation of a Regent had taken up ten times the time the creation of the world did, and we do not seem to be any more advanced than we were on the 12th November'.[40] But on 27 January Pitt again directed Parliament's attention to the knotty problem, moving for a Committee to invite the Prince to accept the Regency with restrictions.[41]

Burke, in a paroxysm of rage, excelled himself in overdrawn imagery. 'If it is intended to erect a republic, why is this not avowed? The Prime Minister wishes to create a mere mummery, a piece of masquerade buffoonery, formed to burlesque every species of government . . . a ministerial spectre, its bones are marrowless, its blood is cold, it has no speculation in its eyes. I reprobate it as a chimera, a monster summoned up from the depths of hell.' He added the improbable assertion that peers did not care 'two skips of a louse for the emoluments of office'; and that one 'might as well look for energy in the mutilated heroes of Italian opera as in this government'.

The House ignored his unseemly outburst, and the invitation was duly conveyed to the Prince who, 'impelled by an anxious concern for the public safety', agreed to undertake the unwelcome trust on the assumption that the restrictions would be only temporary.

Since the King's illness, the two Houses of Parliament, without the Crown, had been sitting merely as a convention with no legislative powers. The question now was, how, in the absence of the King, to open a session at which the decisions made on a Regency could be given legislative effect. Lord Camden, for the Ministry, suggested issuing Letters Patent under the Great Seal authorizing a Commission to open Parliament in the King's name. Similarly to the Regency Bill would be affixed the Great Seal in token of the royal assent. Promptly the Prince and Royal Dukes declined to have anything to do with such an improvisation; and Lord Stormont, the reversionary Secretary of State, pointed out, 'With respect to the two Commissions intended to be issued under the Great Seal, the first is informal, and the second illegal. . . . What is the impediment which has prevented the Ministers from addressing the Prince of Wales to take upon himself the exercise of the whole legislative authority of the Crown?'

Everyone knew what the impediment was, but it could not be mentioned. However, the Opposition preferred not to expose their numerical weakness to a division. Moreover, even more than the Ministry where Thurlow would neither assist, advise nor obey Mr Pitt, the Opposition lacked cohesion.

Nothing was ever equal to the violence of party, *de part et d'autre*, but most on the Prince's side because disappointed. The Duke of Portland* has declared his determination not to act with Mr Sheridan, who is now Prime Minister at Carlton House. Charles Fox, beside ill-health, is dissatisfied with Mr Sheridan's supremacy and not choosing to be questioned by Mr Rolle. Jack Payne is such a favourite he is to be a Lord of the Admiralty, and he leans on the Prince as he walks, not the Prince on him.[42]

* Who was 'as honest as the skin between his eyebrows, but had nothing above them to recommend him'.

The Queen was said to have received from her eldest son a ten-page letter 'to intimidate her against accepting the management of the Household'.*[43]

The King's condition at the end of January was worrying. In the middle of the month there had seemed to be a steady improvement: but although he was not now nearly as bad as he had been at the beginning of his illness, he was agitated, bad-tempered, abusive and hardly improving. On the 27th Greville, making his morning inquiries from the pages, found that the King had had a very bad night and was 'very touchey' that morning. When he passed on the news to Baker and Pepys, they smiled significantly and said Dr Willis had just told them the King was quite calm.

'Well', said Greville, 'I seem to have let the cat out of the bag.'

Later in the day, Greville was taken by surprise on the terrace. 'Greville! Greville!' called the King, and hastened towards him. Taking the equerry's arm, he said, 'You will walk with me, and I shall not part with you again today.'

It was one of Greville's rare personal encounters with the King in January, and may be accepted as strictly true.

'Remember', said His Majesty, 'your promise to be my friend. Now, what will you have? Will you have the Treasurer-ship of the Household?—No! That was your brother! One of you shall be Treasurer, the other Controller: take your choice of these.'

Spicer, one of Dr Willis's attendants, a Warwickshire man, then appeared, and the King said, indicating Greville, 'Spicer! Come and meet your countryman!... Now which do you choose as Member for Warwick? Colonel Greville or his brother? They can't both be Members you know—But they're good fellows, they shan't vote but shall be my friends.'

'The Dear King was as usual', wrote Greville, 'well-intentioned and most kind to me, but alas he was much hurried, and there was much wildness in his countenance and manner.'

---

* This may have something to do with a mysterious letter Colonel Digby and Fanny Burney copied out for the Queen and sent to town on the 30th. 'It was', wrote Miss Burney, 'extremely curious—I am sorry I must make it equally secret.'

A more knowledgeable observer would have taken hope from the King's return to something like his normal hurried, nervous manner. Later the King tried to run away from his attendants because they would not go the way he wanted. 'To what sudden fluctuations of good and bad, of calm and turbulence, does this afflicting illness doom our interesting and unfortunate patient!'[44]

On the 28th the King was quiet and cheerful, but by no means in his right mind, though the irrepressible Willis gave Miss Burney 'a most reviving report of our beloved King, and with a glee so genuine that I think even the Opposition must have sympathised in it'. Dr John, 'a truly amiable character, with admirable good sense and no pretensions', confirmed the good news which Miss Burney passed on to her friends. But to the Queen Dr Willis suggested that the pages should be withdrawn from His Majesty's presence, as their presence agitated him more than Willis's own men. Greville passed on her order to the pages, who said they would obey explicit orders from the Queen. But later the objectionable Ernst made trouble, 'saucily telling Dr Willis that he would obey a written order from the Queen telling him not to got in, and no other. And if he did stay out, though he should hear a bustle in the night, he would not assist'. . . . After this, and it seems with good reason, the pages were relieved of their attendance, and Greville was deprived of his 'regular and correct information of the real state of His Majesty's health'.* The pages were replaced by Willis's men, and Dr John even assumed the duties of the King's Private Secretary. 'The proceedings of the day', observed Greville with acid under-statement, 'mark an evident and rapid move to New Authority.'

Fortunately the other pages were less cantankerous than Ernst: and when that evening the King lost his temper and pulled the hair of one of Willis's men, they went to his help.[45]

The next day the King was calm, but talked too much of Eliza. He suggested that Sir Lucas Pepys negotiate with Spain the exchange of Gibraltar for Minorca. 'Still good news from

* This, and other passages in his diary, clearly disclose Greville's main source of information.

the two good doctors!' rejoiced Miss Burney, with whom the Willises were not entirely frank.

On the 30th Greville heard that the King had struck Spicer, and kicked him on the shin, while he was opening the window shutters. It is difficult to know what really happened, as Dr John writes of the incident:

> Dr Warren accused us of having concealed material circumstances, such as His Majesty having fought with a screen in the night. It so happened that His Majesty having taken up a screen and T. Wynne* another in defence, and there the affray ended. . . . Then about hiding the loss of a hat and wig. His Majesty wishing to go one way and advised another, a little struggle ensued, such as lying down, and hat and wig fell off. Whether Dr Warren meant a compliment or a censure to the way Whigs are kept steady, I know not!

Dr Warren told Greville, 'Not one syllable of his conversation can be mistaken for sense.' Dr Willis was driven to the distasteful necessity of confining His Majesty to the Coronation Chair and giving him a 'severe lecture on his improper conversation, Eliza, etc. His Majesty becoming more loud and impatient under this lecture, Dr Willis ordered a handkerchief to be held before his mouth, and he then continued and finished his lecture.'[46]

* One of Willis's men.

CHAPTER VII

The Royal Recovery

Although nobody at the time realized it, Willis's severe lecture was a turning point in the royal malady. It was the last occasion for coercion. From that day, His Majesty's reason steadily improved.[1] The Opposition, however, at the end of January, still clung stubbornly to their delusions:

> He is certainly much worse than ever. On Thursday he was so furious as to strike, bite and kick at his attendants, and 5 men were with difficulty able to put on his coercing waistcoat. He is dreadfully emaciated, and now sees the Queen without any emotion. When not furious, there is every symptom of fatuity, even that of his tongue hanging out of his mouth. . . . He threw himself head over heels into a shallow pool of water, and has made one or two attempts to knock his head on a chimney-piece.* He gave a kick to one of the pages that laid the unfortunate man senseless.[2]

The day after this nauseating letter was written, the King went for two long walks, played picquet with the Queen, read aloud part of Handel's life and sang some of his favourite musician's choruses. Greville found him 'composed and altogether less deranged than he has been for some time'; and Dr John was well satisfied.[3]

On 1 February Greville heard he was 'quiet and orderly, but talked incessantly'; and Dr John reported, briefly, 'great satisfaction'. On the 2nd he had a long walk in the garden, paying great attention to all the alterations. There he had an unexpected encounter with Fanny Burney.

She saw him among the trees and, 'alarmed past all possible expression', fled. The King pursued her, calling loudly and hoarsely, 'Miss Burney! Miss Burney!'

* Dr Warren informed the Parliamentary Committee that the King 'never showed any intention to injure himself'.

She was frightened out of her wits, for the Queen, a tyrant when crossed, had given strict orders that no one should meet him; yet he might be deeply offended at her flight. But on she ran, too terrified to stop, in search of some labyrinth where she could escape.

The steps still pursued her, the poor, hoarse voice rang in her ears; and behind him she could hear the Willises beseeching him not to heat himself so unmercifully.

Other voices called, 'Stop! Miss Burney, stop!' But in panic she ran on.

'Doctor Willis begs you to stop!'

'I can't! I can't.' Still she fled.

'You must, Ma'am! It hurts the King to run!'

So she halted, panting, in an agony of fear.

The King came up, with the Willises on either side, and three attendants hovering near.

'Why did you run away?' he asked.

Shocked at a question impossible to answer, she forced herself forward to curtsey. As she straightened up, he put his hands round her shoulders and kissed her cheek. For a moment she feared he meant to crush her, but the Willises nodded and smiled, as though it were his usual salutation.

His joy at seeing someone other than pages, doctors and keepers was so great that she lost her terror. He begged her to walk beside him, away from the Willises, and chatted of everything that came into his mind.

'I assure you, Miss Burney, I'm quite well—as well as ever in my life. Now how do you do? Are you comfortable?'

He asked after her abhorred colleague, Madame Schwellenberg. 'Never mind her!' he laughed. 'Don't be oppressed—don't let her cast you down! I'm your friend—I know you have a hard time of it, but don't mind her!' She could only curtsey.

'Stick to your father!' he urged. 'Stick to your family! Let them be your objects!' How readily she assented!

'I will protect you, I promise you that. Depend on me.'

She thanked him; and the Willises, thinking him rather too elevated, proposed that she leave him. 'No! No! No!' the King protested, and they let him have his way.

He then started complaining angrily about his pages, especially Ernst whom he had brought up himself. He asked some very embarrassing questions about his illness, which she tried discreetly to parry.

Turning to music, he made a thousand inquiries about her father's *History of Music*; which brought him to his favourite theme, Handel. 'You know, Miss Burney, when I was a boy, Handel said, "While that boy lives, my music won't want a protector." '

But when he tried to sing some airs and choruses, his voice was so hoarse that the effect was very painful.

Again Willis tried to separate them, but the King would not have it. 'No! No! No! Not yet! I have something I must just mention first.'

He began talking of their mutual friend Mrs Delany, who had recently died. 'She was my friend. I loved her as a friend. I made a memorandum when I lost her—I'll show it to you.'

He rummaged in his pocket-book, but could not find it, and seemed about to cry.

'Come, Sir', urged Willis, 'now do you come in, and let the lady go on her walk—come, now, you've talked a long while—so we'll go in, if Your Majesty pleases.'

'No! No! I want to ask her a few questions. I've lived so long out of the world, I know nothing.'

They spoke of mutual friends; then he startled Miss Burney by confiding that he was far from satisfied with his government, and meant to form an entire new Ministry. He showed her his list. 'This was the wildest thing that passed.'

Again Willis tried to separate them and again the King prevailed, speaking now of Dr Burney and lamenting that he had not been appointed Master of the Band. 'And what has your father got at last? Nothing but that poor thing at Chelsea. But never mind! I'll take care of him. I'll do it myself.'

Of Lord Salisbury, who had used Dr Burney very ill, he assured Miss Burney, 'He is out already, as this memorandum will show you, and so are many more. I shall be much better served. When I get away, I shall rule with a rod of iron!'

Finding that at last they must part, he took his leave, and again begged her not to be bullied by Madame Schwellenberg.

'Never mind her! Depend upon me! I'll be your friend as long as I live! I here pledge myself to be your friend!'

What a scene! Miss Burney hastened to confess it to the Queen, who was astonished, and anxious to hear every particular. Miss Burney told almost all. Some of his distressing questions she could not repeat.

Greville, too, 'Colonel Welbred', had to hear all about it. 'Did he not promise to—do something for you?—take care of you?'

'Oh yes!' Miss Burney laughed. 'Oh yes! If you want anything, apply to me: now is my time.'

On the whole, from what Greville could recollect, this seemed to have been one of the King's best days since he had come to Kew. [4]

On the 3rd the King shaved himself, for the first time for seven weeks. He talked in French to one of his new attendants, a Swiss, who said he had been ordered not to speak French. 'I know', said His Majesty, 'but you can't speak English, so I shall call you Dumbey.'

The Queen and Princesses visited him in the evening. Picquet did not go very smoothly, but with Dr John to give them a lead, they all sang catches and choruses, the King giving a hearty rendering of 'Rule Britannia' and 'Come, cheer up my Lads!' Greville welcomed hilarity where so much gloom had been, 'though in truth it partook more of the jollity of an election than the etiquette of a Court'.

When the ladies got up to go, the poor, lonely King pleaded, 'I might surely stay a few hours with my family, when I must stay so many with footmen.' But 'by not pressing too much at the moment, all came round again and ended well, and the King parted with his family very quietly'. [5]

Greville, pessimistic as usual, was fearful of the effect of this long evening with the Queen; but Dr John was well satisfied with his patient's progress:

Dr Warren, who sees him one quarter of an hour every day, says, as to seeing and asking after sheep on his farm, these were no proofs of being better; and we, who see him through the whole of every day, find in this attention and pleasure to his usual amusements an entirely new power of the mind. If I had not lived so much in the country that I may not have acquired the fashionable powers of judging, I should think the Doctor a damned fool in this business.[6]

Here speaks the specialist, experienced, observant and sincere, exasperated at the bunglers with whom he has to work. This one passage in Dr John's diary goes far to justify everything he and his father said and did.

An unparalleled example of administrative despatch, over the week-end at that, resulted in a Commission being filled in for opening Parliament under the Great Seal on Tuesday, 3 February. The replies of the Queen and Prince of Wales, to the invitations to take up their respective duties in the Regency, were read to the Commons.

Lord North referred to 'false alarms industriously circulated that the Prince had asserted his right to assume the sovereign power independently of the two Houses'.

'I allow', Pitt tartly replied, 'that it was not claimed by the Prince, but it was asserted by others, who now lament their own assertions which they are ashamed to avow and seem desirous to retract.'

This got a gratifying rise out of Burke. 'The Ministers are preparing to create a monster of sin and death: death to the Constitution, sin to the feelings of the country. They are giving birth to innumerable barking monsters, eager to destroy every principle of our constitution. They are about to purloin the Great Seal to commit an act of forgery and fraud, to support violence and to consummate their climax of villainy.'[7]

Despite Burke's eloquence (to which the Commons were now well accustomed) the two Houses met next day as a Parliament.

Meanwhile Carlton House was seething with excited anticipation. By a singularly unhappy inspiration, Regency Medals were struck. On the one side, round a profile of His Royal Highness in a prodigious lace jabot, was written 'Prince Regent of Great Britain, France and Ireland'; on the reverse, with the ostrich plumes:

Born August 12, 1762
Appointed February   , 1789.[8]

Hardly anyone bothered to read the medical bulletins, which varied little from day to day. But steadily now the King's health improved. On the 4th he was better than Dr John had ever seen him. Despite a cold, wet, blustering day, he inspected his sheep and, on his return, for the first time in many years, played on the flute. He had a good game of picquet with the Queen, and joined Princess Mary in singing 'Wind gentle Evergreen' and 'De'il take the Wars'.

'Sir Lucas Pepys did not see the King tonight', wrote Greville, in his captious vein, 'I regret that such opportunities are witheld. . . . I do not quite understand why the King's talking to his shepherd or his gardener should not risk agitation as much as one physician going in with Dr Willis to feel his pulse.'[9]

On 5 February, Greville thought he had never seen the King better: and quoted as an instance His Majesty's listening with attention and interest to a long, involved story about William III. Also he recollected clearly a Quaker he had seen at a Northumberland House masquerade exactly thirty-three years before. 'Would that the latter had not occurred!' lamented Greville—perhaps a discreet reference to rumours of the King's youthful passion for Hannah Lightfoot, the Fair Quakeress.* With Dr Warren, however, the King blotted his copy-book, talking of Eliza and addressing him as Ricardus Warren Baronetus. 'As deranged as ever, poor man!' was Warren's verdict.[10]

On that day, 5 February, a full-scale debate[11] opened on the Regency Bill. It was fought clause by clause, most bitterly over control of the household and physicians.

Burke was in his usual form:

His Majesty is insane: his disease is not intermittent, nor has he any lucid intervals and partial visitations of reason. His faculties are totally eclipsed—not a partial, but an entire eclipse. That bold

* There is a story that, in his youth, George III married and had by her a son, known as George Rex, who was hidden away at the Cape of Good Hope. Were this true, the Prince of Wales, his brothers and sisters would be illegitimate. The Queen was always sensitive about this persistent rumour. Almost certainly, however, the King's admiration for Miss Lightfoot never went beyond a distant and innocent passion. The matter is fully discussed in *Historical Notes and Queries*, Series II, vol. X, 89 et seq.

promiser, Dr Willis himself, cannot venture to fix a time when the King may be able to resume his functions. The Bill is intended to degrade not only the Prince, but the whole Brunswick family, who are to be outlawed and attainted. Until the Queen shall think proper to assert that the King is recovered, the people possess no means of knowing the fact. If her Council shall declare it, and His Majesty shall be capable to sit in a chair at the head of the Council, the Bill provides that he shall be declared capable. What is this, except putting into the hands of Dr Willis and his keepers the whole power of changing the government? A person who has been insane may be so subdued by coercion as to become capable to act the farce appointed, and of appearing for a short time to have resumed his intellect. I maintain the utter impossibility of adducing proof whether a person who has been insane is perfectly recovered or not. The whole business is a scheme, under the pretence of pronouncing His Majesty sane, to bring back an insane King.

By the end of Burke's speech the House was, as usual, three-quarters empty, and no one bothered to reply to him.

It was a matter on which Lord North, blind and prematurely senile, could nevertheless speak with authority. 'Eighteen peers belong to the Household. Do gentlemen recollect that eighteen peers voting on one side make a difference of thirty-six on a division?' It was stated, without contradiction from the Treasury Benches, that there were nearly one hundred and fifty household offices, worth over £100,000 a year—nearly a third of the whole Crown patronage.

Pitt rather feebly suggested a second household, separate from the King's, for the Regent. (Since the offices would be only temporary, they would have little political value.) Sheridan, most extravagant crony of the most spendthrift prince England has ever known, indignantly rejected the offer. 'How does he dare suggest such an idea, when the Prince desires no such establishment created as may occasion fresh burdens on the public?'

The Opposition's arguments were unanswerable—or answerable only by a reply which would give mortal offence to the man who seemed likely within a few days to be, as Regent, in a position to pay off all old scores. But as rumours of the King's amendment raced round London, the Ministerial ranks were steadied, and Pitt won every division by a comfortable majority of fifty or sixty.

On the 6th, the King visited the Observatory and, noticing that the gentleman in charge grew pale at seeing him, said, 'If you're not ill, you're shocked at seeing me, Rigaud. But all will be well by and by.' He fired off at Rigaud a series of rapid questions, quite in his old style, about the astronomical instruments; and then bustled off to discuss the Botanic Gardens with Eaton, his head gardener, and his Merinos with Sir Joseph Banks. He took from the library some books of sermons and old songs; and desired that two large pictures, which had been removed from his room in December, should now be replaced. He shaved himself very well, not only his face but his whole head; and was allowed, for the first time for many weeks, to have a knife and fork. Greville deprecated these indulgences.

In the evening His Majesty was busy with plans for a new Order of Minerva, to reward men of learning. It was a perfectly sensible idea, though it never materialized.

'I own', observed Greville, 'I should be glad that Dr Willis would introduce me, and should be most happy to witness myself these favourable progresses of which we have heard of late such encouraging details.'[12]

Dr Willis made it clear, next day, that the King's condition was still critical, and depended mainly on Dr Willis. 'I could by rash management make him fly out at any time and get angry. And I'd be burned if it wasn't even now in my power to make a fool of him in four days.' When the Willises were there, they checked everything the King said or did wrongly.[13]

The Willises and the King, between them, gave the other physicians a surprise on the 7th. 'Why, Sir', suggested Dr John, 'don't you dismiss them when you have finished with them, as you would have done before your illness?'

Accordingly, after they had been with him a quarter of an hour, the King bowed and said, 'I'll detain you no longer, gentlemen.'

Previously Dr Warren, even before shutting the King's door, used to remark audibly, 'Poor man, how mad he is!' But now,

'as though thunderstruck, they instantly retired, walking out
solemnly one after the other as at a funeral, without uttering a
word'. Unhappily we have only Dr John's side of the story: his
rivals' sentiments are not recorded. In his public bulletin Dr
Warren merely wrote, 'His Majesty passed yesterday in a
composed manner, had a very good night and is composed this
morning.'[14]

On the 8th the King was not quite so well. In order to have
his way and go for a drive in his phaeton rather than a walk, he
shammed lameness until Willis and the surgeon examined his
foot. In the evening, however, he had forgotten his lameness,
and walked as far as his farm.*

The Queen and Princesses visited him. To Greville's relief,
they were not greeted (as on the two previous evenings) by a
cheerful serenade on the flute. The King was reverting to his
old habit, which he had droppped during his illness, of punct-
uating his hurried conversations with 'What? What? What?'
Greville observed that its return, 'though not a grace in
language, yet restoring habits of former days, may be presumed
a forerunner of returning wisdom'. Horace Walpole, who was
generally spiteful about George III, commented sourly on the
news, 'the King has returned, not to his sense, but to his nonsense. Kings grow popular by whatever way they lose their
heads.' But Greville was right, Walpole wrong: the royal
mannerisms, absurd though they might be, as indicators of his
innate nervousness were a sign of normality—their temporary
absence a symptom of derangement.[15] Psychotic patients commonly lose all self-consciousness for the period of their illness.

Withers alleges, without truth†, that

* He was a keen farmer; and, under the pseudonym of Ralph Robinson,
had corresponded with Arthur Young, the agricultural expert.

† If the incident had taken place, it could not have been before 8 February, because that was the first Sunday after the King resumed his flute-
playing on the 4th, and after he was allowed a knife and fork on the 6th. By
that time, the pages had been removed from his presence: so that Withers,
if he was, as he claimed, a page, could not have been an eyewitness. The
King, by 8 February, was just not behaving in this manner. Moreover, Dr
Willis would never have made a fool of himself on the orders of his patient.

The story is certainly a lie: but has been often quoted, without the slightest
critical examination, as though it were true.

the King told his physicians to dance a hornpipe; and when they declined that honour, 'Here is my sceptre', said he, holding a knife in a threatening posture, 'and, by God, the man who presumes to oppose my will shall be instantly—instantly impaled alive!' And the King called for his flute, and Sir George and Dr Duplicate danced until it was dark. And thus ended the Sabbath day.[16]

On the 9th the King played cards and the flute with Dr Gisborne before breakfast, 'innocent pastimes, no doubt, but now appendages to altered and interrupted habits'. He also hinted once or twice at Lady Pembroke. He again welcomed his wife and daughters with the flute, and sang with them in harmony. 'Too unceremonious', considered the hypercritical Greville: but Dr Willis no longer feared a relapse.

As for Dr Warren, 'his general idea is that, when the King is quiet, he is an idiot—otherwise phrenetic, and this opinion he industriously spreads'.[17]

Most people, by now, took Dr Warren's views with a pinch of salt: but the debates[18] on 10 and 11 February, on the delicate question of how, and by whom, the King was to be declared sane, provided Burke with the occasion for his last and most lamentable exhibition of spleen. He was not a good loser. If the King was ever to return to the throne, he shouted, 'it would be a King quietened and subdued by coercion, smitten by the hand of Omnipotence. Do we recollect that the Almighty has hurled him from his throne, and plunged him into a condition that may justly excite the pity of the meanest peasant?'

'Oh! Oh!' roared the outraged Commons. 'Take down his words!' But the thick brogue continued.

'Ought we to make a mockery of him, put a crown of thorns on his head, a reed in his hand, and cry, "Hail! King of the Britons!" . . . I have visited', said Burke, flourishing a medical treatise on the subject, 'the dreadful mansions where these unfortunate beings are confined. Some, *after a supposed recovery*, have committed parricide, butchered their sons, hanged, shot, drowned, thrown themselves from windows.'

176

There were cries of 'Oh! Oh! Order! Order!' and Burke complained of the interruption.

'I never', observed Pitt acidly, 'wish to do away with the impression the Honourable Gentleman's speeches make on the House.'

'Such', continued Burke, somewhat subdued, 'is the danger of an uncertain cure—such is the necessity to see that a sane sovereign is put in possession of the Government. The King's supposed cure would be horrible in the extreme, if a relapse took place.'

Next day, Burke found, in his favourite place in the House, a 'bulletin': 'Very irritable in the evening, no sleep all night and very unquiet this morning.' It was not the sort of joke he appreciated.[19]

Even those on Treasury benches missed Charles Fox. 'You cannot imagine', wrote Wilberforce, 'how insipid and vapid are our debates without Fox. They serve us the same tasteless mess day after day, till one loathes the very sight of it.'[20]

Pitt agreed to limit the restrictions to three years, but added that he had every reason to believe His Majesty would soon recover.

Burke, with vexation and disappointment, was 'almost mad, and will be quite so if the King recovers'. The Prince and the Duke of York were 'quite desperate, and endeavouring to drown their cares and internal chagrin in wine and dissipation'. While in his cups, the Prince promised a regiment to one of his pot-companions, a Captain Macdonald, 'who has not the smallest pretensions to one, but keeps him to his promise'. He also summoned to Carlton House Doctors Warren and Pepys, who there exhibited a degrading public squabble about the King's chances of recovery.[21]

There was a clause in the Regency Bill providing that the Regent should forfeit his rights if he should marry a Roman Catholic. Mr Rolle did not miss the opportunity of proposing that this be made retrospective, forcing from the Opposition a stumbling and unconvincing denial. *A propos* Regency Caps, *The World* reported milliners as recommending that the 'Fitzherbert hat sit rather heavy on the crown'. On a report of Charles Fox returning to Town, *The Times* pointed out that his indisposition 'had just lasted the event of Mr Rolle's motion'; and that his case had been 'concussion, through jolting over the rights of the people'. Gleefully the Treasury-subsidized Press rubbed salt into the Opposition's wounds: 'The favourable report of His Majesty's health has created consternation almost incredible. One rat almost died of fright.' 'We'll be off in a jiffy', said one elegant lady. 'What's that?' asked her friend. 'We'll be off like the new Ministry, on the recovery of the King.'[22]

A by-election at Aylesbury provided the occasion for a *jeu d'esprit* circulated all over the West End, at the expense of the ludicrous Mr Weltjie and his Royal Master:

> To de Gendelmen, de Abbés and de Freholders of de Comté of Ailsbri.
>
> My friend Gerri Lake havin offurd his sarvis's to reprepre-present you in Parlialialiament, I presum to tak de friddom to recumminind um to you, bein my frind and grate frind of my master de Prince. He is ver clever gendelmon and kno de horse ver vell, how to bi for de Prince and how to sel for himselv. But if you tink him two poor, I beg to offer myselv. I am naturalise Inglisman and Wig, and was introduce to de Wig Club by Lord Stormont and Jak Payne. I am no Papis myselv, tho I keeps grate fat Papis hore. My principles are God dam de King and de Quin, and God bles de Prince and all his broders. I say agen and agen dat de Prince be our lawful suvring, and not his fader.
>
> I am, gendelmen,
>
> Your frind and sarvant,
>
> W. WELTJIE.[23]

It was, indeed, the winter of the Prince's discontent. Nothing went right for him. At the same time as this damaging squib, *The Times* reported, with hilarious detail and in language unbecoming the Thunderer, his misfortune in shooting a friend in the rump: 'Lord Clermont, having had too hearty a break-fast, sat in a resting posture behind a furze-bush. Two of the Prince's dogs scented the noble Peer and came to a point. The Prince let fly at the bush and wounded Lord Clermont in the defenceless part of his body. The Prince's gun hung fire, or the snipe would have received the whole charge. 23½ grains of No. 4 shot were extracted from Lord Clermont's bum.'[24]

'Drinking, wenching and gaming', reported *The Times* a few days later, 'are the principal baits with which the Opposition Party furnish their hooks to catch ROYAL FRY; and these baits they dig in the most nauseous stews the metropolis affords.'[25]

The King, meanwhile, went from strength to strength. Greville, however, never himself seeing him, 'often regretted the difficulty there is in obtaining unbiased information'. On the 10th His Majesty began to take an interest in politics, and asked to see the Chancellor. Willis advised, not yet. 'I will not see him', assented the King, 'until you think fit. But I have been ill for seventeen weeks, and have much to inquire about. I must have lost some friends in that time.'

He brooded on the subject. 'For God's sake', he asked Dr John, 'is there really a Parliament or not?'

'You may be sure, Sir', Dr John soothed him, 'that during such an illness as Your Majesty has experienced, care has been taken of affairs of State. But you mustn't think of such matters now.'

'I'll take your advice, Dr John. But I adjourned Parliament, so if it is now assembled, 'tis totally illegal.'

The daily bulletin credited him with 'more than his usual recollection'.

Greville considered it a bad sign that His Majesty 'continues too familiar with his attendants, endeavouring to make them *friends*'. Poor King, he must have been very lonely. But now more visitors were admitted. Lord Herbert wrote that day to Eliza's husband, 'I have been with him at Kew for several hours, and had I not known of his having been ill, I should not even have perceived he was grown thin.'[26]

'Feel my pulse, Dr Warren', said the King on 11 February. 'How does it beat? And how many strokes did it beat three days ago? I think there is some amendment, is there not?'

Warren's reaction is variously recorded. Dr John wrote, 'Dr Warren admitted he saw nothing wrong in his conversation with the King: he foresaw amendment a fortnight ago, and never before discovered symptoms of returning sanity.'

To Greville Warren said, pointing to the best report he had yet signed, 'That's the Bulletin they wanted me to sign weeks ago.' 'Former hesitations on Dr Warren's part rendered Dr Willis sneeringly triumphant.'

In his afternoon walk, the King overheard Eaton, his gardener, promise to make up for Willis a basket of exotic plants. 'Get another basket, Eaton', he ordered jovially, 'and pack up the doctor in it, and send him off at the same time.'

A little later, seeing Willis wave away some workmen in the garden, the King said, 'Willis, you don't know your own business. You ought to accustom me now to see people by degrees, that I may be prepared more for seeing them at large.' Later, seeing the gardeners make up a bonfire, he told them, 'Pray, put out that fire directly. Don't you see it smokes Mrs Boscawen's house?'

Dr Willis told Lady Harcourt there was now only a shade of delirium left. Knowing the King very well, she shrewdly observed, 'I am not very clear whether the shade they talk of may not be merely his own natural manner, which being different from that of the generality of the world, and very unlike what they may expect from a King, may perhaps be considered by them as some remains of disorder.' On another occasion, hearing the attendants lament their patient's 'bustling manner', this observant lady commented, 'This, we know, in his days of perfect health, would not have appeared extraordinary to us.'[27]

The Bishop of Salisbury called to offer his congratulations on the King's miraculous recovery, and to 'sound his panegyric on Dr Willis to whose sole skill he imputed this amendment'. 'His zeal and affection towards His Majesty', wrote Greville, sour with jealousy, 'is well known, but evidently he knows not the true history with us. . . . I confess I am now become desirous of knowing from my own observations what is to be considered as symptoms of that real progressive amendment now so much talked of.'[28]

On 14 February Sir George Baker admitted, 'I believe, i' faith, the King will get quite well.' It was the first time Dr John 'ever heard him speak in favour of the case'. Sir Lucas

Pepys and, less decidedly, Dr Warren, had already pronounced him to be convalescent. The Archbishop of Canterbury, by 12 February, was firm as a rock: 'The last ten days have passed without a single interruption of good accounts from Kew, and signed by physicians whose hopes have hitherto been least sanguine.' The gardeners, the astronomer, Vulliamy the King's watchmaker, all reported favourably, and every word of these experts was eagerly repeated in society.[29] 'Yet no man has a doubt there will be a change of government the moment the Regency takes place. . . . Few opposition people were at the House, and those languid, like men of whom hope deferred has made the heart sick. Sheridan and Co may at all events urge to get possession for the sake of rank, let the possession be ever so short. It is shocking to suppose the Prince will submit to this.' But the Prince swore he would change the Administration, were it only for seven hours.[30]

The Times on the 13th, quoting Dr Willis, reported recovery as certain; and on the 14th declared, a trifle prematurely, the cure complete, the crisis at an end. 'When a rumour arrived at Brooks's, "What news?" asked Surface [Fox]. "Bad news, very bad news. The King is much better." Down went the cards, and a general execration of Dr Willis followed.'

On the same day the *Morning Herald* reported that the King was very agitated, and had no returning recollection. The Opposition industriously spread rumours that he dressed as, and thought he was, a Quaker, in honour of ——* 'His present fancy', said Mrs Crewe, 'is to think himself a Quaker. So much for his amendment.' But Dr John recorded in his diary, 'Now Dr Warren, to try the King, took hold of his coat and said it was very thin. The King said he did not find it so, it was always a favourite coat of his, being the Chancellor's colour. Dr Warren hoped that the King would give him a reason corresponding with that report, in which there is no foundation whatever—a mere story.'[31]

Charles Fox, however, doggedly disregarded every good

* The name in Dr John's diary is left blank, which usually indicates Lady Pembroke. She seems, however, to have had no Quaker connections. It may be another reference to Hannah Lightfoot, 'The Fair Quakeress'. See footnote on p. 172.

report, writing on the 12th to stiffen Portland, 'I have no belief in the King's recovery, but I dare say some of our friends are a bit alarmed'; and, four days later, 'The Bulletins, whether good or bad, ought not to make the slightest difference in the conduct of the Prince or of us.'

But Betsy Sheridan, closer to the centre of affairs, admitted on the 12th, 'the King these last three days has been *certainly* mending, so much as to damp the hopes of the most sanguine people of the party'. To impecunious but optimistic Irish relatives, who pestered her brother for jobs under the new Ministry, she was obliged to explain very frankly that his own situation was now precarious and that 'the King's amendment and the total uncertainty of what the event will be with regard to the Regency, makes any application *impossible* at present'.[32]

The King had still to be frequently dosed with Emetic Tartar, a remarkably disagreeable tranquilliser, hidden in his food; and he kept on making embarrassing references to his old flame, such as 'I shall buy the house on Richmond Green that was Queen Elizabeth's; for you know', he added with a wink to his surgeon, 'everything which was Elizabeth's is dear to me.'[33]

The physicians did not lack advice on their case. 'Amicus', ignorant of His Majesty's somewhat unfortunate addiction to the flute, recommended to Sir George Baker the soothing effects of sweet music. An unauthorized intruder was found in Kew House, a young Scot who had studied physics and wished to offer a cure for His Majesty. A search of his person having produced only an ink-horn, a few shillings and a watch, he was handed over to one of the Secretaries of State. To Greville he appeared 'insane, but quietly so, and I am satisfied he came here with no malicious intent'.

Mrs Thrale recommended the desperate remedy of 'cold water, almost to drowning point': but a Mr Brewin advised Sir George to sit his patient in very hot water, pouring cold water over his head. Another of Sir George's correspondents gave full details of an improvised Turkish bath:

Take a bathing tub and fix some hoops over it (like this drawing), and coverd in with some blankitts or cloths, and so as no air can come in to it, and leave a space for the patient to put his head out,

182

when to hot, or sick, if required. Then place a stool in it with holes in it for to sit upon, and a little stool lower for to set the feet upon, then place a large flat earthun dish and placed at the bottom of the tub, to prevent the patient from burning. Then put in the fire ten or twelve large coggle stons and let them be made very hot, then set on a large copper or boiler, full of water, with a handfull of rosemary, a handfull of sage rue and peppermint each, then seat the patient in the tub upon the stool and his feet on the little stool, then take a hot coggle or two and put it in the dish and take a quantity of wather, 3 or 4 quarts from the copper and pour it on the coggle ston, so as to make a strong steam, and so it must be repeted as often as you think the patient can permit the fomentation, 30 or 50 minutes or longer, and the person must be rubed with some warm cloth as the sweet comes on and so on, carre must be taken that no are can come in tub, and the bed well warm and a medicine given.

Several loyal subjects dreamed of remedies, such as leeches applied to the head, and finely powdered camphor pills. 'No Physician' advised Sir George to 'steep a napkin in hot vinegar, bend it round his temples and let him eat frequently of bitter almonds. Wood roses and primroses, both leaves and root of each a handful, pound all this together with a head of garlic and the powder of a crab's claw. Mix all well together and give one spoonful in the morning fasting and fast three hours after.' But 'A.C.' thought it would be more efficacious to 'boil three large handfuls of ground ivy shred small, in two quarts wine till there is but one third remaining, then strain it and add to it three ounces of the best salad oil, boil it up to an ointment, shave the patient's head, warm this ointment, and chafe the head with it. Then take fresh herbs bruised and apply them plaisterwise, tying it on on top of the head very hard.'

A patient whose 'intellects had quite gone, had obtained wonderful relief from the application of lamb skins to her head every three hours.' Another recommended, with exasperating vagueness, 'electrical treatment'. The Duke of Dorset proposed to dose the King with the blood of an ass: to which another amateur alienist recommended adding the brains of a ram or of a dog. A more enterprising suggestion, emanating from Lord

183

Hervey, was to infect His Majesty with the itch, the eruptions of which would surely carry off the disorder.

We do not, alas, know what treatment was proposed to the Prince of Wales in a letter the composition of which took no less than nine hours, by Dr James Graham, Founder and Principal of the Temple of Health and Hymen. As he had recently been under treatment in a madhouse in Edinburgh, and his main contribution to medical science was the invention of the Royal Celestial Electrical Bed of Patagonia, which guaranteed children of the desired sex to couples making use of it at fifty guineas an hour, his suggestions must have been of singular interest.[34]

The royal pulse rate was now down to 64, the royal avoir-dupois to 12 st. 3 lb., almost three stone below normal; and the routine of Kew was interrupted by a daily influx of visitors inquiring after the royal health. 'The high-trained courtiers seem now to have taken a hint, and are making surpassing inquiries, stealing a march upon others not less anxious in the cause, but not equally accustomed to practising such finesse.'

On Sunday, the 15th, the King as usual played picquet with the Queen. A visitor asked Thomas Willis if he distinguished one day from another.

'Certainly', replied the clergyman.

'I don't think', said the visitor, 'that His Majesty would play cards on a Sunday if he was well, and himself.'

'He knows it's wrong', answered Willis, 'but he says he thinks it may now be excusable, for he has no other way of entertaining the Queen.'[35]

On the 17th the Lords discussed the Regency Bill in Committee; and the bulletin, issued by Dr Warren, announced, 'The King has for some time past been in a state of amendment, and is this day in a state of convalescence.' The Third Reading was imminent: but at the King's request, the Chancellor went to see him. He was a little nervous, but talked sensibly on foreign affairs: his questions about English politics were parried. Greville heard that the Chancellor 'was not well pleased with the appearance of his countenance, and did not think it that of so much health as has been represented by the physicians'.

184

Greville gained the same impression from the attendants' gossip, the King having held up a candle to his own portrait and asked, 'Did you ever see such a hog?'* Kew gossip also said that, when asked by Willis if in a case of a private person he would not now take off the Statute of Lunacy, the Chancellor answered, 'No, but I would have sent him home to his friends, to be seen again in ten days.'[36]

Be that as it may, the Chancellor was sufficiently impressed by the King and by Willis to postpone until the 23rd the Third Reading of the Regency Bill.

Charles Fox, however, the slave of his own hopes, wrote on the 17th to his friend Fitzpatrick:

> I hope by this time all ideas of the Prince or any of us taking any measures in consequence of the good reports of the King, are at an end: if they are not, pray do all you can to crush them; and if it were possible to do anything to cure that habitual spirit of despondency and fear that characterises the Whig party, it would be a good thing; but I suppose that is impossible. I rather think, as you do, that Warren has been frightened; I am sure, if what I hear is true, that he has not behaved well. . . . If you would let me know by return of post on what day the Regency is like to commence, I should be obliged to you.[37]

While Charles Fox was thus deluding himself, Warren was urging Willis to encourage the King to go to Hanover. 'To what end?' asked Dr John suspiciously. Indeed, it seems a curious plan, explicable only if someone wanted the King out of the way.[38]

Having always been interested in watches and clocks, and busying himself much with them lately, the King had a long, cosy chat with Vulliamy, his watchmaker—exactly the sort of talk, with the sort of person, that he used to enjoy when he was well. In the evening, with his wife and daughters, he read

---

* His Majesty's appearance was, indeed, remarkably porcine. Had he made such a remark a year before, it would have been quoted as a pleasing, if eccentric, example of royal condescension.

aloud *The Merchant of Venice*, 'in different tones of voice as suited the characters, attending particularly to the part of Shylock'.

Later (and this was considered a great step forward), when the Queen was about to leave him, the King asked Willis, 'Would it not be a proper attention in me to hand Her Majesty upstairs to her apartment?'

Dr Willis consented, and in a few minutes His Majesty returned to his own room. Greville considered 'his readiness in coming down as a sense of his situation, from which real good may arise'.[39]

On the 19th the King 'spoke with great indifference as to the means which had been used to effect his recovery, thankful to God that by any means he was so well'. To Warren he showed his 'Coronation Chair', with a look, Warren thought, 'of not unpleasant recollections'. Warren's bulletin announced that 'His Majesty continued to advance in recovery.'

He asked if he might go upstairs to invite the Queen to visit him. 'With all my heart', said Willis, and up he went. In the event, he was allowed to pass the evening, very comfortably, in Her Majesty's apartments.

He chatted affably with Greville about a family bereavement. Not having spoken to the King for some time, Greville was the better able to judge any amendment, and was quite satisfied that he was much better.[40]

Pitt called at Kew, accompanied by Dundas who, knowing there was no refuge for him at Carlton House, had been throughout the crisis true as steel, 'sticking to Pitt as a barnacle to an oyster-shell—there was no man who ate Pitt's toads with such zeal, attention and appetite'. That evening the Prime Minister wrote to his mother, 'The King is perfectly well, and if he were a private man, would be declared so.'[41]

Desperately the dwindling Opposition clung to their delusions.

Neither the accounts sent to St James's [wrote Lord Sheffield on the 19th] nor the ministerial account can be relied on, but his mind is more composed. He is much afraid of Dr Willis. Some time ago he used to show the greatest joy when the other physicians came in, Willis being absent. He is not now suffered to see anyone without Willis. He is occasionally outrageous, and on some subjects quite deranged. . . . The four months' delay in appointing a Regent justly provokes the reprobation of all men not heated by party.

'The King', wrote Sir Gilbert Elliott, 'wore a star on his coat, and Sir George Baker congratulated him on appearing like a King. "Hush! Hush!" said the King, "Don't talk of Stars, we must not talk of stars. You know I am Mopsimus and don't like French mottoes." '[42]

Where Elliott got his story cannot be known. Greville's account of the same incident is far less colourful. 'Sir George Baker and Sir Lucas Pepys saw the King this morning [20th] and on the whole spoke favourably of His Majesty. The former perceives some shades. He had played the flute to him; and talking of his Star,* he told him he intended to change the motto.'

He sent for Mr Palmer, the cutler, and examined several cases of razors, presenting a set to Greville, and others to the pages. Greville then walked with the King, who spoke of his enforced removal to Kew. 'That', said the King, 'was indeed a very disagreeable day. . . . As for you, I do you the justice to say that you pledged yourself to nothing—but Harcourt told me to trust to his honour,† and I've not forgot that.'

He talked, 'much like himself', about his hothouse flowers, and of his plan to lay Kew and Richmond Gardens together.

Greville urged him to be in no hurry to return to active politics. 'Believe me', replied the King, 'I have no child's play before me, but all will do well by degrees.'[43]

He was also visited by the Chancellor that day; and after these excitements was given a precautionary dose of Tartar Emetic. 'It is curious, so often has His Majesty now taken it, how little he suspects the cause of his many sicknesses—but this medicine is so cunningly and so variously masked by Dr Willis, that it is almost impossible to detect, or even to suspect the vehicles. At one time it comes in whey, at another in asses' milk,

* Of the abortive Order of Minerva.
† General Harcourt promised him that he should see the Queen and Princesses at Kew.

sometimes in bread and sometimes it becomes successful in bread and butter.'[44]

The King had a long walk with Sir Joseph Banks next day, the 21st, visiting the exotic garden and Merinos, inspecting the new farm-yard and farm offices. When it started to rain, a gentleman's carriage was borrowed: but on the sun coming out, the coachman was dismissed with a guinea, and the King continued his walk.

Dr Warren thought very favourably of him: and a person (possibly Sir Joseph Banks) who saw the King reported that 'though thin, he is not so thin as he has been, looks fresh and healthy and is much handsomer through not being so weather-beaten. Somebody attempted to talk politics with him, but he said, "None yet, for my head is not strong enough for that subject." '[45]

With agonized reflections on lost opportunities, Opposition ladies were sadly consigning their Regency Caps to attics, box-rooms and the deserving poor. 'The embarrassment', wrote the Archbishop of Canterbury, 'of those *qui ont manqués leur coup* is great indeed, and great will be the outcry of those thousands whom they had promised.' Fox, however, though puzzled at the delay in the Third Reading, was still confident, and on the 21st wrote to Portland, 'I cannot believe that a Council of Regency can be thought of. If it is, I own I think it is the best chance of getting the country against Pitt. I rather incline to think that more delay is what they will try, in hopes of a perfect recovery in a few weeks.'[46]

The Chancellor saw the King again on the 22nd, and was very pleased with his progress; though His Majesty hinted at Lady Pembroke and spoke of an attachment thirty years ago. The Chancellor austerely advised him to drop such ideas at fifty.[47]

For several days there had been anxious discussions at Kew about how, when and where the King should meet the Prince of Wales and the Duke of York. This difficult interview was effected on 23 February, in the Queen's apartments, with no one else but her present. On his way to meet his sons the King, wiping his eyes with a handkerchief, observed, 'It was a maxim of my ancestor of the House of Brunswick never to shed a tear.'

He then went upstairs. He stayed half an hour with them talking, they told Greville, on general subjects—how he had taken up Latin again, and learned to play a good game of picquet.

The ordeal over, the King wrote to his Prime Minister, 'It is with infinite satisfaction that I renew my correspondence with Mr Pitt by acquainting him of my having seen the Prince of Wales and my second son. Care was taken that the conversation should be general and cordial. I chose the meeting should be in the Queen's apartment, that all parties might have that caution which at the present hour could but be judicious.' The King then gave Pitt some advice on Supplies, and concluded in words that must have been welcome to his Prime Minister: 'I must decline entering upon pressure of business. Indeed for the rest of my life I shall expect others to fulfil the duties of their employments, and only keep that superintending eye which can be effected without labour or fatigue.'[48] It was a resolution which might better have been made thirty years before: but, however late, it was of great importance. For those vital years in which the eighteenth-century political system disintegrated under pressure of the French Revolution, the Crown was removed from the day-to-day business of government. The ground so lost by George III was never regained by his successors. So the royal malady, coming at a political climacteric, gave a fortuitous, decisive twist to the development of the English constitution.

As for his sons, who to Greville had expressed great satisfaction at the King's amendment, they hastened back to Brooks's and 'amused themselves with spreading a report that the King was still out of his mind, and in quoting phrases of his to which they gave that turn. It is certainly a decent and becoming thing that, when all the King's physicians, all his attendants and his two principal Ministers agree in pronouncing him well, his two sons should deny it.'[49]

'By God!' exclaimed the Chancellor when he heard their stories, 'I suppose they wind up the King when I go to Kew, for he seems always well when I see him.'[50]

There was much discussion at this time of courtiers and others who had trimmed their sails to the wind from Carlton House. One of these was the Duke of Queensberry, 'Old Q.', who was dismissed from his post of Lord of the Bedchamber and positively driven out of the country by 'people calling him a rat for deserting his master to hobble after a young Prince'. Another was 'little Lothian', whom the King later removed from command of the 1st Life Guards, though he generously offered him another regiment in Ireland. The new peer, Malmesbury, had disgraced himself by first assuring Pitt he approved of the proposed restrictions; then rushing off to Fox and recanting.[51]

Of his favourite son the King inquired wistfully, 'Frederick only voted against us once, didn't he?'

'Your Majesty must be aware to what trials one in his situation is exposed.'[52]

'Very true', said the King, 'very true.'

Later, in April, he told a friend, 'They were the boldest rats I ever knew, for all the calculations were against them. Even Warren said it was probable that I should recover.' But the King was not vindictive, and months later had still not looked through the papers to see who had betrayed him. 'I could not do so until I found myself in a disposition to forgive. I took the sacrament today, and shall begin with the papers tomorrow.'[53]

On the 24th the Chancellor formally announced to the House of Lords that he had found the royal intelligence perfectly sound, and the King capable of conversing on any subject. The bulletin of the 25th, issued by Dr Warren and Dr Reynolds, stated, 'His Majesty's progress to recovery has been gradual and regular for some time past, and His Majesty appears this morning to be free from complaint.' On the next day, Sir George Baker and Sir Lucas Pepys proclaimed 'an entire cessation of His Majesty's illness'; and on the 27th, the bulletins ceased.[54]

The Regency Bill was dead, but a grotesque ghost of it walked on 27 February. The Irish Parliament, 'which was to the English Parliament as a monkey is to a man', had seen fit to offer the Prince the powers of Regent *without restriction*. At precisely the moment when the cessation of the bulletins proclaimed the King's complete recovery, a sheepish Hibernian delegation presented their Address to His Royal Highness at Carlton House. He made them a graceful answer, and entertained them to a terrific Opposition beano. People attempted, complained Betsy Sheridan, 'to be witty upon their expedition'.[55]

'Dr Willis and his sons', wrote Greville with evident satisfaction on the 25th, 'must now expect their speedy dismission. If this can be done prudently, all must rejoice. . . . If His Majesty is declared fit to assume his government, surely the continuance of Dr Willis and his sons under the roof would be incompatible with his high functions. I long to know that he sits down to dinner by himself, and not forming a trio as he yet does with Dr Willis and his son.'[56]

The fact was, however, though Greville (with all his attention to servants' gossip) seems to have been at this stage unaware of it, that the King's disorder was still apparent in his frequent and unbecoming references to Lady Pembroke, of whom he spoke with embarrassing freedom. It is ironical that almost the sole remaining symptom of his disorder should be what in most of his contemporaries would have been considered a sign of normality—a wish to commit adultery. But George III had always been unfashionably chaste. He had schooled himself to be faithful to his unprepossessing wife, even to dote upon her, and his affections had never strayed. So when, on the 26th, Dr John observed that the King was 'quite right except a hint or two at Lady Pembroke', Pitt said he could not build anything upon the sanity of the King until this was done away with. The next day His Majesty said to the Queen, in Dr John's hearing, 'If I pay respect to you, why need it affect you, my loving another?' It was, indeed, a not uncommon point of view: many gentlemen at Court had, at one time or another, come to a similar domestic arrangement. But from the King, these words were, as Dr John noted, 'Strange!'[57]

On the 27th Miss Burney ran into His Majesty in the Queen's apartment. He smiled, and assured her, 'I'm quite well now. I was nearly so when I saw you before—I could overtake you better now!' The only gossip Greville heard that day was about dismissing some of the King's pages.* When the King walked on the river bank, some boatmen called across to him, 'God bless Your Majesty! Long life and health to you! We're glad to see you abroad again.' The King pulled off his big shovel-hat and bowed graciously. But Dr John, formerly perhaps more

* Four were, in fact, dismissed for disclosing to the Prince secrets of the King's illness. They were treated well financially.

reticent, wrote, 'Wrong respecting old object, Lady P——, and yet not so wrong as usual. He gave up the former delusion of marrying her, and seemed to listen to my argument which set forth the cruelty of distressing the Queen.'[58]

Why, in Greville's and Dr John's diaries, is there this strange reversal? Before the 26th, Greville often mentions Lady Pembroke, Dr John never. Thereafter her name appears in each day's entry in the doctor's diary, but is conspicuously absent from the equerry's. Perhaps now that the Regency Bill had been scotched, Dr John was more frank in his private diary. Perhaps with the dismissal of the four indiscreet pages, Greville had been deprived of his source of gossip. Wherever there is a discrepancy between the two diaries, it must be remembered that after mid-December Greville hardly ever saw the King, but relied for his information on attendants; while the Willises were with their patient all day and every day.

Sir Joseph Banks brought with him the magazines and registers* for the last four months, so that His Majesty could make himself up-to-date with the news. The King spoke to Greville in the ante-room with as much calmness and propriety as ever he did in his life; and when he met Fanny Burney he seemed not at all concerned with his own health, but only with hers.

'Pray', he asked anxiously, 'are you quite well today, what? what?'

'I think not quite, Sir', she answered.

'She does not *look* well', said he to the Queen, 'she looks a little—*yellow*, I think.'

There were, from this day on, no more private evening parties; the King invited all the gentlemen to join the Royals at cards every evening—an honour which they received, no doubt, with mixed feelings.

Greville 'picked up accidentally this day a very curious anecdote, being told that one of the new attendants lately brought in by Dr Willis was one of Mr Fox's Committee at the Westminster Election [in 1784] . . . a ridiculous introduction to have happened from so violent a partisan against Mr Fox as

* e.g. *Gentleman's Magazine, Annual Register*, etc. etc., monthly newspapers.

Dr Willis has pleasure in showing himself to be.'[59] There are no further clues as to who this man was, or when he arrived. If by 'lately' Greville means in January, he may have something to do with several stories unfavourable to the Willises, or disparaging the King's recovery, for which 'one of Willis's men' is quoted as the source.

While, however, the King was so composed and sensible with Greville and Miss Burney, with Dr Willis he was 'very absurd respecting Lady P——. He said he should be driven mad if he was plagued any more upon the subject. . . . He would now correct an error he had been guilty of all his life. When he professed love for ——, he had always been wrong. The truth was he really had no love for —— but for ——.'[60]

It was a situation of agonizing embarrassment for Pitt, Thurlow and the Willises who had just staked everything on the King being in his right mind again. By a miracle, news of it never leaked out. The Chancellor advised that His Majesty be 'strongly put in mind of the consequences, did he persist in his foolish notions regarding Lady Pembroke'. This must have had a good effect, and frightened the King, for the last mention in Dr John's diary of this amiable lady is dated 1 March: Dundas, the apothecary, was instructed by the Chancellor 'to assure the King that he had never taken messages to or from Lady P——'. It was not long before Lady Pembroke, having perhaps had 'some conversation with the King which entirely destroyed his hopes of succeeding with her', was back in her old position of friend and confidante of the Queen, harmlessly and platonically admired by His Majesty.[61]

The King had set his mind on two projects which his advisers all thought imprudent—a visit to Hanover, presumably for a change of scene; and personal attendance at St Paul's for a Thanksgiving Service for his recovery. It was generally feared that the excitement would result in agitation, even a relapse. Greville, moreover, had a more personal prejudice against *any* sea voyage: 'had he looked at me attentively he might have seen, without spectacles, that I was not a volunteer on such an expedition. . . . On all sea expeditions I hope he will take a more useful sailor than myself.'[62]

With some management, the King was dissuaded from these

rash projects. It is with surprise that we find him undertaking on 3 March, one that appears even more injudicious—a visit to the Richmond workhouse, which was also a lunatic asylum. He lunched off a slice of the workhouse bread and, having seen the quarters allotted to the poor, asked to see those of the mad. He inquired particularly about the treatment of the insane, and discussed without embarrassment the uses and abuses of the strait-waistcoat.

He showed, indeed, remarkable good sense about his illness and its treatment. One day in March, in Kew House, he happened to see the waistcoat hanging on a chair. The spectacle put his equerry into an agony of confusion: but the King said calmly, 'You needn't be afraid to look at it. Perhaps it is the best friend I ever had in my life.' He was also quite unmoved at finding the windows of his apartment still nailed up, a relic of the precautions against suicide.[63]

While at Richmond, the King visited his Apothecary, who had had a bad fall, and sat for two hours by his bedside. 'You took care of my illness', said His Majesty, ''tis my turn to nurse you now.'

On his return to Kew he passed an enjoyable evening listening to a Welsh harpist's rendering of Handel. Dr Willis, that day, laid down *ex cathedra* that 'it was impossible to think of the King's illness any other than as a delirium arising from fever'. But Greville felt that 'risk is still closely connected with agitation. He must be kept from flurry, and must continue to be prudent and on his guard.'[64]

On 4 March, Greville's tour of duty finished: the arrival of 'bustling Colonel Manners' relieved him of a

long waiting so different from all I had hitherto been used to, that much shall I rejoice to return to the more simple duties of an equerry, uninterrupted by His Majesty's illness and unannoyed by those party feuds or jarring politics, which have been so improperly maintained by *some* within the walls of Kew Palace. . . . To the King I owe the fullest acknowledgement of his uniform kindness, nay affection, towards me; but I do not feel that expressions of equal obligation are due from me in some other quarters.*

* Probably the Queen and Pitt; certainly the Willises.

194

The former have my lasting love and gratitude. The latter will never alter a respect due from me, in which I have *at no time* been deficient. . . . The information I possessed might have been usefully extended to some few who had the right to ask it of me—but in such directions to which I now allude, it was not asked.[65]

So passed from the scene an honourable servant of the King, whose sole wish was his master's recovery; whom pessimism and jealousy drove into implacable enmity against those very men to whom that recovery was due.

On the day Greville left, the Duke of York came to Kew. He was in a bad temper and, when refused admission to his father until the Queen had been consulted, threatened to knock Willis down. He insisted on seeing the King alone, and on his return to Town told everyone that his father was 'very deficient in mental powers, fatuity having succeeded to irritation'. He and the Prince of Wales complained bitterly to Fox that they were not allowed even to explain to the Queen their conduct: 'whoever is responsible has, indeed, much to answer for.'[66]

It was, however, only prudent to keep the King and his two sons apart, for nobody irritated him more: when he and the Duke of York next met, on the 12th, there was a terrific row because of three desertions from the Duke's regiment.

On 10 March, the King twice read over the physicians' evidence before the Select Committee. 'If I can stand that', he observed, 'I can stand anything.' This was just as well, for the Queen directed Miss Burney, whose genius seems to have run rather to prose, to compose a verse in honour of her husband's recovery:

> Amidst a rap'trous nation's praise,
>   That sees thee to their prayers restored,
> Turn gently from the general blaze—
>   Thy Charlotte greets her bosom's lord.

The King expressed the utmost pleasure.[67]

On 15 March there was in St Paul's a Service of Thanksgiving for the royal recovery. The Prince, despite the exertions of his hired cheerleaders, was in the worst possible humour.

When White's gave a Grand Fête in celebration, he and the Duke of York not only refused to attend, but sent their tickets (with the Duke's name on them to circumvent the club rules) to Hookham's Library in Bond Street for sale to the first comer.

At the Fête the royal household was vigorously represented by Colonel Manners, who sang 'God Save the King' with such fervour that 'Some of the company', he confessed, 'took the liberty to ask me not to be so loud, because they pretended I was out of tune: but it was in such a good cause that I did not mind that.'

The Opposition sulks were very marked; and one Opposition lady, invited to subscribe to a ball, replied tartly that she by no means considered the King recovered, and would defer her joy on that happy occasion to some future period. The best loser among them was Sheridan, who was actually giving a dinner to celebrate the Regency when he heard the news of the withdrawal of the Regency Bill. His guests could not conceal their mortification, but Sherry at once downed a bumper (never to him, on any pretext, an unwelcome exercise) to His Majesty's long life and prosperity.[68]

The illuminations were glorious: even Brooks's exterior was lit up, whatever the gloom within; and the poorest cobblers decorated their stalls with farthing dips to demonstrate their loyalty and joy. 'And all for what?' asked Betsy Sheridan. 'For truth to say, I do not think the recovery exists.' The Prince of Wales, also well lit up, was stopped in his carriage by a mob who howled at him, 'God save the King!' 'Long live the King', he replied loyally. Next they called on him to shout, 'God bless Pitt! Pitt for ever!' This was too much for the Prince who, whatever his faults, was not afraid of a mob. 'Damn Pitt!' he yelled. 'Fox for ever!'

The Sheridans' butler earned some overtime by waiting at a Grand Ball at the Pantheon. His employers laughed at the idea of him attending Mr Pitt; but their other servants 'considered him a rat for voluntarily engaging in the service of the enemy, so do politics descend. The Duke of York gave a ball to his most intimate friends and twenty of the most beautiful women in London *of no character.*'

Mrs Thrale, the transparency and illuminations of whose house were particularly admired by its owner, rejoiced:

for had the Regent been made without limitations, and his brother appointed Generalissimo of the Army, we had never seen our King again, unless Force had produced him—nor could one have trusted even to *that*, where private assassination would have been facilitated by the nature of his malady and his death laid to his own charge. God forgive me if my suspicions are unjust, but I do think Warren and Sir George were traitors, and that the story of the razor and penknife was prepared artfully to make mankind less surprised *if an accident should happen.* The pages, *we see*, were rascals, and had not Pitt held fast in the House of Commons, and put the person of our monarch under the custody of his *Queen alone*, responsible to *Parliament* only, not to the *Regent*, for her care of him, a sudden extinguisher would have been put upon his sacred life, and his faithful people would have rebelled for him in vain. So may God of his mercy ever preserve virtuous parents from the hands of *their own children.* [69]

Gillray produced a caricature, 'The Funeral Procession of Miss Regency', showing Mrs Fitzherbert as the principal mourner, supported by Burke, Fox and Sheridan.

On 23 April there were further junketings, and a Procession in which His Majesty himself was well enough to take part. The Prince, in the uniform of his regiment, himself escorted his father to his mother's house, and there presented himself 'in a manner which required to be seen in order to be fully felt and understood. It was to the *revered* monarch, to the *beloved* parent that His Royal Highness offered assistance. The tender attachment of the most affectionate of sons—the zealous devotion of the first of subjects—were manifested with an energy and grace that no language can adequately describe.'

As for the procession, the King complained genially to a friend who had a fine view from a balcony, 'You have the advantage of me, for I saw nothing but the backs of the horses.' [70]

The King was thought by most people to be as well as ever in his life; though he himself complained for the next two months of lassitude and dejection. 'Though I am recovering', he informed Mr Pitt, 'my mind is not yet strong enough to stand little ruffles, and still more so when they relate to Lord Buckingham, who does not stand well in my mind.'[71]

However, he was well enough for all the rats to come swarming in to his Levee, where nearly all the ladies wore headdresses embellished with loyal slogans. Even his two eldest sons would have come, had not their mother 'thought it fair to warn them that the entertainment was for those who had supported the King and Queen on the late occasion'.[72] Two of the King's steady friends watched the rats moving up the stairs.

'*Tempora mutantur*', observed one, '*et nos mutamur in illis.*'

To which the other neatly replied, 'The King has got his reason back, thanks to Dr Willis.'

That was the general opinion, whatever doubts Colonel Greville might have had. His Majesty himself had none, and handsomely rewarded the Willis family with £1,000 a year for twenty years to Dr Francis Willis, and £500 a year for life to Dr John.* Sir George Baker, who presumably also received a retainer, got £1,380. As for the others, they were rewarded according to, or perhaps rather beyond their merits: they were paid £30 for each visit to Windsor, and £10 for each visit to Kew. 'Their warrants', observed His Majesty to Mr Pitt, 'seem very large, considering their conduct; but I will not enter upon a subject that cannot but give me pain.'[73]

That was in August 1789. The King had survived the greatest crisis of his reign, and all seemed set fair for many years to come. But, although few people as yet realized its significance, in the previous month there had occurred an event which, by restoring to politics ideals, disinterested aims and honest aversions, had rendered totally obsolete and irrelevant the manoeuvring and the reversionary tactics which had been practised by three generations of English politicians. A shake had been given to the kaleidoscope, and the pieces were never again to resume their former pattern. The Bastille had fallen.

* Dr Francis Willis went on to treat the Queen of Portugal, but without such success.

Appendix

Summary of a statement prepared by Mr John Robinson, Secretary to the Treasury, for the information of Mr Pitt to whom it was shown on 15 December 1783; showing the probable votes in the House of Commons, in the event of Mr Pitt forming a Ministry.

(Figures in parentheses relate to the House of Commons as constituted in December 1783; figures without parentheses to the House as it would probably be after a general election managed, with adequate resources, by Mr Pitt and Mr Robinson.)

	FOR MR PITT			
	Certain		*Hopeful*	
English counties	(18)	22	(19)	18
„ open boroughs	(70)	84	(40)	54
„ close „	(49)	99	(34)	32
Wales	(5)	8	(4)	10
Scotland	(7)	40	(7)	2
TOTAL	(149)	253	(104)	116

	AGAINST MR PITT			
	Certain		*Doubtful*	
English counties	(31)	29	(12)	11
„ open boroughs	(92)	58	(30)	36
„ close „	(76)	31	(18)	15
Wales	(11)	4	(4)	2
Scotland	(21)	1	(10)	2
TOTAL	(231)	123	(74)	66

Bibliography

(Short titles, where used as references, follow the main title in parentheses. The place of publication is London, unless otherwise stated.)

PRIMARY SOURCES, UNPUBLISHED

Sir George Baker's Diary, *(Baker)*.

Miscellaneous letters from the King and others, to Sir George Baker, in the library of Rode Hall, *(Rode Hall Papers)*.

Miscellaneous letters and papers in the library of the Royal College of Physicians, *(R.C.P. Papers)*.

Dr Willis's Journals. British Museum, Add. MSS 41690–1.

PRIMARY SOURCES, PUBLISHED

Auckland, William, Lord. *Journal and Correspondence, (Auckland)*. 4 vols. Bentley, 1860–2.

Buckingham and Chandos, Richard, Duke of. *Courts and Cabinets of George III, (Courts and Cabinets)*. 2 vols. Hurst & Blackett, 1853–5.

Burke, Edmund. *Correspondence*. Vols. I–III. Cambridge University Press, 1958–61.

—— *Works*. 8 vols. Dodsley and Rivington, 1792–1827.

Butler, C. *Reminiscences*. John Murray, 1827.

Combe, William. 'A Letter from a Country Gentleman to a Member of Parliament' (pamphlet). 1789.

—— 'The Royal Interview' (pamphlet). 1789.

Cornwallis, Charles, Marquess. *Correspondence, (Cornwallis)*. 3 vols. John Murray, 1859.

d'Arblay, Frances. *Diary and Letters, (d'Arblay)*. 7 vols. Colburn, 1842–6.

Delany, Mary. *Autobiography and Correspondence, (Delany)*. 3 vols. Bentley, 1861.

Devonshire, Georgiana, Duchess of. *Diary, (D.D.D.)*. Reproduced in Walter S. Sichel, *Sheridan*, q.v.

A Festival of Wit. 1789.

George III. *Correspondence.* Ed. Sir John Fortescue. 6 vols. Macmillan, 1927–8.

Glenbervie, Sylvester, Lord. *Diaries, (Glenbervie)*. Ed. Francis Bickley. 2 vols. Constable, 1928.

Greville, Col. the Hon. Robert Fulke. *Diaries, (R. F. Greville)*. Ed. F. Bladon. John Lane, 1930.

Historical Notes and Queries, (H.N. & Q.).

Leeds, Francis, Duke of. *Political Memoranda, (Leeds)*. Camden Society, 1884.

Malmesbury, James, Earl of. *Diaries and Correspondence, (Malmesbury)*. 4 vols. Bentley, 1844.

Minto, Sir Gilbert Elliot, Earl of. *Life and Letters from 1751 to 1806, (Minto)*. 3 vols. Longmans, 1874.

Papendiek, Charlotte. *Court and Private Life in the Time of Queen Charlotte, (Papendiek)*. 2 vols. Bentley, 1887.

Parliamentary History, Vols. XXIII and XXIV.

The Pembroke Papers, 1780–94. Ed. Lord Herbert. Jonathan Cape, 1950.

The Report from the Committee appointed to examine the Physicians who attended His Majesty, (Examination of the Physicians). 1788, 1789.

Report of the Historical Manuscripts Commission, (H.M.C.).

Rose, George. *Diaries and Correspondence, (Rose)*. 2 vols. Bentley, 1859.

Sheridan, Betsy. *Journal*. Ed. W. Le Fanu. Eyre & Spottiswoode, 1960.

Thrale, Hester. *Thraliana*. Ed. Katharine Balderston. 2 vols. 2nd edn. Oxford University Press, 1951.

Walpole, Horace. *Letters, (Walpole, Letters)*. Ed. Mrs Paget Toynbee. 19 vols. Oxford University Press, 1903–25.

—— *The Last Journals, (Walpole, Journals)*. Ed. A. Francis Steuart. 2 vols. John Lane, 1910.

Withers, Philip. *A History of the Royal Malady, by a Page of the Presence.* 1789.

Wraxall, Sir Nathaniel W., Bt. *Historical and Posthumous Memoirs, (Wraxall).* 5 vols. Bickers, 1884.

Wyvill, Christopher. *Political Papers, (Wyvill).* 6 vols. York, 1794–1802.

SECONDARY SOURCES

Aspinall, Arthur. *Politics and the Press.* Home & Van Thal, 1949.

Butterfield, Herbert. *George III and the Historians.* Collins, 1957.

Campbell, John, Lord. *The Lives of the Lord Chancellors.* 8 vols. John Murray, 1845–7. 1869.

Fitzmaurice, Edmond, Lord. *Life of William, Earl of Shelburne, (Shelburne).* 3 vols. Macmillan, 1875–6.

Guttmacher, Manfred S. *America's Last King, (Guttmacher).* C. Scribner's Sons, New York, 1941.

Hobhouse, Christopher B. *Fox.* New edn. Constable and John Murray, 1947.

Holt, Edward. *The Public and Domestic Life of George III, (Holt).* 2 vols. Sherwood, 1820.

Huish, Robert. *The Public and Private Life of George III, (Huish).* Kelly, 1821.

Jesse, John H. *Memoirs of the Life and Reign of George III, (Jesse).* 5 vols. John Nimmo, 1901.

Lascelles, Edward C. P. *The Life of Charles James Fox.* Oxford University Press, 1936.

Melville, Lewis. *Farmer George.* Pitman, 1907.

Namier, Sir Lewis B. *England in the Age of the American Revolution.* Macmillan, 1930.

—— *Structure of Politics at the Accession of George III, (Structure of Politics).* 2nd edn. Macmillan, 1957.

Pares, Richard. *King George III and the Politicians.* Oxford University Press, 1953.

Petrie, Sir Charles. *The Four Georges.* Eyre & Spottiswoode, 1935.

Porritt, Edward and Annie G. *The Unreformed House of Commons.* 2 vols. Cambridge University Press, 1903.

Ray, I. 'The Madness of King George III'. *American Journal of Insanity,* Vol 12, 1855.

Rhodes, Raymond C. *Harlequin Sheridan.* Basil Blackwell, Oxford, 1933.

Richardson, Joanna. *The Disastrous Marriage.* Jonathan Cape, 1960.

Robinson, John. *Parliamentary Papers 1774–84.* Ed. W. T. Laprade. Historical Society of Great Britain, 1922.

Russell, Lord John. *The Life and Times of Charles James Fox.* 3 vols. Bentley, 1859–66.

—— (Ed.). *Memorials and Correspondence of Charles James Fox.* 2 vols. Bentley, 1853.

Sichel, Walter S. *Sheridan, (Sichel).* 2 vols. Constable, 1909.

Stanhope, Philip, Earl. *Life of the Right Honble William Pitt, (Stanhope).* 4 vols. John Murray, 1861–2.

Thackeray, William M. *The Four Georges.* Smith, Elder, 1861.

Trevelyan, Sir George Otto, Bt. *George III and Charles Fox.* 2 vols. Longmans, 1912–14.

Vulliamy, Colwyn E. *Royal George.* Jonathan Cape, 1937.

Watson, John S. *The Reign of George III, (Watson). Oxford History of England,* Vol. 12. Oxford University Press, 1960.

White, Terence H. *The Scandalmonger.* Jonathan Cape, 1952.

Notes

INTRODUCTION

1. John Adolphus, *History of England, George III* (7 vols., J. Lee, 1840–5), I, 175; *Guttmacher*, 75.

2. *Guttmacher*, 283–7, 311, 343, 377.

CHAPTER I
The Onset of the Royal Malady

1. Particulars of the King's summer tour are in: *Stanhope*, II, App. i–ii; *Huish*, 495–8; *Wraxall*, V, 154; *d'Arblay*, IV, 1–91; *Holt*, I, 304–7; *Auckland*, II, 225; *Pembroke Papers*, 392; *Guttmacher*, 189–93; Daniel Lysons, *History of the Three Choirs* (Gloucester, 1812); Richard W. Binns, *A Century of Potting in the City of Worcester* (Quaritch, 1865), 141; *Gentleman's Magazine*, 1778, II, 758, 883, 1075; *Gloucester Journal*, 11 Aug. 1788; *Rode Hall Papers*; most contemporary newspapers and magazines.

2. White, *The Scandalmonger*, 91 et seq.

3. *Letters from George III to Lord Bute* (ed. Romney Sedgwick, Macmillan, 1939), throughout.

4. *H.N. & Q.*, Ser. X, vol. VII, 87; *Auckland*, II, 236.

5. *Wraxall*, V, 157; *Guttmacher*, 191; Adolphus, *History of England*, I, 175.

6. Withers, *History of the Royal Malady*, 9–11.

7. Ibid., 16.

8. *Auckland*, II, 223; *d'Arblay*, IV, 25, 34, 39, 50, 76, 80; *Baker*.

9. *Rode Hall Papers*.

10. *Jesse*, IV, 188; *d'Arblay*, IV, 117–8; *Guttmacher*, 193; *Baker*.

11. *Baker.*

12. *Stanhope,* II, App. iii–iv.

13. *Courts and Cabinets,* I, 428; *Baker.*

14. *Jesse,* IV, 198; *Examination of the Physicians,* 68–71; *Guttmacher,* 194–5; *Baker.*

15. *Jesse,* IV, 198.

16. *Papendiek,* II, 5–12.

17. *Rode Hall Papers.*

18. *Courts and Cabinets,* I, 428; *Stanhope,* II, App. iv; *Guttmacher,* 105–6.

19. *Wraxall,* V, 188; *Jesse,* IV, 200.

20. *Stanhope,* II, App. iv.

21. *Baker.*

22. Melville, *Farmer George,* 209; *Baker.*

23. *Jesse,* IV, 201–4; *d'Arblay,* IV, 120–2.

24. *Baker.*

25. Ibid.

26. *D'Arblay,* IV, 120–2.

27. *Minto,* I, 225–6.

28. *Auckland,* II, 255; *Courts and Cabinets,* I, 364; *Papendiek,* II, 9.

29. *Minto,* I, 228.

30. *Stanhope,* II, App. v.

31. *Baker.*

32. *Jesse,* IV, 203–4; *d'Arblay,* IV, 126; *Baker.*

33. *Jesse,* IV, 203–4; *d'Arblay,* IV, 127–33.

CHAPTER II
The Political Scene

1. Pares, *King George III and the Politicians,* 148–52.

2. *Correspondence of George III,* nos. 3699, 3700.

3. Burke, *Works,* II, 260.

4. Earl of Ilchester, *Henry Fox, First Lord Holland* (2 vols., John Murray, 1920), II, 203; *The Life and Letters of Lady Sarah Lennox* (ed. Countess of Ilchester, 2 vols., John Murray, 1901), I, 76.

5. *Wyvill*, I, 460.

6. Namier, *England in the Age of the American Revolution*, 262; Robinson, *Parliamentary Papers*, 14–17.

7. Ibid., 66.

8. Petrie, *The Four Georges*, 118; *Structure of Politics*, 181–9.

9. Philip Yorke, *Life of Lord Chancellor Hardwicke* (3 vols., Cambridge University Press, 1913), II, 238.

10. Robinson, *Parliamentary Papers*, 135–73.

11. Ibid., throughout.

12. Add. MSS 32870, f. 431.

13. *English Historical Documents*, 1783–1832, II, 253.

14. Robinson, *Parliamentary Papers*, throughout.

15. Burke, *Works*.

16. Namier, *England in the Age of the American Revolution*, 219–32; Burke, *Correspondence*.

17. Chesterfield to Desrolles, 18 Nov. 1753; John, Lord Hervey, *Memoirs of the Reign of King George II* (ed. Romney Sedgwick, 3 vols., Eyre & Spottiswoode, 1931), III, 702.

18. Add. MSS 32922, f. 60; Burke, *Works*.

CHAPTER III
The King, Mr Fox and Mr Pitt

1. *Jesse*, III, 342–7, 356; *Huish*, 417; *Correspondence of George III*, No. 3566.

2. *Jesse*, III, 431, 442–3; *Auckland*, I, 9, 11, 28–9, 33, 36; Lascelles, *The Life of Charles James Fox*, 112.

3. Ibid., 71; *Jesse*, III, 364.

4. William Mason, 'Heroic Epistle to Sir William Chambers'; *H.N. & Q.*, Ser. I, vol. X, 123: Ser. III, vol. V, 74; vol. VI, 381: Ser. V, vol. II, 415.

5. *Jesse*, III, 474; *Stanhope*, I, 19.

6. *Wraxall*, V, 348–62; *Jesse*, III, 389; *H.N. & Q.*, Ser. I, vol. XII, 313: Ser. III, vol. IV, 522.

7. *Jesse*, IV, 12–15; *Holt*, I, 258–9; Add. MSS 47560, ff. 4–6; Lascelles, *The Life of Charles James Fox*, 124–6.

8. *Jesse*, III, 475–6.

9. *Jesse*, III, 470–1; *Courts and Cabinets*, I, 208, 218–19; Butler, *Reminiscences*, I, 75.

10. *Jesse*, III, 378–89; *Shelburne*, II, 106–7.

11. *Jesse*, III, 378–89, 394; Pares, *George III and the Politicians*, 67; *Memorials and Correspondence of Charles James Fox*, I, 267; *H.M.C., Carlisle MSS.*, 598–9; *Leeds*, 66.

12. *Shelburne*, II, 87–8.

13. *H.N. & Q.*, Ser. II, vol. VI, 90: Ser. III, vol. IX, 275: No. 194, 261; *The Rolliad*.

14. *H.N. & Q.*, Ser. II, vol. VI, 118.

15. *Glenbervie*, 143; *Stanhope*, I, 133.

16. Pares, *King George III and the Politicians*, 126–8; *Stanhope*, I, 139; *Wraxall*, V, 320; *Parliamentary History*, XXIV, 24; *Annual Register*, 1789, 114.

17. *Jesse*, IV, 15–28; *Stanhope*, I, 140.

18. *Minto*, I, 89; *Auckland*, I, 68–9.

19. Russell, *The Life and Times of Charles James Fox*, II, 40; *Courts and Cabinets*, I, 288–9.

20. *H.M.C.*, X, 6, pp. 520, 523, 527–8; *Courts and Cabinets*, I, 285; *Rose*, I, 47–8; *Auckland*, I, 67; *Walpole, Letters*, XIII, 103; *Memorials and Correspondence of Charles James Fox*, II, 220.

21. Robinson, *Parliamentary Papers*, 66–105.

22. *Ibid.*, 149–65.

23. *Auckland*, I, 68–9; *Jesse*, IV, 25–8.

24. *Correspondence of George III*, no. 4546; Russell, *The Life and Times of Charles James Fox*, II, 49; *Memorials and Correspondence of Charles James Fox*, II, 221.

25. *Stanhope*, I, 156–7; *Minto*, I, 91.

26. *Stanhope*, I, 149–53; Russell, *The Life and Times of Charles James Fox*, II, 55.

27. *Stanhope*, I, 161, App. iii.

28. *Parliamentary History*, XXIV, 366; *Stanhope*, I, 166, 170.

29. Ibid., App. vi; Add. MSS 47561, ff. 66, 68, 74–6; Russell, *The Life and Times of Charles James Fox*, II, 59; *Parliamentary History*, XXIV, 218, 222, 286, 310, 365–6, 371, 381, 387, 442, 466, 663, 677, 690, 706, 709–10, 717, 736, 740–2.

30. *Memorials and Correspondence of Charles James Fox*, II, 282; *Stanhope*, I, App. iv, vi.

31. *Auckland*, I, 72.

32. *Stanhope*, I, App. vii.

33. Ibid., 193.

34. Ibid., 197; *Malmesbury*, II, 61.

35. *Stanhope*, I, 202; *Walpole, Letters*, XIII, 141; Pares, *King George III and the Politicians*, 199; Robinson, *Parliamentary Papers*, 66–105.

36. Hobhouse, *Fox*, 194; *Jesse*, IV, 73; *Betsy Sheridan's Journal*, 143.

37. Add. MSS 47561, ff. 81–4.

38. *Stanhope*, I, 205.

39. Lord Cornwallis to Lord Ross, 17 Feb. 1784.

40. *Jesse*, IV, 90–7.

41. *Malmesbury*, II, 126–31.

42. Russell, *The Life and Times of Charles James Fox*, II, 182, 185–6; Lascelles, *The Life of Charles James Fox*, 194–7; *Courts and Cabinets*, I, 391; Add. MSS 47560, f. 13; Combe, 'Letter from a Country Gentleman to a Member of Parliament', 8.

CHAPTER IV

The Royal Patient at Windsor

1. Thomas Moore, *Life of Sheridan* (2 vols., Longman, 1825), II, 21–2; *Wraxall*, V, 100; *Huish*, 500; *d'Arblay*, IV, 138–40; *Guttmacher*, 199–200, 216–17; *Baker*.

2. *Guttmacher*, 197; *Baker*.

3. Moore, *Life of Sheridan*, II, 19–25.

4. *D.D.D.*, *Sichel*, II, 403; *d'Arblay*, IV, 127; *Guttmacher*, 198.

5. *Courts and Cabinets*, I, 433–5; *H.M.C.*, Ser. II, 14, p. 14.

6. *Guttmacher*, 202, 241–2, 258–9, 401.

7. *Courts and Cabinets*, II, 12; *Betsy Sheridan's Journal*, 131–2; *Minto*, I, 230.

8. *D.D.D.*, *Sichel*, II, 420; *H.M.C.*, XV, 6, p. 658; Campbell, *Lives of the Lord Chancellors*, VI, 189–95; Moore, *Life of Sheridan*, II, 23.

9. Oliver Warner, *The Glorious First of June* (Batsford, 1961), 89, 107, 108.

10. Moore, *Life of Sheridan*, II, 25.

11. *Jesse*, IV, 206; *Papendiek*, II, 13; *d'Arblay*, IV, 132–5; *R. F. Greville*, 79–80; *Baker*.

12. *R. F. Greville*, 79–80; *d'Arblay*, IV, 132–5.

13. *Jesse*, IV, 206; *d'Arblay*, IV, 136, 147, 229; *R. F. Greville*, 80; *Huish*, 503.

14. Campbell, *Lives of the Lord Chancellors*, VI, 188–9; *Guttmacher*, 201.

15. *Papendiek*, II, 11–12; *Guttmacher*, 201.

16. *Guttmacher*, 205; Withers, *History of the Royal Malady*, 35–8.

17. *Courts and Cabinets*, I, 439: II, 2; Combe, 'Letter from a Country Gentleman to a Member of Parliament', 44.

18. *R. F. Greville*, 81–3.

19. Ibid., 86–7; *Guttmacher*, 204; *Courts and Cabinets*, II, 6–7; *Betsy Sheridan's Journal*, 131; *R.C.P. Papers*, 43.

20. *R. F. Greville*, 81–3; *d'Arblay*, IV, 163–5, 169.

21. *D.D.D.*, *Sichel*, II, 403–4.

22. Ibid., 405.

23. *R. F. Greville*, 94–6.

24. *Courts and Cabinets*, II, 9–10.

25. Ibid., 14–15; *D.D.D.*, *Sichel*, II, 409.

26. *Auckland*, II, 242–3.

27. *Wraxall*, V, 295; *H.N. & Q.*, Ser. II, vol. I, 94; Harriette Wilson, *Memoirs* (2 vols, Eveleigh Nash, 1909), I, 20; *D.D.D., Sichel*, II, 400; Campbell, *Lives of the Lord Chancellors*, V, 583; *Memorials and Correspondence of Charles James Fox*, II, 291–9.

28. *Wraxall*, V, 197–8; *H.M.C.*, Var. Coll., 6, p. 278; Campbell, *Lives of the Lord Chancellors*, VI, 583; *Guttmacher*, 224; Moore, *Life of Sheridan*, I, 313: II, 19–20; J. Nicholls, *Recollections and Reflections* (2 vols., Longman, 1824), 71; *Courts and Cabinets*, II, 14–15; *D.D.D., Sichel*, II, 411.

29. *Wraxall*, V, 193.

30. *H.M.C.*, XV, 6, 655–6; *Jesse*, IV, 210–11; *Examination of the Physicians*, 5–8; *Minto*, I, 234; *Huish*, 502–5.

31. *Auckland*, II, 242–4; *Jesse*, IV, 224.

32. *Papendiek*, II, 11–12; *R. F. Greville*, 90–3.

33. Ibid., 101–2.

34. Ibid., 104–14.

35. Withers, *History of the Royal Malady*, 31–2.

36. *D.D.D., Sichel*, II, 408–11.

37. *Auckland*, II, 240–6.

38. Ibid., 240–4.

39. *Papendiek*, II, 15–19; *Jesse*, IV, 220; *Courts and Cabinets*, I, 445; Moore, *Life of Sheridan*, II, 29.

40. *H.M.C.*, XV, 6, p. 656; *Papendiek*, II, 18; *Jesse*, IV, 213; *Courts and Cabinets*, II, 17; *Rose*, I, 96; *d'Arblay*, IV, 160, 184, 336–7; Lee Papers in Aylesbury Record Office.

41. *Wraxall*, V, 202–3; *Jesse*, IV, 232–7; *Courts and Cabinets*, II, 23; *Betsy Sheridan's Journal*, 132; *Guttmacher*, 214.

42. *Papendiek*, II, 5–9, 25; *Leeds*, 120–3; *Huish*, 504–5; *Jesse*, IV, 252–6; *Courts and Cabinets*, II, 20; *R. F. Greville*, 107–14, 236–8; *London Chronicle*, 29 Nov. 1788; *d'Arblay*, IV, 184–91, 199, 202.

43. *Morning Herald*, 6 Dec. 1788.

44. *D.D.D., Sichel*, II, 410; *Auckland*, II, 280.

45. *Auckland*, II, 251.

46. *Public Advertiser*, 27 Dec. 1788.

47. *D.D.D., Sichel*, II, 409–11; *H.M.C.*, XV, 7, p. 659; *Leeds*, 129.

48. *H.M.C.*, VI, 278; *Leeds*, 122; *D.D.D., Sichel*, II, 411; *Auckland*, II, 251; *Minto*, I, 244.

49. *Holt*, I, 317; *Walpole, Letters*, XIV, 110; *H.M.C.*, XIII, 3, p. 377: 7, p. 81; *Auckland*, II, 251; *Minto*, I, 238; *Guttmacher*, 215.

50. Peter Pindar, *Works*.

51. *Stanhope*, II, 1–3.

52. *R. F. Greville*, 114–17.

CHAPTER V
Dr Willis and Sons

1. William N. Massey, *History of England* (4 vols., Longmans, 1855–63), III, 376; *Jesse*, IV, 265–6; *London Chronicle*, 25–7 Dec. 1788; *d'Arblay*, IV, 205, 215; *Guttmacher*, 217.

2. *D.D.D., Sichel*, II, 410–13.

3. *Auckland*, II, 256–7.

4. Peter Pindar, 'On Messrs Pitt & Co.'

5. *Jesse*, IV, 257–62; *Papendiek*, II, 92; *Examination of the Physicians*.

6. Melville, *Farmer George*, 216–17, quoting F. Reynolds, *Life and Times*; *R. F. Greville*, 145; *London Chronicle*, 27–30 Dec. 1788.

7. *Examination of the Physicians*, 42.

8. Add. MSS 41690–1.

9. Add. MSS 41691, ff. 167–76.

10. *Wraxall*, V, 206.

11. *Papendiek*, II, 20–1.

12. Ibid.

13. *R. F. Greville*, 118–20.

14. Ibid., 120–1.

15. *Papendiek*, II, 23.

16. *Examination of the Physicians*, 62, 73–4; *Papendiek*, II, 23; *Wraxall*, V, 263; *Jesse*, IV, 267–8.

17. *H.M.C.*, XV, 7, p. 297.

18. *D.D.D., Sichel*, II, 412.

19. *Courts and Cabinets*, II, 35.

20. *Gentleman's Magazine*, 1789, 171.

21. *Examination of the Physicians*, 7–8; *Jesse*, IV, 267.

22. *Examination of the Physicians*, 8–9; *Guttmacher*, 220.

23. *H.M.C.*, XV, 7, p. 298; *D.D.D., Sichel*, II, 412–13; *Examination of the Physicians*, 62; *Guttmacher*, 219–20.

24. *Auckland*, II, 255.

25. *H.M.C.*, XV, 6, p. 661.

26. *D.D.D., Sichel*, II, 422–3.

27. *Leeds*, 130; *Wraxall*, V, 207.

28. Particulars of the debates can be found in any contemporary newspaper or magazine, and in: *Wraxall*, V, 208–17; *Stanhope*, II, 4–6; *Courts and Cabinets*, II, 56; 'Debates in the House of Lords on the Subject of a Regency' (pamphlet), 9–11; *Guttmacher*, 215.

29. *Courts and Cabinets*, II, 49–54.

30. *Auckland*, II, 257; *Courts and Cabinets*, II, 64; Lascelles, *The Life of Charles James Fox*, 207; *D.D.D., Sichel*, II, 414–15; *Thraliana*, II, 721.

31. *Auckland*, II, 258.

32. Russell, *The Life and Times of Charles James Fox*, II, 199.

33. *D.D.D., Sichel*, II, 415.

34. Campbell, *Lives of the Lord Chancellors*, V, 585.

35. *Leeds*, 127; *H.M.C.*, Var. Coll., 6, p. 278; *Thraliana*, II, 721.

36. *Holt*, I, 318–19; *Auckland*, II, 260.

37. *D.D.D., Sichel*, II, 414–16.

38. *Examination of the Physicians*, 63.

39. *H.M.C.*, XV, 7, p. 299.

40. *Examination of the Physicians*, 75.

41. *Massey*, III, 387, quoting Locker MSS; *R.C.P. Papers*, 2, 41.

42. *Jesse*, IV, 249–51; *H.M.C.*, XIII, 7, p. 142; *Courts and Cabinets*, II, 57–9; *Wraxall*, V, 219–20; *Stanhope*, II, 9.

43. *Stanhope*, II, 9–10; *Guttmacher*, 225.

44. *D.D.D.*, *Sichel*, II, 417; *Memorials and Correspondence of Charles James Fox*, II, 299–300.

45. *Auckland*, II, 259; *Stanhope*, II, 16.

46. Accounts of the debates, and of Willis's intervention, are to be found in all contemporary newspapers and magazines, and also in: *Stanhope*, II, 11–13; *Wraxall*, V, 226–30; *Huish*, 500–1, 516; *Auckland*, II, 257–60; *R. F. Greville*, 123; *Examination of the Physicians*, 12–18; *Betsy Sheridan's Journal*, 139.

47. *Auckland*, II, 260; *Minto*, I, 246.

48. Add. MSS 41690–1.

49. *R. F. Greville*, 80 et seq.

50. Ray, 'The Madness of King George III.'

51. Add. MSS 41691, f. 3.

52. *Examination of the Physicians*, 83; Add. MSS 41690, ff. 11–12: 41691, f. 3.

53. *R. F. Greville*, 125; *Jesse*, IV, 271; *Examination of the Physicians*, 64.

54. *R. F. Greville*, 123; *Examination of the Physicians*, 12–18; Add. MSS 41690, ff. 11–12; *D.D.D.*, *Sichel*, II, 419–20; *Betsy Sheridan's Journal*, 139.

55. *R. F. Greville*, 123; *Examination of the Physicians*, 65; *Huish*, 516; Add. MSS 41691, f. 9.

56. *R. F. Greville*, 125; Add. MSS 41690, f. 12.

57. Add. MSS 41690, ff. 11–12: 41691, ff. 4–5.

58. Add. MSS 41690, f. 15; *Morning Herald*, 22 Dec. 1788; *R.C.P. Papers*, 7.

59. *R. F. Greville*, 125–6.

60. *Minto*, I, 252–3; *D.D.D.*, *Sichel*, II, 418; *Morning Herald*, 20 Dec. 1788; Combe, 'A Letter from a Country Gentleman to a Member of Parliament', 13, 47; Combe, 'The Royal Interview', 54; Peter Pindar, *Works*; *H.M.C.*, XI, 7, p. 56; *Guttmacher*, 256.

61. *Jesse,* IV, 249–52; *D.D.D., Sichel,* II, 418–19; *Betsy Sheridan's Journal,* 136.

62. Ibid.

63. *Auckland,* II, 261.

64. *Wraxall,* V, 231–5.

65. Accounts of the debates are in all contemporary newspapers, and in: *Wraxall,* V, 231–40; *Stanhope,* II, 13–15; *Courts and Cabinets,* II, 71; Campbell, *Lives of the Lord Chancellors,* VI, 206; 'Debates in the House of Lords on the Subject of a Regency' (pamphlet), 53.

66. *Stanhope,* II, 18; *Betsy Sheridan's Journal,* 134.

67. *Huish,* 522; *D.D.D., Sichel,* II, 421–3; *Leeds,* 137; *Minto,* I, 269; *Betsy Sheridan's Journal,* 134-5, 143.

68. *Leeds,* 141; Add. MSS 47560, f. 16.

69. *Holt,* I, 321–3.

70. Add. MSS 41690, f. 13.

71. *R. F. Greville,* 127; *R.C.P. Papers,* 7.

72. *R. F. Greville,* 129; Add. MSS 41690, f. 14; *R.C.P. Papers,* 8.

73. *R. F. Greville,* 130; Add. MSS 41690, f. 14.

74. *R. F. Greville,* 130–2; Add. MSS 41690, ff. 14, 18–20; *R.C.P. Papers,* 11.

75. *R. F. Greville,* 132–3; Add. MSS, ff. 18-20.

76. *R. F. Greville,* 123; *d'Arblay,* IV, 213; *D.D.D., Sichel,* II, 420.

77. *R. F. Greville,* 136–7; Add. MSS 41690, f. 21.

78. Add. MSS 41690, f. 22.

79. *R. F. Greville,* 142; *D.D.D., Sichel,* II, 421.

80. Add. MSS 41690, f. 24.

81. Ibid., f. 27; *R. F. Greville,* 143.

82. Add. MSS 41690, f. 27; *R. F. Greville,* 144–8.

83. Add. MSS 41690, ff. 31–2; *Guttmacher,* 230.

84. *Examination of the Physicians,* 18–19, 20–7, 30–1, 52–4; *R. F. Greville,* 148.

85. *D.D.D., Sichel,* II, 422–3; *Minto,* I, 259; *Auckland,* II, 270; *Guttmacher,* 230.

86. *R. F. Greville,* 150–3.

87. Ibid., 153–4; Add. MSS 41690, f. 36.

88. *Rode Hall Papers; R.C.P. Papers,* 44.

89. *R. F. Greville,* 154–5.

90. Withers, *History of the Royal Malady,* 45.

CHAPTER VI
In the Balance

1. *Auckland,* II, 263.

2. *Leeds,* 137; *H.M.C.,* XIII, 3, p. 377; *D.D.D., Sichel,* II, 423.

3. *Wraxall,* V, 259.

4. Aspinall, *Politics and the Press,* 77, 271–8; *The Times,* 30 December 1788, 30 Jan. 1789; *D.D.D., Sichel,* II, 420.

5. *Jesse,* IV, 274-80; *Auckland,* II, 292; *Guttmacher,* 240.

6. *Pembroke Papers,* 401.

7. *Wraxall,* V, 255–8.

8. *Gentleman's Magazine,* 1789, I, 427–9; *Wraxall,* V, 253–5.

9. *Examination of the Physicians,* 3–18.

10. *D.D.D., Sichel,* II, 424; *R. F. Greville,* 156.

11. Ibid., 156–7.

12. *Examination of the Physicians,* 20–7; *D.D.D., Sichel,* II, 424.

13. *R. F. Greville,* 158; Add. MSS 41690, f. 41.

14. *Examination of the Physicians,* 34–42; *D.D.D., Sichel,* II, 424; *Guttmacher,* 234.

15. *R. F. Greville,* 158–9; Add. MSS 41690, f. 42.

16. *Examination of the Physicians,* 49–58; *D.D.D., Sichel,* II, 424–5.

17. *R. F. Greville,* 159–63; Add. MSS 41690, f. 44: 41691, f. 85.

18. *Examination of the Physicians,* 63, 68–71; *D.D.D., Sichel,* II, 425.

19. *R. F. Greville,* 164–6; Add. MSS 41690, ff. 50–1; *Holt,* I, 325; *Glenbervie,* 394; *Auckland,* II, 273.

20. *Examination of the Physicians,* 75–82.

21. Add. MSS 41690, f. 51; *D.D.D., Sichel,* II, 425; *Stanhope,* II, 20; *Thraliana,* II, 726–7.

22. *Wraxall,* V, 260–1.

23. Accounts of the debate are in all contemporary newspapers and magazines, and in: *Stanhope,* II, 21–2; *Wraxall,* V, 263–71.

24. *The Times,* 3, 11 Feb. 1789.

25. *Wraxall,* V, 274–5.

26. *Morning Herald,* 20 Jan. 1789.

27. *D.D.D., Sichel,* II, 426; *Auckland,* II, 277; *H.M.C.,* XIV, 4, pp. 526–7.

28. *Auckland,* II, 268–70.

29. Ibid., 267; *Betsy Sheridan's Journal,* 145.

30. *R. F. Greville,* 166–9; Add. MSS 41690, f. 52.

31. *R. F. Greville,* 170–1; Add. MSS 41690, f. 53.

32. *R. F. Greville,* 174; Add. MSS 41690, f. 55.

33. *R. F. Greville,* 175; William Roberts, *Memoirs of Hannah More* (4 vols., Seeley, 1834), II, 141; Add. MSS 41690, f. 56.

34. *R. F. Greville,* 178–9; Add. MSS 41690, f. 57; *Holt,* I, 323; *Huish,* 523.

35. Add. MSS 41690, f. 58; *Guttmacher,* 234; *R.C.P. Papers.*

36. *R. F. Greville,* 184–5; Add. MSS 41690, f. 60.

37. *R. F. Greville,* 187–90; *d'Arblay,* IV, 232–3; *R.C.P. Papers,* 15.

38. *Pembroke Papers,* 403.

39. Add. MSS 47561, ff. 91–6.

40. *Auckland,* II, 268.

41. Accounts of the debates are in all contemporary newspapers and magazines, and in: *Wraxall,* V, 277–85.

42. *Auckland,* II, 279; *The World,* 3 Feb. 1789. *Betsy Sheridan's Journal,* 135.

43. *H.M.C.,* XV, 7, p. 300; *d'Arblay,* IV, 241.

44. *R. F. Greville,* 192–4.

45. *R. F. Greville*, 195–7; Add. MSS 41691, f. 121; *Holt*, I, 324; *d'Arblay*, IV, 238.

46. *R. F. Greville*, 198–9; Add. MSS 41690, f. 69.

CHAPTER VII
The Royal Recovery

1. Add. MSS 41691.

2. *H.M.C.*,XIII, 7, p. 87.

3. *R. F. Greville*, 200–1; Add. MSS 41690, f. 70.

4. Ibid., f. 71; *d'Arblay*, IV, 243–50; *R. F. Greville*, 203.

5. Ibid., 203–5.

6. Add. MSS 41690, ff. 70–3.

7. *Wraxall*, V, 286–9.

8. Ibid., 291–2.

9. Ibid., 295; *R. F. Greville*, 206; Add. MSS 41690, f. 74.

10. *R. F. Greville*, 202–7; Add. MSS 41690, f. 75.

11. Accounts of the debates are in all contemporary newspapers and magazines, and in: *Wraxall*, V, 296–7, 300.

12. *Huish*, 525; *R. F. Greville*, 209–11.

13. Ibid., 213.

14. Add. MSS 41691, f. 132; *R.C.P. Papers*, 44.

15. *R. F. Greville*, 212–13; *Guttmacher*, 242.

16. Withers, *History of the Royal Malady*, 45–6.

17. *R. F. Greville*, 214–15; Add. MSS 41690, f. 76.

18. Accounts of the debates are in all contemporary newspapers and magazines, and in: *Wraxall*, V, 301–2; *Jesse*, IV, 284–5: V, 4–5; *Auckland*, II, 291.

19. Ibid.

20. *H.M.C.*, XIV, 4, p. 527.

21. *Auckland*, II, 291.

22. *The World*, 7, 9 Feb. 1789; *The Times*, 6, 9 Feb. 1789.

23. *Wraxall*, V, 308.

24. *The Times*, 6 Feb. 1789.

25. Ibid., 26 Feb. 1789.

26. *Auckland*, II, 286; *R. F. Greville*, 217; *Pembroke Papers*, 405.

27. *Wraxall*, V, 320; *R. F. Greville*, 219; Add. MSS 41690, f. 81; *Jesse*, IV, 280–1; William Roberts, *Memoirs of Hannah More*, II, 142; *Guttmacher*, 242.

28. *R. F. Greville*, 220–1.

29. Add. MSS 41690, f. 84; *Auckland*, II, 284–6.

30. Ibid., 287; *Pembroke Papers*, 407.

31. *The Times*, 13, 14 Feb. 1789; *Morning Herald*, 14 Feb. 1789; Add. MSS 41691, f. 143; *R. F. Greville*, 207; *Betsy Sheridan's Journal*, 147.

32. Add. MSS 47561, ff. 107–9; *Betsy Sheridan's Journal*, 148–9.

33. *R. F. Greville*, 221.

34. *The World*, 28 Jan. 1789; *Thraliana*, II, 727; *R. F. Greville*, 222–3, 246; *Guttmacher*, 205–6; *Rode Hall Papers*.

35. *Guttmacher*, 225.

36. Ibid., 229–31.

37. *Memorials and Correspondence of Charles James Fox*, II, 302.

38. Add. MSS 41691, f. 151; *R. F. Greville*, 232.

39. Ibid., 233.

40. Ibid., 234-5; Add. MSS 41691, f. 155; *R.C.P. Papers*, 32.

41. *Stanhope*, II, 25; *Courts and Cabinets*, I, 364.

42. *Auckland*, II, 288; *Minto*, I, 274.

43. *R. F. Greville*, 235–8; *Betsy Sheridan's Journal*, 153.

44. Ibid., 238–9.

45. Ibid., 239; *Auckland*, II, 292.

46. Ibid., 289, 292; Add. MSS 47561, f. 111.

47. *R. F. Greville*, 241.

48. Ibid., 244; *Stanhope*, II, App. vi–vii.

49. *R. F. Greville*, 246; *Courts and Cabinets*, II, 125–6.

50. *Huish*, 31.

51. *Cornwallis*, I, 406–7.

52. *Jesse*, V, 293.

53. *Holt*, I, 328; *Jesse*, IV, 295.

54. *Wraxall*, V, 323; *R.C.P. Papers*, 38–9.

55. *Wraxall*, V, 324–5; *Betsy Sheridan's Journal*, 152.

56. *R. F. Greville*, 248–50.

57. Add. MSS 41691, ff. 167, 170.

58. *R. F. Greville*, 251–2; *Jesse*, IV, 280; *Holt*, I, 324; *d'Arblay*, IV, 263.

59. *R. F. Greville*, 252–3; *d'Arblay*, IV, 265.

60. Add. MSS 41691, ff. 173–4.

61. Ibid., ff. 173–4, 177; *Pembroke Papers*, 407; *Guttmacher*, 257.

62. *R. F. Greville*, 254–6.

63. Ibid., 256; *Wraxall*, V, 331; Add. MSS 41691, f. 181.

64. Ibid.;*Betsy Sheridan's Journal*, 153; *R. F. Greville*, 257–8.

65. Ibid., 259–60.

66. *Holt*, I, 324–5; Add. MSS 47560, f. 43.

67. *Holt*, I, 328; *Jesse*, IV, 295; *d'Arblay*, IV, 269–70.

68. Ibid., 303; *Courts and Cabinets*, II, 149, 152–3; *Cornwallis*, I, 406; *d'Arblay*, IV, 283.

69. *Huish*, 531; *Guttmacher*, 249; *Minto*, I, 283; *Betsy Sheridan's Journal*, 156–7; *Thraliana*, II, 732.

70. *Holt*, I, 320.

71. *Pembroke Papers*, 407; *Stanhope*, II, App. vi–x.

72. Add. MSS 47560. f. 17.

73. *Stanhope*, II, App. xi; *Rode Hall Papers*.

Index